HISTORY

OF

ECONOMICS

or

Economics as a Factor in the Making of History

By

Rev. J. A. DEWE, A.M.

Late Professor of History in the College of St. Thomas,
St. Paul, now Professor of History at the
University of Ottawa

Nibil Obstat.

REMY LAFORT,
Censor Librorum.

Imprimatur.

✠JOHN M. FARLEY,
Archbishop of New York.

NEW YORK, NOVEMBER 30, 1907.

INTRODUCTION

HISTORY is no longer a study of isolated events, but rather of the workings of unseen laws and influences. As the different phenomena of chemistry and physics receive their orderly arrangement and their power to interest only from their association with certain laws, so, in history, the facts that make up the narrative are but the material or medium through which are conveyed the workings of laws both universal and ever constant.

The study of history has thus lost much of the dryness, and, perhaps, also some of the disregard in which it used to be held. No longer is it a mere committal to memory of battles and sieges, of alternating wars and treaties, of the rise and succession of dynasties. It is now a scientific research into the influences that bring about all these different results. The action of the motor power of certain laws is now seen in all the pages of history, and every event that takes place can be attributed to the action of some law.

The study of history, therefore, has been raised to the dignity of a science, a science that specially interests the mind of the seeker after true wisdom. None other, perhaps, deals so effectively with the mainsprings of human conduct. It reveals the future by means of the past, and shows to mankind what particular environment it must seek after in order to achieve the greatest happiness of the greatest number. Moreover, to the student who has emerged from the embryo condition of the small boy, this scientific study of history should hold out most fascinating attractions, since it presents the key with which to unlock some of the most actual, pressing problems of our present civilization.

The influences or laws that shape the events of history are many and various. They may, however, all be summed up under three great categories, namely: Physical Surroundings, Religion, and Economics.

From time immemorial, the physical surroundings of a nation have vitally determined its history. Climate, whether hot or cold, the configuration of the country, whether it be an island or a part of a continent, the resources of the soil, whether agricultural or mineral, have their share in determining the political place and habitual occupations of a nation. Athens, Carthage, Venice, England, all became great maritime and commercial powers on account of their proximity to the sea. Small frontier nations, on the other hand, like Phenicia and Prussia, have been forced into a condition of hot-bed artificial strength, owing to the necessity of constantly providing against danger from their more powerful neighbors. To an almost equal extent have the productions of the soil been instrumental in determining the whole character and history of a nation. The abundance of precious metals, the bountiful supply of iron, or the exuberant fertility of the soil, all determine the average occupation of the citizen and the wealth of the nation and the power of the State.

Religion is another very important influence in the shaping of history. Man's conduct is swayed, to a great extent, by his religious belief. If we leave aside the influence of religion, the history of the Eastern peoples is an insoluble enigma. If, in Greek history, we leave religion out of account, the old Greek oracles with their inspiring utterances, obeyed alike by all classes of society, would no longer appear on the pages of history, and the Greek religious assemblies, such as those of the Amphictyonic Councils, which at one time seemed likely to bring about the unity of Greece, would likewise vanish. Indeed, Greek history, without the religious element, would be cut down by at least one half, and even the remaining half would be void of meaning.

The same might be said of Roman history. There every important transaction of the State is blended with some religious act. The taking of the auspices, the consultation of the augurs, the offering up of sacrifices, accompanied all the acts of Roman life, whether public or private. Even down to the time of Cæsar, an unlucky omen might thwart the action of the most powerful magistrate.

If we turn over the pages of modern history, bright with the rays of dominant Christianity, we find religion still a most important factor in the shaping of history. The Mohammedan invasions, the Crusades, the wars against the Albigenses, the Thirty Years' War, the War in the Netherlands, were all brought into being by the religious element. Then, again, was it not the struggle between empire and Papacy that practically dominated the theater of European politics for three centuries? We might mention, as well, all the different institutions molding society that have been started by the spirit of religion: the monasteries and convents of the Middle Ages, the universities, the guilds, and all the different ordinances that have regulated man's public and private life.

Finally, we come to the third category of formative causes, namely, economics. This element, as we shall see, is also of the greatest importance, and this not only on account of its own intrinsic activity, but because it is so intimately bound up with the other two important formative influences in history, namely, physical surroundings and religion.

By economics is meant the science of wealth, and this, again, means the knowledge of the laws that govern the production of wealth, and its distribution. We might, perhaps, express this definition in simpler terms by saying that economics is the science of how a man makes his wealth, and how he gets it.

It is evident, then, that economics must have an almost unbounded influence on human conduct, both public and private. For the great majority spend the greater part of their time either in producing or distributing wealth, and, from the point of view of extension, the time that an ordinary man has to employ in earning his daily bread is greater than that which he can possibly expend in explicit acts of religion.

This all-pervading activity of economics is still more apparent in the State or commonwealth. In the whole course of ancient and modern history, there is scarcely any single important political event that has not been caused, either directly or indirectly, by some economic influence. Religion and physical causes may also have been present, but the economic factor seems to have been the most constant and the most pervasive.

Although we shall be anticipating what will come afterwards, a few examples taken from typical nations will serve to illustrate this statement.

In ancient history, the great revolution that was followed by the rise of the people to political power was occasioned directly by economic causes. In Greece, it was the misery of the debtor, combined with the depressed condition of trade, that occasioned the reforms of Solon—reforms which, in their turn, led up to the completely democratic constitution of Clisthenes. Indeed, one remarkable feature of the genius of Solon is the way in which he saw that his legislative reforms, in order to be effectual, must also be accompanied by economic reforms. He saw that any concession of political power would be useless if the people were still left to groan in misery, and to starve by inches, and hence the great part of his reforms not only relieved the misery of the debtor, but tended generally to further industries of all kinds and the expansion of trade.

In Rome, we find exactly the same parallel. For years there was serious friction between the Patricians and the Plebeians. And the main causes of this friction were likewise economic. The people were cut off from the land, while the laws of debt were unjustly severe. Indeed, the great socialist leaders in Republican times, according to Mommsen, all took their stand on some economic question. Cassius endeavored to deal with the agrarian question, Manlius with the law of debt, while Mælius tried to introduce the custom of distributing, gratis, cereal foods among the poorer classes.

In modern times, the relation between politics and economics is still closer. Hostilities between nation and nation, the formation of alliances and treaties, the good or bad understanding between rulers and their subjects, can nearly all be traced to economic causes.

We might quote, as an illustration, the Hundred Years' War between England and France. During the whole of that war, England had on her side the faithful assistance of Flanders, and of the two duchies of Gascony and Guienne. The reason of this alliance was the constant interdependence of England and these countries, which was mainly economic. England was, during the Middle Ages, essentially an agricultural country, fleece being her most important product. Flanders, on the other hand, had the art of manufacturing the fleece into wool. Thus, the two countries were mutually dependent, one upon the other. Neither could have repudiated the alliance without great inconvenience.

Gascony and Guienne, also, carried on extensive trade transactions with England, but in a different way. England was dependent mainly on these two duchies for her imported wines. Then, again, although England had salt mines, she had not discovered the art of working them, so that, for salt, she also had to depend upon these two duchies, and thus, all during the vicissitudes of the Hundred Years' War, there was a natural and effective tie between these countries and England.

Another example which illustrates in a different way the importance of economics as an influence in the shaping of history, we find in the rise and fall of the political power of Venice. It was commerce that first made Venice so powerful in the arena of European politics. The sea trade routes from the East to the West converged through Venice, which thus became the clearing-house of the world. Merchants from all parts thronged the Rialto, while through her was exchanged the wealth of nations. Venice thus became also the center of distribution. In the wake of this material prosperity soon appeared a power that, in European politics, was colossal. Her ambassadors were found in all the capitals of Europe, while she rapidly became the focus of the manifold activity of European politics. When, however, the old trade routes were done away with, the cause of her power was obviously undermined. Her political influence began to wane with the decline of her trade, and she quickly became reduced to the condition of an insignificant power.

In more modern times, it would be no exaggeration to

say that the great majority of wars and revolutions have been brought about by economic causes. The War of Louis XIV, the Seven Years' War, the War of the American Revolution, were mainly struggles for the possession of wider markets. The overthrow of the monarchical dynasty in France was occasioned mainly by economic discontent aroused by heavy taxes and enactments, while, in America, the great war between North and South was brought about by the different economic conditions prevailing in the two sections—conditions which made slavery favorable to the Southerner, and unfavorable to the Northerner.

All these are but casual examples, selected at wide intervals of time and place, which illustrate the important connection between economics and history. This illustration, however, is only partial, but in the course of this work we shall find constant proof that it is impossible to understand clearly the sequence of political events without considerable knowledge of the economic factor.

Even the intervention of the religious and physical elements is blended with economics. As a great writer has pointed out, all great religious movements are connected with the material well-being of the people. And with regard to the physical element, the advantages or disadvantages of soil and climate are closely dependent for their importance upon the economic activities of the people themselves.

The study, therefore, of the economic interpretation of history is all-important for a right understanding of history. Historical events are grouped together by such close ties of natural connection as to aid the memory considerably. Most distant periods are found to present most interesting parallels, and this gives cohesiveness to the structure of historical knowledge, while the scientific mind also receives full satisfaction in viewing the ultimate causes of the historic phenomena that are so numerous and otherwise so perplexing.

We are now brought to the final justification of the economic treatment of history. Surely, only that is really worthy of the name of knowledge that contributes to the welfare of the individual man and of society. While the knowledge of a past that has no bearing on the future is a useless encumbrance upon the mind, the economic study of history is full of salutary lessons for the present and guidance for the future.

How many arduous questions are facing the statesman of to-day! Questions essentially economical, and upon the solution of which depends the fate of statesmen and the rise or fall of nations. Such questions as Protection, Free Trade, the power which the government has to interfere with corporations and trade-unions, and the expediency of so doing, the problem of providing for the poor and the unemployed, the problem of peacefully reconciling with one another the colonial aspirations of the countries of Europe, and also of the United States; all these are vital problems, and to many seem new. But, as we shall see, they are all, or most of them are, old problems dressed up in a different form. They have appeared over and over again in the pages of history, ancient and modern, and with them has also often appeared the key to their solution.

To the student of history, to the statesman, to the citizen desirous of contributing his share to the well-being of the State, to the intelligent man, who wishes to discourse with authority on modern problems, the economic study of history will prove as advantageous as it is interesting.

Nothing now remains by way of introduction except to indicate briefly the main divisions of the subject.

The first part deals with the economics of the ancient period of history; the second treats of the economics of the medieval period; and the third has to do with the economics of the modern period.

During the preparation of this work, much assistance and unfailing courtesy have been tendered me by the chiefs of different libraries in foreign countries, in the United States, and in Canada, notably the libraries of Harvard and Yale Universities.

Also, I wish to make mention of my indebtedness to Mr. Martin O'Gara, of the University of Ottawa, for valuable time generously given in the reading of the proofs and especially the compilation of the index.

J. A. DEWE.

CONTENTS

Contents

PART III

MODERN PERIOD

PART I
GREEK AND ROMAN PERIOD

HISTORY OF ECONOMICS

CHAPTER I

ECONOMIC CONDITIONS IN GREECE

THE Greeks had no conception of political economy as a science. They did, however, busy themselves with certain facts and data that constitute the material of this science, namely, with the production and distribution of wealth. They raised crops, breeded cattle, extracted the precious metals, traded with one another and with foreign nations; but they did all this without having any established formulæ or principles, and without any sight of those tendencies that constitute the laws of political economy.

One of the reasons of this would arise from the nature of the subject itself. The phenomena that make up the material of political economy seem vague and indeterminate. Only after much patient reflection does it become apparent that what seemed to be so many heaps of facts are really produced and regulated by constant and undeviating influences. The Greek mind, therefore, especially in its infancy, would naturally shrink from striving to reduce to the condition of a science such indefinite and apparently inappropriate material.

Moreover, even if the material of political economy had seemed all that could be desired, the Greek mind itself had not received the necessary previous training.

It was still in an infantile condition. It was ruled chiefly by instinct and imagination. The habit of careful observation and of the use of deduction and induction, so necessary for constructing a science, was at first wanting. It is not surprising, therefore, that, owing to the apparent want of adequate material, and the deficiency of any previous scientific training, the Greek mind should have failed to construct a science of political economy.

And yet the ancient Greeks had some theories regarding the production and distribution of wealth. These theories, it is true, were not drawn up in scientific form, but they constitute the germ of the science of political economy, and they foreshadow some of the latest political economic theories.

The treatise written by Xenophon on "Wealth" clearly shows that, even in his time, there had sprung into existence a considerable number of ideas regarding the production and distribution of wealth—and these ideas had been slowly developing from the earliest times. His ideas regarding the nature of agriculture, the importance of manufactures and trade, could have been discerned already in the legislation of Solon as far back as 594 B.C.

Both Plato and Aristotle held opinions on economic subjects, though these opinions are speculative and academic, and chiefly regard the ethical side of political economy. Thus, they extol the value of labor in the ideal city, a city whose inhabitants are of absolutely sound moral principle. But they decry its use in the real city, on account of the sordid love of wealth that so often results.

Not only Xenophon, but nearly all the Greek writers, agree in upholding the value of agriculture, one of the reasons alleged being that agriculture, unlike other pursuits, takes away from no man, and they all agree in maintaining the right of the State to regulate trade and commerce. These important theories, it is interesting to note, were very predominant during the last two centuries, and when first originated were regarded by many as new.

There was, however, one remarkable feature in which the Greeks differed from the Teutonic nations, and rather resembled the Romans, and that was the views which they held regarding private property. Among the early Germans there was no such thing as absolute private property, all land being held in common, and distributed afresh at the beginning of every year. Even in modern times, some trace of this is to be seen in the recognized principle that land may be appropriated for the public service of the State, providing that compensation be given to the owner, while, by the law of attainder, a criminal's goods may still be confiscated. But, amongst the early Greeks, the idea of private property was deeply rooted. Even though the fruits of the ground were not considered as the right of the owner or producer, yet the ground itself was held to be absolutely the property of the owner. Religion itself defended the rights of private ownership, and no law could be passed infringing upon such rights.

This notion of the inviolability of property affected considerably the economic life of Greece. Since the land remained to the family, and could not be alienated from the family, either by sale, or by the debt of the owner, or even up to later times by confiscation, the Greek husbandman remained more or less fixed to the soil. There was very little mobility in agricultural labor. At the same time, one can easily perceive how the occupation of agriculture, on account of its ancient traditions, and its intimate connection with the sacredness of private property, was always held in the highest esteem.

Such were the main general ideas held by the Greeks regarding economics. These ideas were of the simplest kind, and formed the basis of no constructive system. They did, however, give a certain kind of continuity to the economic activity of the Greeks, and explain many things in their economic legislation that would be otherwise inexplicable.

We will now briefly review the economic condition of ancient Greece. For the sake of clearness and method, the production of wealth will be considered first, and then its distribution.

Section I

The Production of Wealth in Ancient Greece

The southern position of Greece would lead to the natural supposition that the climate, the soil, and natural products are sub-tropical, yet this is not the case. Only in Messenia can anything like sub-tropical vegetation be found. The climate, generally, is mild, and the soil is far from being luxuriant. This is easily explained by the configuration of the land. Mountains and hills everywhere abound, while numerous arms of the sea penetrate far into the heart of the country.

Great variety is to be found in the different parts of Greece. Thessaly was always celebrated for its rich pastures and the breed of its horses. The Bœotian mountains were noted for their pleasant groves and verdant slopes, and the Bœotian plains for rich soil and abundant crops. Attica, in spite of its poor soil, can produce wheat, oil, and timber; Messenia, on the other hand, is noted for its semi-tropical fruits and flowers, a strange contrast to the barren soil of neighboring Elis.

Under the soil of Greece were also various deposits that added materially to her industrial wealth. Near Athens, there were the great clay pits from which the Athenians derived the material for their exquisite pottery. In Mount Pentelicus were the celebrated Pentelic marbles, so largely used for building purposes. Nor were there lacking the precious metals. The silver mines of Laurium were known even at the time of Themistocles, and were a great source of wealth. Gold could be found in Siphnos (Cyclades) and in far-off Colchis, and in the Pangean mountains were both gold and silver mines.

The natural wealth of Greece, however, must not be measured only by what could be found strictly within her borders. There were also her numerous colonial settlements, all renowned for some kind of product. Along the Black Sea were the huge wheat-fields and timber districts. The lands of Asia Minor could furnish the fruits with which to grace the tables of the rich. If we turn to the Western colonies, there was scarcely a town in Italy and Sicily not famed for some specialty. Thus, Acragas was famed for its soil, Syracuse for its horses, Tarentum for its oyster fisheries.

Of all these different products, there could be no doubt that wheat was the most important. Upon it depended the very existence of the citizen, and agriculture, therefore, received a very careful study. Even in early times, we find in Attica an acquaintance with the different methods of irrigating the soil, and improving its condition by means of fertilizers.

The grain was procured from the country through jobbers. In small places it was crushed in small mortars, but in the larger towns it was handed over to the miller, his apparatus consisting of a huge millstone revolving on a cylinder of iron. The miller then sold the flour to the bakers, who baked it into loaves, the weight and size of which were all carefully regulated by statute, and examined by special commissioners.

The greatest care was taken to regulate the supply of grain. For example, in the period that followed the war with the Persians, the supply of this essential commodity became scarce, and a law was passed limiting its exportation under severe penalties. Attempts were also made to prevent merchants from unlawfully enriching themselves by sharp methods of trade. No dealer was allowed to take more than one obol per measure of corn for what he had originally given. Special commissioners were also appointed to regulate the sale of corn (*sitophulaces*). Unfortunately, however, all these precautions were often unavailing, and artificial means were often used to raise the price of breadstuffs.

After grain, perhaps, the olive received in Athens the greatest attention. The olive was valued more for its oil than for the fruit itself, which was dried and sold in its skin.

Besides the cultivation of grain and of the olive, that of the vine was also perfected to a considerable extent. Trenches were carefully dug around for the sake of moisture, and the tree was propped up by artificial supports. The juice of the grape was procured in much the same way as it is in certain parts of Italy to-day, the grape being pressed by the feet and the juice collected into vats. There were many different kinds of wines, the principal being the red wine procured from the grapes on the hillside, and the white wine from the grapes grown on the plains.

Besides agriculture, there were also other important industries, which appeared even from the earliest times. Already, in the Iliad and the Odyssey, we read of carpenters and masons, and in certain trades the principle of division of labor soon became fully recognized. In two respects, however, Greek manufacture differed considerably from our modern system. First, in early times, the family was largely self-sufficient. That is to say, the members of the family manufactured all its own necessaries; some, for example, preparing the food, others making the different pieces of furniture and articles of apparel. Even when, by the eighth and seventh centuries before Christ, manufacturing industries became more diffused, certain occupations were still confined to certain families owing to the fact that the son generally followed the trade or profession of the father. Also, certain trades were confined to certain particular streets; one street would contain all the bakers, another all the butchers.

Besides this local distribution of trades, another respect in which the Greek system differed from our own was that guilds and trade corporations were quite unknown. No doubt, this was partly owing to the strong connection between the family and the trade. It is thus curious to observe that, while the family element was prejudicial to the quick formation of the State, it was also a very successful check to the formation of any artificial combination of trade.

Although, however, there were no combinations of trades, or of members of the same trade, there appeared by the fifth century before Christ factories of a very considerable size. Some of these contained hundreds of workmen, who performed their tasks under the super-vision of a kind of foreman.

This was especially so with regard to the manufacture of clothes. By the sixth and fifth centuries, one single factory often had the exclusive production of some particular kind of dress. One factory, for example, manufactured men's hats exclusively, another women's hats exclusively, while another again manufactured nothing but tunics. It is evident from this that there must have been a great number of employees even in one factory.

The same principle of division of labor, of allotting one particular task to certain people, exclusively trained for that task, is also found in the building industry. The quarryman extracted the stone or other building material from the quarries. Then one class of men cut the material into the required shape, while yet another set of men had the exclusive task of placing the blocks of stone, or marble, one above the other. Finally, the carpenters made the doors, and other frames, and a special set of men placed the tiles on the roof.

In the construction of ordinary dwellings the builder superintended all the different arrangements, but in large public edifices architects were employed, who often enjoyed considerable repute, and were admitted into familiar intercourse with the great.

This division of labor always brings into existence men of remarkable genius and long experience. Athens, in this, was no exception, and perhaps in no industry is this so well illustrated as in the pottery industry. It is true that the earthenware destined for ordinary use was rough and clumsy, but, on the other hand, the artistic kind of earthenware displays the greatest talent and technical skill. Certain traditions of the art seem to have been handed down from father to son, and their splendid results can still be seen in some of our museums.

Altogether, the manufacturing industries of the Greeks display a great amount of organization and industrial skill. And it is not to be wondered at if in later times the position of the manufacturer received the recognition it deserved. What seems at first to have belittled the position of the manufacturer was that he sometimes exhibited greed for money. Nothing seems to have been more repellent to the Athenian mind than an open display of avarice. In the writings of Plato and Aristotle nothing is more evident than the fact that the manufacturer, as such, was deemed worthy of respect, but that he too often degenerated into a seeker after mere material gain, and thus came to occupy a lower place in the public esteem.

There is one element in the production of wealth in ancient Greece that must not be overlooked, namely, the use of slave labor. Evidently, this must make a considerable difference in the rate of wages, average of prices, and especially in regard to the relation between the free laborer and employer. Most of the lower forms of labor, such as working in the mines, rowing the galleys, and many of the tasks in the different factories were done by slaves; nearly all domestic work in the private houses was also done by them.

The result was that the greater part of the citizens were free to devote themselves to the care of the State, and to cultivate their own individual perfection. A high degree of culture supposes leisure, and this leisure was conditioned by the fact that the slaves did a great part of the manual labor, and thus enabled the citizen to devote himself to the cares of State.

SECTION II

DISTRIBUTION OF WEALTH

The distribution and interchange of wealth naturally follow upon the production of wealth. But the process is usually slow. This is especially the case in ancient times, when money, the common medium of exchange, and such means of transport as ships and good roads were still wanting. Hence, we find that, in Homeric times, the family was self-sufficient, and made its own necessaries. And even when the town took the place of the family as the unit of distribution, goods still passed directly from the producer to the consumer.

It was the sea, more than anything else, that hastened the advent of wealth. The first traders were the Phenician captains, who, at first, cautiously hugged the coast and made their wealth as much by piracy as by honest trade. But the place of the pirate was soon taken by that of regular traders. These naturally visited the places with the best harbors, and thus Corinth, Miletus, and Athens quickly appear as the great centers of commerce and trade.

At the same time as the circumference of trade was enlarged, the appearance of money as a common medium of exchange greatly facilitated the progress of the wheels of commerce. At first the coins were measured by weight, but afterwards by tale, and each coin had stamped upon its surface its own proper value.

Another element in the progress of the commerce of Greece was the banking system. Even in comparatively early times, there were bankers in Greece. Owing, however, to the multiplicity of their functions they somewhat differed from our modern banker. The Greek banker was at once a money changer, a money lender, and a receiver of deposits. As money changer, he exchanged the coins of the different nations—an important function, when we remember that almost every important city minted its own coins.

He also loaned money at interest. It was in this way that capital and labor were brought together. No doubt the rate of interest was high, but, on the other hand, money was plentiful, the risks were great, and the banker had all the privileges of a monopoly. However, it must be admitted that there were also usurers of the worst kind, who were a source of danger to the commonwealth and of ruin to individuals. Plutarch speaks of instances where the usurers would subtract the interest immediately after the loan was made, and lend it out again, also on interest.

In contracting debts, there would seem to have been in vogue two different systems. First, there was the informal handshake; second, there was the formal contract, in which the debtor pledged something valuable as security of payment. In very early times he pledged even his own body, but this was forbidden by the laws of Solon.

The banker was also a receiver of deposits. In this respect he most nearly resembles our modern banker. But the Greeks were slow to make such deposits. The jars of money that are still found from time to time, while they contribute to our knowledge of Greek numismatics, also testify to a strong tendency to hoard.

Together with the banking system there were other appliances of commerce. There were the importers, whose duty it was to carry the different merchandise from shore to shore. There were also consuls *(proxenoi)* in different States, who looked after the interests of commerce, and who were likely to bring together seller and buyer.

Even to this day there still remain the ruins of what were once two typical centers of Greek trade. These are the ruins of the *deigma* or exchange, and the *agora* or marketplace.

The *deigma* was the place where sellers exhibited samples of their wares. Such a custom would naturally save the expense and trouble of securing the services of a commercial traveler. In Cuba, at the present day, there is still some kind of exchange very similar to the old Greek *deigma,* and many traders have expatiated upon its advantages.

Another center of commerce was the *agora.* This was the marketplace, where the goods were exposed for retail sale. Fully Greek citizens were allowed, without any condition, to expose their wares for sale, but *metics* or foreign citizens had to pay duty, such sums of money going to swell the coffers of the treasury. In the center of the *agora* was an open space surrounded by a portico, and this, like the Roman forum, served as a kind of lounging or general meeting place for the well-to-do. Each part of the *agora* was apportioned to its own particular trade. Thus, the lamp sellers would be in one part, the fruit sellers in another. This, perhaps, was meant to harmonize with the general custom of setting apart certain streets for particular trades.

But business was not conducted only in the *deigma,* the *agora,* or even in the street shops. The narrow streets of Athens resounded with the strong and strident cry of the petty huckster or hawker, and such goods, even more than those exposed for sale in the *agora,* were disposed of only after a considerable amount of haranguing and altercation.

It was not long before the importance of commerce came to be fully realized by the State, and of this the severe laws of debt are more than a sufficient proof. Commerce is essentially based on credit and good faith. If this is shaken, all falls to the ground. At all costs, the lender must be put in a position of safety, for, in the words of Demosthenes, "Commerce emanates, not from the borrower, but from the lender;" hence the severity of the early laws of debt. Even the reputation of the personal integrity of the merchant was secured by law, which inflicted severe punishment on whomsoever should falsely accuse him. State recognition also showed its activity in the appointment of commercial courts to decide cases involving commercial laws, all means being used to arrive at a prompt decision.

SECTION III

STATE ADMINISTRATION OF FINANCES

It was not long before State recognition of commerce led to interference for good or evil with every detail of commercial life. For the principle that the citizen was absolutely subordinate to the State, and must seek his own perfection through the collective perfection of the State, naturally applied to commerce as well as to every other department.

From some points of view the State regulation of trade was highly beneficial. The overseers of the harbor, of whom there were ten appointed every year, the inspectors of weights and measures, and the inspectors of the different goods that were sold, performed tasks both useful and necessary. Such officials were a means of

checking wrong-doing and commercial robbery. Almost
equally beneficial was the care shown by the State for the
poor. There was a special fund set aside for the children of those who died in war. Pisistratus, the Tyrant,
illustrated one phase of the paternal nature of tyrannical
governments by causing special provision to be made for
those who were mutilated in war. If, in the early years
of Greek history, no mention is made of other classes of
needy persons, the presumption is that there were none.
It must have been after the Peloponnesian war that des-
titution became common. After that time, bounties or
alms were sometimes awarded by decrees of the people.
This, however, was only done when the Senate had
carefully examined into the merits of the case, and the
amount never exceeded two obols (about eight cents).
At the same time, mention is also made of the education
of orphan children by the State.

Besides looking after the poor and needy, the State
also busied itself with the task of regulating the course
of trade in the interests of the general welfare.

Thus, it was forbidden to kill sheep and goats before
the lambing season was over, the object of this being to
prevent the depletion of these animals. A similar intention underlay the laws that forbade the exportation of
certain articles, such as wheat, and even forbade the
loan of money to any vessel that did not return to Athens
with a cargo of corn. It was also in the interests of the
consumer that the price of salt was carefully fixed by
statute, and that, as we have already seen, the profits of
dealers in grain were prevented from colliding with the
welfare of the citizen buyers.

On the whole, State interference with trade does not
seem to have been productive of very evil results in
Greece, for a considerable margin of liberty was allowed

to buyer and seller, and there seems to have been very little dishonesty on the part of overseers and other public officials.

Certain defects, however, became somewhat apparent in the management of the State's own finances. In an absolute democracy, where the ultimate control of the money is vested in the great body of the citizens, and when all, one after another, try to get into positions of financial trust, defalcations are sure to be found. It is true that the actual administration of the public treasury was confided to the Senate, which received the dues and other sources of revenue, and paid out whatever sums were necessary. But under the Senate were various officials who were responsible for collecting and distributing the revenues, and it was among these that dishonesty was sometimes to be found. Among these officials was the board of ten, called *poletai*, one member being elected from each of the ten tribes. These *poletai* regulated the levy of taxes. There were also the officials who collected the tribute from the allies, and, finally, a special set of officials who collected the arrears of tribute. All these found abundant opportunities for dishonesty.

The money thus taken in was handed over to the receivers or treasurers (*apodecteres*). Their chief duty seems to have been that of erasing the debtors' names in the presence of the Senate, and distributing the sums of money that were paid.

Naturally there must have been a considerable amount of bookkeeping and auditing. In the keeping of ordinary private accounts slaves were employed as clerks, because they could be forced, by torture, to give evidence. But only citizens could be employed as clerks in the public service. These clerks had to render an account to a set of officials, called the *logistai,* or public auditors. These officials, however, could often be bribed. It thus came to pass that the only means of correcting the balance between receipts and expenditures and of checking the dishonesty of public officials was partly reduced to a helpless condition.

Altogether, peculation became a crime extremely common among Greek officials. Even Pericles himself, in this particular, was not exempt from suspicion. Nor is this a matter of surprise. The elaborate apparatus necessary for the prevention and detection of public fraud is an invention of comparatively modern times.

A brief survey of the production and distribution of wealth in ancient Greece will have revealed much of the same good and evil that we find even in our own modern system. As time went on, the organization of industry became more and more complex, and presented many of the problems that still press for solution even at the present day. We must now consider the way in which this economic system determined some of the important crises of Greek history.

CHAPTER II

INFLUENCE OF THE ECONOMIC ELEMENT IN MOLDING GREEK HISTORY

OF ALL the Greek City-States, Athens stands forth as typical of everything that is greatest and noblest in Greek history. It was Athens that headed the Greek States in the successful resistance to the Persian invader. It was Athens that, through her colonial empire, offered at one time the best prospects of effecting the unity of Hellas. It was Athens that, owing to her peculiar circumstances, has been able to offer to us the purest type of democracy. It is in Athens that we find unified and summarized the history of all the Greek States.

In studying the critical turning points of Athenian history, we can not fail to notice how the economic element has always been a preponderating influence. During the early years of her existence, Athens had to face three important economic problems. She had to deal with the appalling decline of agricultural industry, with the extreme poverty of the lower classes, and with the stagnation of trade. These three problems, if left unsolved, might easily have led to the overthrow of Athens in the times immediately preceding the reforms of Solon, and it was only the prompt remedy that he applied that led, not only to the removal of grave economic evils, but to the formation of a full and perfect democracy. First, there was the agrarian problem. The land was worked on the tenant system. This means that the proprietor of the land would let it out to somebody else who agreed to pay rent in return for the occupation of the land. The rent paid was no less than five-sixths of the produce. This arrangement left only one-sixth for the support of the tenant and his family. Possibly, if the holding was unusually large, the one-sixth part might prove sufficient. But, in the majority of cases, it was not. Moreover, if the division had been more equitable, if it had been what it usually now is, one-half, or, as in some parts of Italy, two-thirds, even then the interests of agriculture would have suffered. For the knowledge that so large a proportion of any profits on the improvement of the land must go to the landlord always acts as an effective brake on the energies of the cultivator.

In addition to the evil effect of this abiding cause, there had also been a succession of bad harvests. The produce was reduced to microscopic proportions, and yet, even of this, the five-sixths had to go to the landlord. Only one resort was left to the wretched tenant, and that was to borrow—often giving as security his own body. Such a remedy, however, only delayed the ruin, to make it still more final and overwhelming. Multitudes of peasants, unable to pay their debts, were reduced to the condition of slavery, the land was left to go out of cultivation, and there was fast rising in the State an ever increasing number of men whose misery and starvation were a constant thunder-cloud hanging over the nation.

The second problem was the extreme disproportion of wealth between the upper and lower classes. Capital was congested in the hands of a few rich men. It failed to circulate freely, and this always produces a dangerous state of things in the body politic. This was especially so in the ancient City-State. The whole area of the Athenian City-State did not exceed thirty-six square miles. Even within this area, the active pulsating life of the State was limited to Athens itself and the country immediately surrounding. Wealth and rags were constantly encountering each other, and the results were ever increasing pride on the one hand, and, on the other, ever increasing jealousy and discontent.

The third great problem was stagnation of trade. Free commercial intercourse between nation and nation is greatly dependent upon a convenient means of exchange; in other words, a common currency. Up till now, Athens had adopted the old-fashioned Bœotian system of currency, and this had the effect of cutting her off from the more lucrative commerce with the prosperous cities and fertile plains of the Asiatic seaboard. There were also other subsidiary causes of stagnation of trade, such as the faulty incidence of taxation, by which is meant that taxes fell unequally and unjustly on the various classes of society; and, finally, there was the want of the capital necessary in order to initiate certain industries. Owing to these different causes, trade in Athens, as also her whole commercial prosperity, had dangerously declined.

Such were the three great problems confronting Athens at the time of Solon. An immediate solution of them was urgently necessary. Elements of disruption were fast manifesting themselves in the State, and even the political existence of Athens seemed on the point of being submerged by the rising waters of sedition and discontent.

No doubt political causes of discontent were also present, but these were as yet inarticulate. Demands for political reform presuppose a certain development of political knowledge, and the Athenian populace, in such early times, could hardly have been conscious of their exclusion from political power, and, still less so, of the means of removing such exclusion.

It was Solon, who, with a sagacity far ahead of his age, perceived clearly the root of the evil, and, what was more important, applied a remedy that was not worse than the disease. His first measures of reform were partly economical and partly political, and were so interwoven with one another as to furnish an interesting object lesson of the connection between economics and history.

The intolerable condition of the people was at once alleviated. Debtors were placed in a position where they could once more labor for their daily bread. Pledges, whether in the way of land or of bodies, were at once restored to the debtor. While, even previous to Solon's time, it was considered sacrilegious to pledge the land that was the sacred property of the family, it was now made illegal also to pledge one's own body as security for debt. At the same time the rate of interest that could be legally demanded was considerably reduced.

Some historians, following the new Aristotle, have asserted that Solon abolished all outstanding debts. Such a drastic measure, however, would have been quite contrary to the sane reasonableness of Solon's reforms. If any further disproof were needed, we find it in the dissatisfaction of the extreme radical party. The probability is, however, that Solon, recognizing the natural limits of the jurisdiction of the State, absolved from their liability all the creditors of the State.

Solon then turned his attention to the betterment of the condition of the trading classes of the community. This he did in the first place by substituting for the old antiquated system of coinage the new coinage already in use by the great commercial centers of Chalcis and Corinth. What the exact nature of this change was, we can conjecture only from Plutarch, who says that Solon made the *mna* to consist of one hundred *drachmas,* whereas before it consisted of only seventy-three. The general result seems to have been to lower the value of the monetary standard, and thus make it easier for debtors to discharge their debts. Such an advantage, however, would be comparatively slight, in comparison with that of assimilating the Attic currency with that of Eubœa and the other leading localities.

In other ways, also, did Solon encourage industry. He forbade all exports save that of the olive, which was so plentiful. No doubt, to many modern economists, this might seem most prejudicial to the best interests of trade, but we must remember that the necessities of life in Athens were few in number, and that the idea was not to barter the essential for what was only of secondary and immaterial importance. Solon also encouraged certain industries that would otherwise languish for want of support. In this he was only anticipating the modern system of bounties in which the manufacturer is paid for every amount of goods that he produces. In Athens, such a policy was signally successful. Industries that were perishing for lack of initial support speedily began to revive, and to acquire an independent and flourishing existence.

Such were the most important of the economic reforms of Solon. They arrested famine and starvation, warded off the danger of a revolution on the part of starving fanatics, and gradually brought about the formation of a strong middle class. Perhaps it was the last result that was the most important of all. No State can exist long or healthily without a strong middle class.

History shows that it is the middle class that saves society both from the despotism of monarchs and the
caprices of the lower classes.   And it was owing to the
strength of the middle class that Athens was able to present to the world the flower of a perfect democracy, as
well as to lead for so many years the onward march of
Greek progress and civilization.

Even the political reforms of Solon rested mainly
upon the solid bedrock of an economic foundation.
First in importance was his division of Athenian society
into four classes, according to the amount of wealth
which they possessed.   The first class was called *penta-
kosiomedimnoi,* whose annual income ranged from five
hundred *medimni* upward; the second class was called
hippeis, and comprised all whose income was between
three hundred and five hundred *medimni;* the third
class, *zeugitai* (or owners of a yoke of oxen), required an
income ranging between one hundred and fifty and three
hundred *medimni,* while the fourth class, *thetes,* consisted of all whose income fell below one hundred and
fifty.   Since only the members of the two upper classes
were eligible to the high offices of State, such an arrangement substituted an aristocracy of wealth for that
of birth.   In other words, it substituted an economic for
an hereditary qualification for office, and thus introduced
a general tendency in the direction of democracy.   For
a barrier of birth is absolutely insurmountable, while the
barrier of wealth is an obstacle that can be overcome.
A poor man, endowed with unceasing industry, and
helped by good fortune, might rise from the lowest to
the highest class, and thus become a candidate for the
supreme offices in the State, even for the office of
archon.

The reforms of Solon had the immediate effect of

introducing equality into the State, and of preparing the way for future reforms. The people were relieved from their intolerable economic condition, and at the same time were entrusted with just so much political power as to prevent them from ever again being oppressed, and to allow them a safe opportunity for self-education. The power which the people now had of electing their magistrates, and of trying them at the end of their year of office, effectually prevented an attempt on the part of the rulers to trample upon their newly acquired political and economic rights.

The reforms of Clisthenes, a few years afterwards, supplied what was wanting in the reforms of Solon, and still further perfected these on the same lines of democracy. Fierce factions in the State still continued after Solon's time. The chief causes of these were tribal exclusiveness and tribal jealousies — in other words, the family unit of organization interfered with the solidification of the State as a whole. Such an obstacle was now removed by the reforms of Clisthenes, who substituted ten for the old four tribes, and carefully distributed the townships among the ten tribes so that the old local interests should not again revive. As a consequence, the old senate of four hundred was also superseded, and another senate formed, consisting of five hundred members, fifty being elected from each of the ten tribes.

Finally, Clisthenes completed the democratic reforms of Solon by the more frequent meetings of the *ecclesia*, or popular assembly, and by vesting all the practical supreme power in the hands of this sovereign body of the people.

By this time, the City-State of Athens was fast rising toward the zenith of her economic and commercial

prosperity. Athens was fast becoming the emporium of
Greece. Her marketplace was the largest and the most
central in Greece. Crowds of foreign merchants from
most distant parts thronged the Piræus, and wealth was
now pouring fast into her lap.

It is no wonder that Athens, after the reforms of
Solon and Clisthenes, was able to head the Greek resistance to the Persian invader. It was the money of
Athens that built the most important ships of its navy
and thus dealt the decisive blow at the battle of
Salamis. And it was the wonderful fecundity and recuperative power of Athenian capital, under all shapes
and forms, that enabled Athens, after the devastating
visits of the Persians, to build another city, fairer and
far stronger than before.

But, after the Persian wars, there entered a new element into the economic life of Athens—an element that,
at one time, seemed to promise to her the sovereignty
of the whole Grecian world, but eventually brought
about her ruin. This was the colonial empire of
Athens, an empire that was formed out of the confederacy of Delos.

It was owing to the guiding hand of Pericles that the
confederacy of Delos became transformed into a maritime empire so vast that it practically turned the waters
of the Ægean and the Hellespont into an Athenian lake.
It was also under Pericles that Athens attained its full
economic development. Some of the features, however,
which were introduced by him mark not only the turning point, but also the beginning of the decline of
Athenian greatness.

The assertion of Athenian supremacy was in itself a
cause of discontent to the allies. The loudest note in
the general chorus of disapproval at the assertive policy

of Athens was that Pericles used the contributions of the allies for the purpose of strengthening and beautifying Athens. The allies complained that this was a case of misappropriation, for the contributions had always been made for the purpose of a common defense against the Persians.

Even from the very beginning, the allies had shown sensitiveness on this point. Thus, they objected to the term *phora,* as applied to the common contribution, and insisted on its being called *suntaxis.* Their chagrin, therefore, can easily be imagined when Pericles directed their contributions wholesale to the personal adornment and utility of Athens.

Pericles, however, excused himself by saying that Athens had sufficiently fulfilled her duty in defending the allies from any possible attack from the Persians, that, so long as this was the case, the purpose of the contributions had been fulfilled. This statement, however, seemed to the allies an excuse rather than a reason. They bitterly resented the high-handed policy of Pericles, and their discontent soon became chronic.

It must be admitted that the administration of the contributions of the allies does great credit to the self-restraint of Athens, and the sagacity of Pericles. Many other States would have wasted the funds in wide profusion and wasteful extravagance; whereas Pericles spent the money on worthy objects, such as the advancement of art and culture. Moreover, Pericles, in his distribution of the funds, showed remarkable sagacity and economic forethought.

According to Plutarch, he did not wish that the Athenian citizens should go without their share in the wealth that had been accumulated through the conquests and progress of all the citizens. Pericles, ac-

cording to the same author, laid the foundations of
great edifices, which would require multitudes of industries of every kind in order to complete them. "Different materials," to use the words of Pericles, "such as
stone, brass, iron, ebony, cypress wood, etc., would require special artisans for each, such as carpenters,
modelers, smiths, stone-masons, painters, embroiderers,
and makers-in-relief, and also bring men into the city,
such as sailors and captains of ships, and for those which
came by land, as carriage builders, horse breeders, rope
makers. Each trade, moreover, would employ a number of unskilled laborers, so that there would be work
for every person of every age and class."

These words of Pericles are full of significance.
They show the mental economic development of his
time, as well as his broad sympathy for every class of
industry. His last sentence is especially worthy of attention. It shows his acquaintance with the economic
distinction between skilled and unskilled labor, and the
need of providing for both classes.

Surely his popularity was founded on something else
besides a majestic presence and a gift of sonorous language. His deeds speak as eloquently as his words for
the good of the State. At no time in the history of
Athens was money so plentiful and so well distributed.

His policy of paying those who took part in the service of the State requires, however, some explanation.
Already there had been precedents for such a policy,
but Pericles carried it to its fullest extent. According
to Plutarch, he extended the payment for public service to the *dicastai,* namely, to those who were serving as jurors; but this really meant the payment of all
those who took part in the public service of the State.

Taking these into account, there must have been a

considerable number of men in the receipt of public pay. At one time, there were no fewer than forty-eight hundred and eighty men engaged in military duties of a remunerative kind, while there were also seventy-nine hundred employed in civic duties, also receiving pay from the State.

During the time of Pericles, however, no evil consequences seem to have resulted from such a system. Moreover, even according to our modern views, it is only just that those who contribute their time and labor to the service of the State should receive some compensation.

We must now turn to the consideration of the weak points in the economic system existing at the time of Pericles. They are important, as showing that not only the rise, but also the fall of Athenian greatness must be sought for in economic facts.

One of these defects we have hinted at already. Extreme dissatisfaction had been expressed by the allies at the way in which Pericles had appropriated the funds of the League of Delos. Another defect, rather similar to this, might also be mentioned, namely, the nature of the Athenian *Cleruchy*. The *Cleruchy* was not an independent colony, but a settlement of Athenian citizens still depending upon Athens. The chief *Cleruchies* were at Chalcis, Naxos, Andros, and Lemnos. There were various reasons for such foundations. One would be the natural desire of having outside lands brought under the direct contact of Athenian influence, especially such a close and important territory as was the island of Eubœa. A second reason was the desire to establish outposts on the trade route between Athens and the Black Sea.

The inhabitants of the *Cleruchies*, however, became

a source of danger rather than of advantage to the Athenians. Their pride and arrogant interference with the natives of the country were intolerable. In fact, the countries in which the *Cleruchies* were planted became even more zealous than the allies to cast off the yoke of Athenian rule.

Another and, perhaps, the most fatal defect in the economic administration of Athens was that the citizens themselves generally held aloof from the trading and commercial movements of the time. Labor and commerce were, for the most part, in the hands of slaves and alien residents. It is true that, with regard to the slaves, they were treated, for the most part, kindly. Indeed, their comfortable condition would surpass that of many of our modern workingmen. It was only in remote districts, where the slaves were herded together in great numbers, that we find anything like merciless severity.

The resident aliens were also of service to the State, not only on account of their loyalty, but because by their taxes they contributed to the wealth of the State. Not only, as we have seen, were the resident foreigners obliged to pay a tax for selling their wares in the marketplace, but each family had to pay a yearly tax, and then, again, it was their increasing industry that went to swell the trade and commerce of Athens.

But, all this time, the Athenian citizens themselves were living on the labor of others. They were not the producers of the wealth that they so lavishly distributed, and it was this that formed one of the main fundamental differences between Athenian and modern democracy. The modern democracy has all the energy and recuperative powers of the living workman. It can produce its own capital. It is not a parasite, living on others and dependent on others, and thus, when danger and misfortune threaten, it is capable of exhibiting both wisdom and fortitude. Even though calamities may happen, it can reproduce all the capital it may have lost.

Such was not the case with the Athenian democracy. Culture and refinement alone do not make up the strength of a nation. When, for its material comforts and necessities, it has to depend upon others, then it becomes weak and hampered. The economic grandeur and splendor of Athens were after all only borrowed from others. They were not built upon the solid bed-rock of economic industry and resourcefulness, and when the waves broke against the edifice it was bound to fall.

It is here that we find the explanation of the speedy downfall of Athens after the death of Pericles. Owing to his genius, the plan of campaign against the Spartans was successful, but when he died the Athenian democracy began to show itself in its true character. It showed a complete want of ways and means. It was wanting in the mental qualities that come only from the presence of industry and self-initiative.

Nor was this all. Great, indeed, had been the re-sources of Athens at the beginning of her long war with Sparta. Besides all her naval and military resources, she had in the treasury no less than six thousand talents. But even with all this, she could not stand the continual drain upon her resources. She was continually spending without reproducing. This condition of internal weak-ness was hastened by the dissatisfaction of the allies. The long war of seventeen years was at length brought to a close by the complete and final triumph of the mili-tary forces of Sparta.

The next few years of Greek history mark the rapid decline of the Greek States, one after another. Sparta for a time has the ascendency, then Thebes. It is not till the time of Alexander the Great and the Macedonian conquests that we step out from the murky atmosphere of petty strifes and factions into the salubrious region of great events.

When Alexander succeeded to the throne he seemed to have solved the task of forming a united Greece. The whole of Greece proper was brought under his control, while powerful Macedonian fortresses would have checked any revolution if such were attempted.

Even during this period, however, economics as a theory was still undergoing a gradual evolution, but in a new direction. Hitherto the Greeks had busied themselves with political economy more as an art than as a science; now they begin to regard it from the scientific point of view. Definitions are made and discussed, and theories elaborated.

The writer who, perhaps, more than any other expresses the advance of Greek thought in this respect is Aristotle. Some of his theories are important as furnishing the basis of many speculations, and even of active policy during the Middle Ages.

Many of the treatises of medieval writers are permeated with Aristotelian views. St. Thomas Aquinas incorporated many of Aristotle's views regarding the conditions justifying the demand for interest and regarding the lawfulness of trade. While, for example, Aristotle praises trade *per se,* he condemns it in the real city, because it leads to sordid avarice. So, also, St. Thomas declares that trade is only lawful when a merchant seeks moderate gain for his household.

Mere speculation, however, could have little effect, whether for good or bad, at a time when the civilized world was torn asunder by constant discord and strife.

It is not till the time of the supremacy of Macedonia, and of the conquests of Alexander the Great, that history pursues once again its broad course of development, and that the economic factor becomes a real and important factor in that development.

After the completion of his conquests, Alexander's desire was to consolidate what he had gained by social and economic means. He strove to amalgamate the Greeks and Orientals by intermarriage. He built large cities, which were intended to become great centers of commerce. He made and improved the roads which connected all the important towns. He also increased the circulation of wealth and furthered the interests of commerce by his wide distribution of the hoards of gold that were found in the Persian treasuries. This had the effect, not only of making capital more accessible, but also of substituting gold for the baser metals as a medium of exchange. Such a reform in the currency was highly desirable, owing to the greater value of gold, and the ease with which it was carried about.

He also bestowed great attention upon the improvement of agriculture, as is shown by his attempts to irrigate the fertile plains of Babylon. And, what would be little expected from a military leader, he endeavored to put together an efficient navy, and to circumnavigate the Arabian peninsula.

Had he lived longer, success might have crowned all his efforts. As it was, the course of subsequent history showed that the most lasting part of his achievements was his efforts on social and economic lines. Many of the cities that he built became, like Alexandria of to-day, great emporiums of commerce and trade. The blending together of the Greek and Oriental element is still conspicuous even in our own times. And the whole of the trade between the East and the West received a remarkable impetus, both during and after his time.

After the death of Alexander, however, we are passing over the last period of Greek economic history—the period marked by the domination of Rome. During this period the history of Greece proper presents very little that is attractive. We discern, still more clearly than ever, the utter incapacity of Greece to manage her own affairs. Only one little State, compact and solid, seems still to survive as heir to all the culture and wealth of some of the City-States of ancient Greece. This is the Island of Rhodes.

Even by nature this island was signally favored. The air is mild and balmy; perennial sunshine is said to prevail, and the soil is remarkable for its exuberant activity. Also the abundance of such natural products as glue, pitch, honey, and saffron ointment enabled her to carry on an extensive trade with both Greeks and Romans, while her position made her the center of the trade between Europe and the Levant.

Her political power acquired a corresponding importance. By 357 B.C., she had shaken off the fetters of her subjection to Athens. Though for a time she was subdued by Alexander the Great, she became free again after his death. Then after successfully repulsing the sieges of the powerful Demetrius of Macedonia, she showed herself in her true light as a great and very formidable power. The Romans themselves were glad to form an alliance with her against Attalus, King of Pergamus, and on another occasion it was chiefly by means of the Rhodian fleet that the Romans defeated Antiochus III, King of Syria.

Unfortunately, however, the Rhodians, in 168 B.C., abandoned their alliance with Rome, and joined the falling cause of Perseus of Macedonia. They, therefore, shared in the defeat of that prince and were subjected to the severest penalties. The naval supremacy that Rhodes had enjoyed in the Ægean Sea was completely taken away from her and her trade crippled by the declaration of Delos as a free port. Thus Delos, not Rhodes, now became the center of the Levant trade, and the result was the commercial and political extinction of the last prosperous and powerful Greek City-State.

CHAPTER III

ECONOMIC CONDITION OF ANCIENT ROME

THE Romans, like the Greeks, had in the early stages of their political existence no conception of political economy as a science. Economic problems of a very urgent nature did, indeed, present themselves to Roman statesmen even from the earliest times, but their manner of dealing with such problems was essentially practical and not theoretical. Nor was there any time for speculation and cool, scientific inquiry. Hence, while many attempts were made to handle economic subjects in a practical manner, we come across very few discussions and theories.

But after the middle period of Roman history, in fact almost when Rome was in its decline, various Roman philosophers and jurists began to discuss certain economic theories. Nor was this remarkable, when we consider that the masterpieces of Greek literature were beginning to find their way into Roman society, and especially that the elaborate system of Roman law, strong even on its commercial side, demanded many interpretations.

Most of these theories are remarkable for their pessimistic character. Occasionally they resemble the lamentations of some of our own modern writers. They complain generally of the neglect of agriculture and the decay of industry. Chief among the writers of this sort were Cicero and Seneca, while Virgil, in later times, echoes the same strain more melodiously and more sweetly, when he sings in the Georgics of the oppressiveness of congested city life, with its vain pleasures and empty formalities, as contrasted with the innocent and healthful delights of country life.

Such writings showed a just observation of the economic evils of the times, but they did not attempt to point out any radical remedy. Even when other writers, like Cato and Varro, busy themselves with the agricultural industry, they concern themselves almost exclusively with its practical details. There is no broad generalization, no formal enunciation of principles. If they do rise above the consideration of the mere concrete, it is only to utter platitudes regarding the benefits of farming life in fostering the natural virtues and begetting honest citizens.

There were, however, certain thinkers of a different type who did seriously discuss some very important economic theories. Foremost among these was Columella. He was born in Spain, about 40 A.D., and wrote a treatise, *De Re Rustica,* in twelve books. One of the interesting questions that he raises is whether large or small farming is to be preferred. He decides in favor of the small farming. Perhaps his decision was partly influenced by the fact that in Italy there were so many huge estates badly managed, and worked by slaves to the general detriment of the free laborer.

Also among the jurists, as we have already said, were raised certain economic discussions. These afford most interesting glimpses of the views entertained by the Romans regarding the absolute and relative value of money, the advantages and disadvantages of slave labor, and the way in which governments might advantageously interfere in such matters as encouragement of population, and curtailment of public and private extravagance.

In one respect the Roman jurists seem to have held

quite a different opinion from the Greek writers, and this was their view regarding interest on money loans. Already in 451 B.C., the rate of interest had been carefully kept in check by the Twelve Tables. Not satisfied with this, the Romans afterwards entirely prohibited all lending on interest. Possibly this antagonistic attitude had no small share in the discussion, raised during the Middle Ages, on the lawfulness of lending money on interest. And this seems all the more likely, when we consider that the provisions of Roman law, and the opinions of Roman jurists, formed a considerable part of the European code.

The debt, however, that modern political economy owes to ancient Rome is not very great, at least from the theoretic point of view. There were very few principles and theories elaborated, and these were not put together so as to form a science. It is rather from the active and concrete side that Roman economics influenced posterity, and as we shall soon see, many of our most important commercial and financial institutions find their precedent in Roman times.

We shall now give a brief survey of the economic condition of Rome, considering, first, its production of wealth, and then its distribution.

ROMAN PRODUCTION OF WEALTH

The rich fertility of Italian soil has been much spoken of by Italian writers, both in prose and verse. Dionysius says that it compares very favorably with all other countries. According to him, the country is so capable of supplying all the necessities of life that it is scarcely at all dependent upon other countries. He speaks of the luxuriant grain-fields of the Campania, of the Messapian and Sabine olive lands, of the rich vineyards called the Tuscan, Albanian, and Falernian. Nor does he omit to speak of the great pasture lands, of the extensive forests, whose wood is so excellent for building purposes. His catalogue of praises also finds room to mention the warm springs, so delightful for bathing, and so efficient in chronic diseases, the many kinds of metals that are under the soil, and finally the delightful temperature of the air.

Much of this is, no doubt, true, but travelers who are practically acquainted with Italy well know that some distinction will have to be made. A great difference exists between Northern and Southern Italy. In the northern parts of Italy the climate more resembles that of England and Scotland, except that it is very much drier. It is only in the Italian lake district that the orange and lemon are found, and even then only in sheltered places.

It is in the middle and southern parts of Italy, and especially in Sicily, that sub-tropical vegetation is to be found. These districts are able to produce corn, rice, oil, silk, and all sorts of fruits, while in striking contrast with the severe winters of the northern region are perennial sunshine, and, during the summer, severe droughts.

Altogether, Italy, even more than Greece, is an agricultural country, and, in fact, from time immemorial, agriculture has been one of the two chief occupations of the Romans, the other being that of war.

It is no small wonder that the greatest writers of ancient Rome are more in favor of agriculture than of the other industries. Cicero, for example, says that there is nothing better, more pleasing, more delightful, and more befitting a well-bred gentleman, than the pursuit of agriculture. The same writer, however, showers disdain on mechanical occupations, and even hurls his denunciations against butchers, cooks, and others of kindred occupations, to whom he himself, however, must have been often indebted for many an hour of pleasure.

Partly, therefore, owing to natural circumstances, partly owing to prejudice, agriculture was the absorbing industry of the time. Other industries there were, but they occupied a position comparatively unimportant.

Naturally such industries were chiefly connected with the actual necessaries of life. From the earliest days, there was need of clothing, and since large numbers of sheep were on the spot it was inevitable that some kind of woolen industry should be established. But this was carried on only in the private family, generally by the slaves under the supervision of their mistress. Only in later imperial times was the wool spun in the public factories. The great Augustus himself wore woolen clothing made in his own family.

Later on, other material for clothing was introduced. We hear of linen, cotton, and even silk being used for articles of apparel, but, of these industries, the home factories were, for a long time, exceedingly few. Nor was there given a stimulus of any kind to the starting and development of such industries, the reason of this being that goods could be so easily imported from abroad, even from such far-off countries as India and China.

Besides the clothing industries, there were also others, which, from their very nature, were more or less indispensable. These were, for example, bakers, fullers, cobblers, carpenters, goldsmiths, coppersmiths, dyers, and even flute-blowers, for flute blowing was considered in those days a branch of industry. All these formed themselves into guilds, called by the Romans *collegia*. These associations were, however, very different from our modern guilds. They were not exclusive, anybody outside being allowed to practise the same trade. What seems to have constituted the main object of their existence was for the purpose of handing down the technique of the trade from one generation to another. Most of them had their own rules and forms of worship. In later times the guilds had to receive a license, and only those guilds could be licensed that could prove extreme antiquity.

One industry, in particular, deserves mention, partly on account of its contribution to the magnificence of the city of Rome, and partly on account of the great numbers of workmen to whom it must have been the means of furnishing employment. This was the building industry. Even the ruins of Rome to-day show the size and greatness of some of the public buildings of ancient Rome, such buildings as those that were in the Roman Forum, and the various temples and baths whose ruins now are scattered throughout the city. In addition to these must also be borne in mind the splendid villas of later Rome, and the great public works that were set on foot by the imperial rulers. Indeed it was Cæsar's avowed object to furnish by these means work for the unemployed, and this policy was continued under later emperors. One example of their care in this regard was the harbor which was built by Claudius near Ostia. This harbor was contained within two jetties stretching far out into the sea and having a lighthouse at the extremity. Another undertaking of the same emperor was the construction of a three-mile tunnel to carry away the overflow of the Fucine lake.

Other great undertakings of a similar nature were the restoration of the Capitol under Vespasian, the building of the Coliseum under the same emperor, while the new Forum in Rome, the new port near Ostia, and the Trajan aqueduct were all colossal undertakings.

All these building operations must have constituted a considerable and never-failing industry, for although many of the employed were slaves, yet many freemen must also have thereby found work.

Such, then, were the main industries of ancient Rome. As we have seen, she had nothing except the building industry to rival the extent and development of the industries of ancient Greece. For most of her goods, Rome depended mainly upon importation. She received everything, and gave nothing back. So profuse, indeed, were the importations of goods, even from such countries as India and Arabia, that the inhabitants of these countries had to ask back some of the exports that they had so lavishly and so expectantly sent over.

Agriculture, then, was the main industry of ancient Rome. From the beginning to the end, it was considered to be the cause of the peculiar virtues of the Roman character and, more than any other industry, it was blended with the political fortunes of the Romans.

It will not be out of place, therefore, if we give some details regarding some of the most important sections of this industry.

First in importance comes the cultivation of grain. In very early times the grain was pounded in mortars, and, after being mixed with water, must have rather resembled our porridge. Soon, however, an improvement took place. The pounding was done, not in mortars, but in public mills. In these mills the grain was poured into a large funnel, and, after reaching the bottom, was well ground by a powerful millstone, which was set in motion by the labor of horses or slaves.

The next step was to improve the preparation of the grain when thus crushed. This was done by baking and the result was the real equivalent of our bread. As yet, however, there were no loaves, only thin cakes. Moreover, all the baking was done at first in private families; not till about the end of the second century before Christ were there public bakers, who, like the members of the other industries, formed themselves into guilds.

The bread from these bakeries must have closely resembled in taste our modern bread. It contained a little salt and water and was also fermented with yeast.

There was also much the same variety that we find in our modern baking. For there were loaves made of the best pure white flour, called *panis siligneus,* and there were loaves made of a coarse flour, called by such names as *panis plebeius, panis sordidus.*

The second branch of agricultural industry practised in ancient Rome, and which, even to-day, is conspicuously flourishing in Italy, was the vine. This, perhaps more than any one branch of industry, is spoken of by Italian writers, both in prose and verse. Some, like Virgil, regard it from the practical and industrial point of view; others, like Horace, regard it rather on its convivial and pleasurable side. The instructions given by Virgil in the two Georgics show a most intimate acquaintance with all the details of the cultivation of the vine, and, as for variety, the taste of Horace must have evidently been tickled by samples of all the choicest wines, not only from Italy, but from the Greek Isles.

A few words in detail must be said regarding the treatment of the grape when arrived at maturity. This treatment differed from the methods adopted by the

Greeks in being more refined and in giving rise to greater variety of wine.

First of all there was the juice that descended from the bunches when they were simply brought in contact with one another after being gathered. This kind of juice naturally came from the over-ripe grapes. It was carefully collected apart and was called *protropium*.

Then the grapes were subjected to the same kind of treatment that we read of among the Greeks; the grape, that is to say, was trodden under the naked feet, pressure was applied, and the exuding juice was then collected. This went by the name of *mustum,* and is the same as our modern *must*. Nor did the process of extraction end even here. By means of powerful pressure the juice was even extracted from the stalks and husks, and made to form a coarser kind of beverage.

Only the *mustum* was reserved for fermentation, and was carefully preserved in vats coated with pitch. Then, as now, the value of a brand of wine depended greatly upon its age. A vat having on its label the names of consuls who had held office years before would be reckoned in great esteem.

The olive was almost as popular in Italy as it had been in Greece. And the ways of preparing it were more numerous and varied. Sometimes it was sprinkled with salt, allowed to remain a few days, and then dried in the sun; at other times the olive was preserved in boiled must. Perhaps the most curious method was that of putting the olive, together with the stalks, into an earthenware vase, and pouring oil on the top. In this condition the contents were allowed to remain, with the result that the flavor of the fresh fruit would last for half a year or more.

The Romans had no butter, but they had another

kind of condiment, of which the olive formed an important ingredient. The other ingredients were coriander seeds, cummin, fennel, and mint; all these, after being mixed with oil, forming what the Romans called *epyterum,* a substitute for our modern butter.

The fruit of the olive, however, was chiefly valued for the oil that was obtained in considerable quantities. Enormous quantities of the olive oil must have been used by the Romans. Not only was it in fashion as an article of diet, but even for such a diversity of purposes as fuel for lamps, and for anointing the body, either after bathing or before any violent physical contest, it was in use everywhere.

Such were the main branches of agriculture, the grain, the olive, and the vine. They furnished occupations that were most suited to the ancient simplicity and rugged character of the Romans, and they were also the main sources of the wealth that Rome herself was able to produce.

CHAPTER IV

DISTRIBUTION OF ROMAN WEALTH

WE HAVE seen that the greater part of the natural wealth of Rome was derived from the land through the industries of the grain, the vine, and the olive. There remains to be seen how this land was divided, and also into whose hands flowed the spoils of Rome's vast conquests.

The original territorial settlement of the Romans was very small. It comprised only Rome itself and the neighboring district. Enterprise and good fortune, however, extended the power of Rome by leaps and bounds. Latium, Campania, Etruria, Sicily, Africa, Greece, all fell under her dominion, even during Republican times.

The land taken from the enemy was, even from an early period, divided in the following manner: A part was reserved for the State, another part for the Roman colonists, a third part was distributed among the poor in small allotments, while yet another part was rented out to rich citizens, who paid a more or less nominal rent.

The part that was reserved to the State generally consisted of mines, forests, and great pasture lands. The profits from these were a source of considerable revenue to the State.

The land allotted to the colonists became absolutely their private property. When a colony was formed in any district, a law was passed stating the amount of land to be given over, and what burdens should be imposed upon the colonists. Anybody wishing to form part of the colony could then hand in his name, and when all arrangements had been made, the colonists all marched out of Rome with great pomp and solemnity. Naturally, these colonies were very useful for extending Roman influence. Not only did they diffuse the knowledge of Roman usages and civilization, but they acted as military outposts. Hence we find that many of the colonies were placed in dangerous and exposed districts.

Another portion of land was often distributed among the poor citizens in small allotments. The soil of such lands was generally very rich and did not entail many initial expenses. Another advantage was that the land so distributed was absolutely the property of the person to whom it had been granted. As was to be expected, the poorer classes were always anxious that as much of the land as possible should be disposed of in this way. But this wish was not always gratified, and much discontent resulted.

We now come to the land that was let out to the rich citizens. Such land was generally of the kind that required a considerable outlay of money. Hence only the rich citizens applied for lands of this description. Moreover, a rent had to be paid which varied in value, but, on the average, may be reckoned at one-tenth of the produce of the corn land and one-fifth of the produce of the vine and fruit trees. In other words, such citizens became *metayer* tenants of the State. Besides this rent, another disadvantage was that the occupant was only a tenant at will of the State. Any moment he might be dispossessed of his holding.

The land in the conquered provinces was subjected to rather different treatment. There, all the land was considered to be the property of the conquerors. But in practice only a portion went directly into the Roman treasury. A great number of private persons were allowed to retain their possessions on condition of paying a land tax. The remainder was treated in various ways. Part of it was sold or rented out, the proceeds in either case going directly into the *ærarium* or Roman treasury. Another portion was retained by the governing elements of the province or by the corporations and in various ways was made subservient to public utility.

Trade and commerce soon found some place in the economic activity of Rome. Already, by the time of Servius Tullius, coined money became the means of exchange. Before the use of money, the standard of wealth seems to have been cattle. Of this circumstance the figure of an ox, stamped on the early Roman coin, seems to be a clear indication, while the later word *pecunia* also points to the same conclusion.

As was the case in Greece, the introduction of a common medium of exchange must have greatly facilitated commerce, both inside and outside of Rome. Moreover, as Roman conquests expanded, her markets became proportionately widened. It is true that Rome, herself, produced very little, but, on the other hand, she was able to pay for her imports by the treasure that poured into her coffers from foreign sources.

The chief part in the commercial activity of Italy was taken by the *Equites* or Roman Knights. Owing to the senatorial Patrician being debarred from extensive trade transactions, and owing to the poverty of the poorer classes, the *Equites* enjoyed almost the entire monopoly of trade. All the great business transactions were in their hands, and they were also indirectly aided by having the monopoly of the State contracts. It was to them that the State farmed out the taxes, which means that the State, instead of collecting the taxes, agreed to receive from the Knights a certain sum of money, and allowed them to collect and appropriate the taxes for themselves. Such an arrangement had its obvious convenience for the State, but the disadvantages were many. The Knights were frequently guilty of a great deal of dishonesty and extortion and it was owing to this that the term "Roman Knight" afterwards incurred so much infamy.

They also had a monopoly of the slave trade. As Rome's conquests considerably increased, this became a source of unlimited wealth. Delos seems to have been one of the chief marts of the trade. According to Strabo, no fewer than ten thousand slaves were often received and transported in the same day. From Pliny we also learn that the average rich man could easily maintain a whole legion of them on his yearly income.

The great part of Rome's industry was dependent upon slaves. Not only were there slaves in domestic households and in the big workshops, but in later times the vast landed estates in Italy were worked chiefly by slaves. The Knights, therefore, must have enjoyed a very valuable monopoly.

But there was, also, another privilege which they enjoyed, perhaps even more important. This was the monopoly of the banking system. From the very earliest days in Rome a systematic method of keeping accounts seems to have prevailed almost everywhere. It was a custom for the father of the household to keep a register in which he wrote in ten different columns the receipts and expenditures. These columns were called, respectively, *codex accepti et dispensi.*

The same custom was followed, but with greater development, by the Roman banker. Each banker had what was called the *liber rationum,* much resembling the

big ledgers of our modern banks. In these books were
written the names of the banker's clients—all drawn up
in alphabetical order. Two divisions were then made,
one for the balance, and the other for the entries of expenditure. To quote the exact words of Pliny, *"huic
omnia expensa, huic omnia feruntur accepta."* At
certain times, the banks drew up in their books a written
account of the finances (*rationes redditæ*) and gave a
note to their clients of their exact standing. Nor were
these transactions merely a matter of private business;
they were all carried out under the supervision of some
State official. In Rome, it was the prefect of the city;
in the provinces, the governor. Often it would happen
that there was a balance or *reliquum,* which could be
paid over at once, or reinvested, according to the will
of the client.

A still more curious parallel between the Roman
banks and our modern banks we find in the check system.
Clients who kept a running account were entitled to use
a written mandate, called *tabulas annulo obsignatis,* and
this practically fulfilled the same function as the
modern check.

The Roman banker also fulfilled another very important function in the economic system. He used to advance money for important enterprises. He thus became, like the modern banker, the means by which capital is at once distributed to the parts where it is most
needed. Without such a contrivance capital and labor
would be separated far apart, to the great detriment of
each other.

Great, indeed, must have been the importance of the
banking system in Roman times, and from it we can
measure the importance of the Knights, who monopolized this business. It is no wonder that they had be-

come, by Cicero's time, one of the most powerful bodies in the State, upon whose action depended the balance of political power.

This power may have been exerted wisely or unwisely, but there is little doubt that the *Equites,* with their command and distribution of capital, maintained the trade and commerce of ancient Rome. As in our own times small retail traders depend indirectly upon the great commercial undertakings, so, in Rome, the retail dealers in the shops, and also the petty huckster, owed their property, and even existence, to the capital of the *Equites.*

FINANCIAL ADMINISTRATION OF THE ANCIENT ROMAN
STATE

The revenues of the Roman State were at first few and simple. First, there were the different lands and mines belonging to the State, and forming part of its domain. All the profits arising from these went to the treasury. Then, as time went on, taxes were imposed upon the people. Some of these taxes were direct, others indirect, the former being levied on the very people who were destined to bear the burden, and the latter being exacted from the payer of the tax only in an indirect way. The most lucrative of the Roman taxes were direct, and consisted of the following:

a. The tribute. This was a tax imposed on all citizens. It depended upon the amount of property at which each person was assessed. After being introduced at the reforms of Servius Tullius, it remained in force until 116 B.C. During this year, owing to the great wealth of Rome, it was suspended until the beginning of the reign of Augustus.

b. The land tax that was levied on the owners of the allotments of the public land.

c. The taxes that were laid upon the inhabitants of the provinces, who were allowed to remain in possession of their holdings. Such inhabitants had to pay either a sum in proportion to the produce, and were then called *stipendarii,* or to pay a fixed sum, and then went by the name of *vectigales.*

d. The general tribute that was levied on each province as a whole. This, generally speaking, amounted to about one-tenth of the general produce, but was collected in different ways.

e. The tax of the supply of corn that all the provinces had to contribute for the maintenance of Rome itself.

f. The *portoria,* or customs duties, which, as trade increased, became very considerable.

Other taxes of later introduction might also be mentioned, such as the tax of five per cent. levied on the manumission of slaves, the tax of one per cent. on articles of sale, the tax of five per cent. on all legacies, near relations being exempted, and, finally, the tax on all sums about which there was a dispute in a court of justice.

All these taxes must have furnished a considerable source of revenue. On the whole, however, they were not very burdensome. In no period of Roman history do we read of any disturbance being caused by taxation. Indeed, there would seem to be almost a disproportion between the profuse expenditure, together with the later extravagance of Rome, and the smallness of the taxation. Such disproportion is diminished, however, when one takes into account the other subsidiary sources of revenue—the confiscations and indemnities inflicted upon the conquered peoples, the forfeiture to the State of unclaimed legacies, and of the property of condemned criminals, the appropriation of the *ager publicus* in the provinces, and, we might even add, the magnificent bequest that was made to the Roman people by Attalus, King of Pergamus.

There now remains to be considered the way in which all this revenue was administered.

In the early times of the kings of Rome, the king, himself, was head of the financial department. Under his control was the *ager publicus,* out of which were defrayed public and private expenses, while the treasurers were his own ministers. Some limit, indeed, was placed upon his administration by the Senate, but the Senate then had very little real power.

Later on, during the time of the Republic, there began the treasury of the Roman people, called the *ærarium,* which was situated in the Temple of Saturn. The ultimate control of this was supposed to be vested with the people, but the Senate formed the actual governing body with the consuls as administrators, and the *questors* as paymaster-generals.

Such was the early construction of the Republican financial administration. It soon underwent great development. A complete separation came to be made between those who received, and those who disbursed the revenues, and a whole hierarchy of officials was established, each with some allotted task in the financial administration.

The Senate enjoyed great control over the provinces. It was the Senate that authorized the imposition of new taxes, and their power was exclusive. Although Livy, in certain passages, seems to attribute to the consuls the power of imposing the tribute, and to the censors the power of imposing indirect taxes, yet the authorization of the Senate was always presupposed.

On one occasion the people, meeting in their centuries, voted a tax. This, however, afterwards received the Senate's approval. With the Senate, also, rested certain powers over the expenditure of finances, such things as the appropriation of funds, the alterations of the assessments, the examination of the budget, and the allowance of credit to public officials in the performance of their duty. During emergencies their power became enlarged so that by sale or otherwise they could dispose, by a special decree, of the public land.

After the Republican times, the emperors gradually usurped the place of the Senate in financial administration. The imperial treasury took the place of the *ærarium*. It was the emperor who eventually drew up the yearly budget (*breviarium*). Whatever nominal power still remained to the Senate was nullified by the emperor's power to choose the members of the Senate, and the great influence which he had in guiding and regulating its proceedings.

While, however, the supreme power over the finances changed hands from the Senate to the emperor, the subordinate officials, and the practical working of all the details, remained very much the same. During the early days of the Republic, the officials were comparatively few in number, but afterwards, with the growth of finance, they considerably multiplied. The following were the most important officials to whom was confided the actual working of the financial administration:

1. *Questors.* These existed even from the earliest times. At first there were two *questors* in charge of the treasury, then, later on, there were appointed one *questor* for each of the two consuls, and another to superintend the taking of the customs at the harbor of Ostia. Finally, when the provinces were classified and organ-

ized, each governor had a *questor* attached to his own household.

The duties of the *questors* were to take charge of the *ærarium,* or treasury; to receive all the money, and, on the authority of the Senate, to make all the disbursements from the treasury.

2. *Ædiles.* The duties of these officials were many and varied: to superintend the supply of provisions; to arrange the public games; to inspect the weights and measures; to inquire into the condition of baths, taverns, and eating houses; to prosecute those who had more than their share of the public land, and who allowed more than the legal number of cattle to graze in the public pastures—all these duties pertained to the jurisdiction of the *ædiles.* It was also owing to the activity of the *ædiles* that trade and commerce were carried on for the benefit of the ordinary citizen. Besides inspecting the weights and measures, the *ædiles* also looked after the markets, and prosecuted those who demanded more than the legal rate of interest, as well as those who hoarded their stock in order to raise arbitrarily the price of goods.

3. *Censors.* These officials made out the register of Roman citizens, and assessed the property of each one with a view to the imposition of the corresponding tribute or property tax. It was also the *censors* who farmed out the taxes, and gave out important contracts.

The administration of Roman finances was, generally speaking, highly beneficial. In spite of some mistakes and abuses, it led to the public and private prosperity of Rome. The erection of magnificent public buildings, even during Republican times, the construction of good military roads, the successful completion of many serious wars, are, in themselves, ample evidence of the efficient administration of Roman finances. In imperial times, we find that the financial administration contributed even more widely to the general prosperity of the community. Under Augustus the old-fashioned system of farming out taxes had been displaced in favor of the collection of the taxes by imperial officers. The appointment of a *Præfectus Annonæ*, in order to keep the Roman market supplied with cheap corn, and the institution of public servants to maintain the aqueducts and water pipes in good repair, and to keep down conflagrations, were of great benefit to the city of Rome. Nor were the means of communication between Rome and the other cities neglected. Under a class of officials called the *curatores viarum*, the roads were kept in constant repair. Even as early as the reign of Augustus, there was established a postage system, which consisted of relays of vehicles along the different roads. At first, the post was only intended for imperial messengers, but, under the Emperors Nero and Hadrian, it was extended and improved.

Another interesting and important feature was the care taken by the Roman government in providing for the poor. This was done in the first place by the corn laws of the Gracchi. By this law all the citizens of Rome were entitled every month to a certain measure of corn below the market price. A great deal has been said in condemnation of such a system, which eventually had the fatal effect of pauperizing the people. It must be remembered, however, that precisely the same plan was adopted in England during the Stuart period, and with signal success. What made such evil effects apparent in Rome was that no distinction was made between genuine and fictitious cases. Such a lamentable oversight, however, was remedied by Julius Cæsar, who appointed certain inspectors to investigate the merits of the applicants, the result being that the number shrank from three hundred and twenty thousand to one hundred and fifty thousand.

Another way was that of providing work for the unemployed. In this, also, Julius Cæsar was conspicuous for his practical sagacity and energy. The widening of the streets of Rome, the building of the Basilica Julia, the site of which cost four million dollars, the erection of the first public library, the draining of the Pontine marshes—all these works were undertaken not only for the sake of their intrinsic utility, but also for the sake of the unemployed. And, later, Roman emperors still followed the same policy by the repairing of roads and building of costly places of amusement.

Yet another way of providing for the poor was that of lending money without interest. Already in Cæsar's time, legislation had been made regarding the rate of interest on borrowed money. In the reign of Tiberius, no fewer than one hundred million sesterces were floated on a public loan. Any debtor might borrow from this fund for three years without interest, on giving to the State security for double that amount.

A fourth means was emigration and colonization. This was thought of even as early as the days of the Gracchi, but Julius Cæsar gave the idea definite and tangible shape. The colonies of Corinth and Carthage were both his creations, and perhaps still more practical was his plan of relieving the congestion of the city by removing whole groups of unemployed from thence into the country.

Finally, there was the education of poor children. Education in Rome was general, though not compulsory. It was carried on in two sets of schools, the advanced and the elementary. In the elementary schools the cost of attendance was very low, not more than four dollars a year. Yet, in addition to this, a special provision was made in imperial times for the education of children in Northern Italy.

Quite enough has been said to show the activity and the beneficent character of Roman financial administration in Republican and especially in imperial times. According to abundant evidence, the vast revenues of Rome were administered wisely and well. Trade and commerce were promoted and the tendency of financial legislation was to check fraud, to promote all branches of industry, and to benefit all classes of society.

We have now to consider the effect of the economic condition of Rome on her political history. In doing so we might conveniently pass in review the following important periods or crises: (*a*) the claims of the Plebeians, (*b*) the rise of the capitalists and the reforms of the Gracchi, (*c*) the Catilinarian Conspiracy, and the advent of Julius Cæsar.

CHAPTER V

INFLUENCE OF ECONOMICS ON ROMAN HISTORY

EVEN from the earliest times, there had been in Rome a class of people called clients. These were not really Roman citizens, since they had not the full privileges of such, being unable to vote at the assembly of the *curiata,* or to hold magisterial office. They lived with the families of the Roman citizens, and the fathers of these families stood to them in the position of patron. Between the clients and the patron to whom they belonged were close and intimate relations. The patron looked after his client's interests, especially in money matters and in making contracts, and also defended his client in the courts of justice. The client, on his part, was liable to such burdens as helping to pay the dowry of his patron's daughter, and to defray the ransom, if his patron or his patron's children were taken prisoners. He also had to share in certain other expenses of his patron, such as those entailed by the holding of offices having connection with the magistracy and the priesthood.

After a time, these clients became freed from any connection with their patron. This generally happened by the extinction of the patron's family. In such cases the position of the clients was most peculiar. Being already part of the State, they could not be turned out of Rome, yet, on the other hand, they had no legal position in the State, no organized religion of their own, and, at the same time, they were utterly unacquainted with the procedure of Roman law, under whose jurisdiction they still remained.

Such clients formed a distinct party by themselves and went by the name of *Plebeians*.

Soon the ranks of the Plebeians were augmented from other sources. During the reign of Tullius Hostilius a number of Latins were forcibly transplanted to Rome, while others, again, came to Rome of their own accord. All these, added to the freed clients, swelled considerably the number of the Plebeians.

Before long their number made it desirable that they should contribute their share toward the burdens of the State, and Servius Tullius, by his celebrated reforms, raised their status to the extent of incorporating them in the army, and enrolling them in the ranks of citizens liable to pay duty.

These things, however, were duties rather than privileges. They were still not fully citizens. They were excluded from all share in the State religion; they could not take the auspices, or perform the other sacred rites, which accompanied every important act of State; they could not perform the rite of marriage in a proper way and could, therefore, marry no Patrician. Even from the protection of the law they were almost completely debarred. The Plebeian might accumulate wealth, it is true, but, if he entered into dispute with a Patrician neighbor, the dispute would have to be decided in a Patrician court before Patrician magistrates, while the decision would be determined by a law of the terms of which he was absolutely ignorant.

Such was the condition of the Plebeian class. No matter whether the Plebeians had previously been clients, or whether they were strangers from another city, they all suffered from the same grievous disability. Not all the Plebeians, however, suffered in the same way. There were rich Plebeians, and there were poor Plebeians.

Those who were rich naturally pined and grasped for more political power; those who were poor thought only of procuring the necessities of life.

It is precisely here that the economic element intervened. It was the want of wealth that made the lower classes of the Plebeians discontented and turbulent, and that gave such fierce energy to the bitter strife between the Plebeians and the Patricians.

This economic element must be analyzed.

A careful examination will show that the cause of the misery of the Plebeians was twofold. First of all, their circumstances prevented them from coming into touch with capital, upon whose assistance labor absolutely depends.

By capital is meant, not merely money, but all the appliances that are necessary for a continuance of labor, such as food, lodging, implements of trade. It is true that many of the small Plebeians had little farms of their own, but the severe and constant wars in which Rome was engaged prevented them from engaging in rural occupations. Ever since the reforms of Servius Tullius that had made them a part of the Roman army, they had been continually called upon to fight the battles of their country. The results, as far as the individual himself was concerned, were often disastrous. After the battles were over, he would return to his farm only to find it deserted and neglected, and even in a state of ruin. If, indeed, he had been allowed to share with the Patricians in the spoils of victory, then there would have been some little capital to enable him at least to begin work. But, unfortunately, this was not so. He too often returned in a penniless condition, and was desperately driven in every direction to seek for capital.

His only resource was to borrow, and borrowing,

especially in the early days of Roman history, spelled ruin.
Until the Twelve Tables of the law were promulgated
no limit had been placed on the rate of interest, and so
unscrupulous were the Patrician money lenders that
often the debt would multiply itself threefold in the
course of two or three years. Solvency became impossible and the result was that the security or pledge had
to be forfeited.   In the great majority of cases, the
pledge was the debtor's own body, in which case the
debtor became the absolute property of the creditor.   It
is true that slavery was not the direct consequence of
punishment of insolvency, but that the debtor, when he
borrowed, went through a form of sale by which he sold
his body to the creditor, who agreed to abide by his share
of the contract until the money was paid back.   But the
distinction was purely legal.   In any case the debtor's
only resource was to borrow, and insolvency meant
slavery.

This was the first element of the economic discontent:
namely, the deprivation of capital, and even of the use
of one's own labor, owing to the constant wars and to
the severe laws of debt.

The second element of the economic discontent was
the land hunger of the Plebeians.   Some, it is true, had
small holdings of their own, but others had not.   Naturally those who were cut off from the land asked themselves the reason why, and the answer was far from
satisfactory.

Most of the wars waged by Rome were successful,
and most of them brought enormous accessions of territory.   Some of these, like the mines, could not be conveniently either sold or rented to any individuals; the
private profits would have been so enormous and so
manifestly unfair.   These were, therefore, retained and

worked by the State. But there were also vast tracts of land, either arable or pasture, or used for garden purposes. These, the State, as we have already explained, either distributed in small holdings among needy Plebeians, or rented out to rich capitalists. These last were not absolute owners, but only possessors of the land, and had to pay every year a certain rent.

Naturally there was a struggle between the poor Plebeians and the men of wealth as to whether the *ager publicus* should be distributed among the poor, or rented out to the rich. In the reign of Servius Tullius, this question was decided rather in favor of the Plebeians. Later on, Spurius Cassius tried to enforce and carry out the legislation of Tullius, but he met with an untimely death at the hands of the hostile Patricians. Altogether, as time went on, the poor Plebeians saw themselves more and more cut off from the land.

This deprivation of land was incidentally accompanied by another evil. This was an unjust incidence of taxation. For the capitalists, in so far as they were in possession of the *ager publicus,* were exempt from the burden of taxation. The result was that the burden became all the heavier, not only for those Plebeians that had no holdings, but even for those who had, since even these were subject to taxation.

The land question, however, was not peremptory in the early stages of the struggle between the Plebeians and the Patricians. The first immediate cause of the Plebeian agitation was their poverty and misery, engendered by want of capital.

Their discontent in 494 B.C. assumed tangible shape. After a successful campaign against the highland tribes near Rome, the Plebeians refused to return to their former state of misery. Taking up a position on the Mons

Sacer, a few miles from Rome, they declared their intention of setting up a separate City-State of their own. Their threat, if carried out, would have been unfortunate, both for themselves as well as for the Patricians, for the Plebeians were quite lacking in the experience of an organized government.

A compromise, however, was effected between the two orders. The Plebeians were allowed to choose two magistrates of their own, called tribunes of the people. If any Plebeian found himself unjustly molested by any Patrician magistrate, he could fly for protection to these tribunes, who, for this purpose, were to keep their doors open both day and night.

The tribunes thus became to the Plebeians living altars of refuge, and the immediate grievance under which the Plebeians had suffered was removed. Nor was the institution of the tribunate merely temporary. The inviolability of the tribune was secured by a special compact between the two orders, while a curse was invoked on all who violated the privilege and person of the tribune. Besides this strong wall of defense, there was yet another safeguard to the permanence of the tribunate, which was that the tribune could call together the assembly of the people. Such a power not only backed up the authority of the tribunes by the support of the Plebeians, but it also gave to the Plebeians themselves a unity and solidarity that they never enjoyed before.

Soon the tribunes acquired fresh powers, such as that secured to them by the laws of Publius Volero, allowing them to take action with the people. Then their freedom of action was still further guaranteed by a law that none should interfere with the tribune while transacting business with the people. Thus, even to attempt to interrupt a speech of the tribune was an offense. No doubt many a modern political orator would be glad of the same privileges that were accorded to the Roman tribunes. In not more than forty years after their institution the tribunes were allowed to be present at the meetings of the Senate, and, according to Dionysius, could even assemble the Senate in opposition to the consuls, in order to discuss the merits or demerits of any bill. Their power was finally and supremely established when the law of Hortensius allowed them to propose resolutions to the people that should be binding on the whole State, and also allowed any tribune to veto the proceedings of any other magistrate, even of the consul himself.

Such then was the full significance of the great Plebeian strike of 494 B.C. In satisfying the economic necessities of the moment the Plebeians had laid the foundation of economic power in Rome.

So far, however, there had been no agitation on the part of the Plebeians in the direction of more political power. They were still debarred from holding offices of State, and from taking any share in the government of the country.

It was the economic element that again caused an agitation among the Plebeians. Evidently the appointment of tribunes was only a partial remedy. It only protected the Plebeian from actual individual oppression at the hands of the Patrician, or from another Plebeian like himself. It did not bring the Plebeian closer to the capital upon which his labors and efforts depended.

This time it was the agrarian element of the economic discontent that attracted attention. The Plebeians had been debarred from their lawful share of the land. It is true that much of the public land was unsuited for let-

ting out in small allotments, but it was the general principle, that the land was for the Patricians alone, that
excited the anger of the lower classes. And this was
increased by the apparent tendency on the part of the
State not to insist too severely on the payment of Patrician rents.

In 487 B.C., therefore, after a campaign against the
Hernici, Spurius Cassius proposed that the land taken
from them should be divided among the poor Plebeians,
both Roman and Latin. Some such proposal had, as we
have said, been made in the time of Servius Tullius, but
this differed by the inclusion of the Latins among the
beneficiaries. No doubt, Cassius, who had successfully
arranged a league between the Romans and the Latins,
was naturally disposed to benefit the latter. But his
good intentions were bad policy. His liberality gave an
excuse to the Patricians to refuse his request, and even
to hound him to death, while it also partially deprived
him even of the support of the Plebeians.

Though Cassius thus failed in 487 B.C., yet, about
thirty years later, a concession was made to the people in
the matter of sharing the public land by the *Lex Icilia*
(456 B.C.). This law provided for the division of the
land on the Aventine Hill among the poor Plebeians.
Such a measure, however, was only extremely partial in
its effects. The people were still substantially cut off
from their birthright, and, in the later periods of Roman
history, we shall see that this was mainly responsible
for the downfall of the Roman Republic.

Incidentally, however, the proposed distribution of
land on the Aventine Hill led to the drawing up of a
written code of law, which was the germ of the Roman
system of jurisprudence, the most priceless inheritance
that Rome bequeathed to the civilized world. The con-

suls did not carry out the law providing for this distribution of land and it was their consequent impeachment
that led to the compromise by which the Patricians allowed a commission to be formed for the purpose of
framing a written code.

In the year 385 B.C., we find the question of debt and
poverty still pressing for a solution. The recent invasion
of the Gauls had caused a great deal of poverty and
hardship. Again were the needy Plebeians compelled
to borrow, and again were great numbers of them reduced to the condition of slavery. Livy relates how
Torquatus Manlius, the savior of his country, who had
defended the Capitol from the Gauls, was walking
through the Forum, and there saw a pale and haggard
old man, the veteran of many wars, being led off by his
creditor. Manlius came to the rescue. He paid the
debt and set the old man free. But he was not content
with this; he proceeded to denounce the Senators for
keeping in their possession the gold that had been taken
from the enemy. The results were fatal for him, and
for the cause that he was upholding. He was tried for
treason and condemned to death, while the treasure still
remained in the hands of the Patricians.

Yet another attempt, however, had been made to
alleviate the condition of the poor, not by any settled
change in the economic conditions, but by temporary
measures for relief. This was the action of Spurius
Mælius, who, in 440 B.C., sold corn to the citizens at an
exceptionally low rate. This, also, was denounced by
the upper classes. He was accused of exciting a revolution, a dictator was appointed, and his master of horse,
Ahala, slew Mælius in the open Forum.

During these years, however, the upper classes of the
Plebeians had been slowly attaining the object of their

desire, namely, the abolition of the social distinction between the orders of the Patricians and the Plebeians, and
the right to share in political power.   In 449 B.C. were
passed the Valerian Horatian laws, which made the
resolution of the Plebeians binding directly on themselves, and indirectly on the whole State.   In 445 B.C.,
the *Lex Canuleia* gave the Plebeians the right to contract a full and lawful marriage with the Patricians,
thus depriving the Patricians of all excuse for exclusive
usurpation of authority on the ground that the Plebeians
had not the secret of performing those sacred rites with
which were blended all the acts of State.   In 444 B.C.,
the Plebeians obtained the compromise by which in any
year, instead of the two consuls, there might be six military tribunes with consular power, among whom
Plebeians might be elected; and finally, in 421 B.C., the
important office of *questor* was thrown open to the
Plebeians.

Thus by rapid steps the Plebeians were mounting to
the highest offices of the State.   It is important, however, to bear in mind that in this progress there were
two distinct movements, one being the desire of the
lower Plebeians to remedy their economic condition, the other the ambition of wealthy Plebeians to
aspire to the highest offices of the State.   Occasionally,
as in the appointment of tribunes of the people, we
find the two movements, and, even afterwards, these two
movements must have considerably aided one another.

It was, however, at the passing of the Licinian
(367 B.C.) laws that we find the evident signs of the
active cooperation between the two classes of Plebeians.
On this occasion, the richer Plebeians openly allied
themselves with the poorer Plebeians with the express
purpose of obtaining their support.   The result was a

complete victory over protracted opposition and the presence in these laws of the two elements, the political and the economical.

There were four changes in all. Of these, two were of a political, and the others of an economic nature. The political clauses were: (1) the restoration of the consulship, with the provision that one at least of the consuls must be a Plebeian; (2) the admission of the Plebeians to one of the three great colleges of priests, namely, that of the keepers of the Sibylline books. Hitherto there had been two Patricians enjoying this charge; now ten were appointed, of whom five had to be Plebeians.

The economic clauses were: (1) a remission of debts to the extent that interest already paid should be deducted from the capital, and the rest paid off in three years by equal instalments; (2) that no citizen should hold more than five hundred acres of public domain, or pasture upon them more than one hundred oxen nor five hundred sheep. According to Appian, another clause also insisted that no landholder should employ more than a certain number of slave workmen, but this seems hardly probable, for, so far, no mention had been made of any agitation regarding the excessive use of slave labor.

Such were the provisions of the Licinian laws. The political clauses were the signal for the rapid admission of the Plebeians to all the offices of State, including the censorship and dictatorship. Thus, all political difference between the two orders had ceased. They now practically formed one political body.

The economic clauses absolutely gave to the poor Plebeians all that they had been striving after for so many years, and were an attempt to deal with the ever present problem of the prevalence of debt and of the distribution of public land.

Unfortunately, the alleviation of the distress caused by the burden of heavy debts was purely a temporary measure. It did not go to the root of the evil. There was no clear insight into the real economic difficulty of the times, which was that the poor Plebeian was cut off from land and capital. Moreover, the provision regarding the distribution of public land remained unheeded, and so, while the population was continually increasing, we find the estates of the rich growing bigger and bigger, and the bulk of the people becoming poorer and more discontented.

The economic agitations of the Plebeians, however, had vital results on the political fortunes of Rome. Without them, the amalgamation of the two orders would never have been completed, or at least it would have been deferred to a much later date. As the economic reforms of Solon inaugurated a new kind of aristocracy, so it was in ancient Rome. An aristocracy of office was substituted for that of birth, and as Athens presented to the world the purest type of Democracy so Rome was now to present to the world the spectacle of the most perfect Oligarchy that has ever been realized, a form of government that was Republican in appearance, but in which the reins of power were placed in the hands of a few families, who, by long experience and tradition, were the most competent to guide the ship of State.

CHAPTER VI

THE RISE OF THE CAPITALISTS AND THE FALL OF THE GRACCHI

ALL during the conflict between the Patricians and the Plebeians, Rome had been gradually extending her sway over the Italian peninsula. In this she was helped, partly by her own prowess, partly by good fortune. For at no time had Rome to face a universal hostile combination. She was always able to win over to her side, at least temporarily, one or more of the surrounding States.

By 265 B.C. the whole of the peninsula from the Sicilian straits to the north of Etruria was in possession of Rome. And the expedients adopted by Rome, in order to retain what she had won, were signally successful. By giving to the territories unequal rights, she produced mutual jealousy, but drew closer the bonds of attachment to herself, while, by military roads and colonies, she gradually extended over all her territory Roman civilization and Roman culture.

In 252 B.C. Rome even extended her sway over what is now the northern part of Italy. Liguria and Cis-Alpina were added to her possessions, and these, also, were secured by the same policy which was at once as strong as it was sagacious.

The war with Carthage became the signal for a career of foreign conquest. Corsica, Sardinia, Sicily, even Carthage itself, became Roman provinces. To these, also, were quickly added Spain, Macedonia, Greece, and a considerable portion of Asia Minor.

Meanwhile, after the laws of Sextus and Licinius

had been passed, the Roman constitution had been undergoing a rapid development. The old aristocracy of the Patricians had been swept away. Names that had been familiar in high places of trust no longer appeared. New names came to the front, some of them being names of Patrician, others of Plebeian families.

It was these who now monopolized the reins of government. While the sovereign power nominally rested with the people, who in their public assemblies had supreme authority, it was the Senate that actually carried on the administration. In the Senate sat all those who had held important offices in the State. Ex-consuls, ex-ædiles and other former officials occupied the benches of the Senate-house. The Senate was the one competent, the one experienced body of men in Rome.

Moreover, the very wars in which Rome was engaged tended to emphasize the growing importance of the Senate. The Senate alone was always on the spot, and could apply at once all the sagacity, power, wealth, and resources that Rome could command. While, therefore, the power of the people was nominal, the power of the Senate was real, and was accompanied by a glamour and a splendor that made the Roman Senate the object of world-wide respect and admiration.

There were, however, certain economic forces that were now working their way, and threatening to undermine the stability of these political elements.

The old economic questions regarding the misery of the poorer people, the prevalence of debt, and the unequal distribution of land had remained still unsolved.

In fact, the conquests of Rome and all the superabundance of wealth that she was now acquiring only accentuated these problems. The public wealth was indefinitely enlarged, but the number of small and prosperous peasant farmers was getting smaller also in indirect ratio. Enormous, indeed, was the wealth that now circulated through Roman society, but the circulation of such wealth was confined only to certain channels.

At this particular period only one section of Roman society was growing wealthier, and that was the *Equites* or Knights. Partly by the prohibition which prevented Senators from engaging in any extensive trade, partly owing to the lower classes being kept aloof from any lucrative contact with the commercial movements of the time, only the *Equites* were able to acquire enormous sums of wealth. They, alone, were the capitalists. Great landed estates may still have been in the hands of the Patricians, but all trade and all banking, and especially all financial undertakings connected with the government, were in the hands of the *Equites*.

Both the agrarian problem and the problem of unequal distribution of wealth came to the front during the agitation roused by the celebrated reforms of the Gracchi. There was also at the same time a political element, and nothing can be more instructive than to see how here, as in so many other cases, the political fortunes of Rome were determined more by the economic than by any other factor.

A brief survey, however, of the general movement started by the Gracchi will be necessary to remind us who the Gracchi were, what they proposed, and how far their measures were successful.

Tiberius and Caius Gracchus were, according to Plutarch, two brothers endowed with great natural gifts, which were still further developed by the care and skill of their mother, Cornelia. Alike in many virtues, in temperance, in fortitude, in liberality, and greatness of mind, they differed in such a way that one seemed to compensate for what was lacking in the other. Tiberius Gracchus in his outward deportment, in his voice and gestures, showed the calmness and even balance of his disposition. Caius Gracchus, by his vehemence of speech and force of gesture, betrayed the tumultuous rushing of the many thoughts that thronged into his mind.

Tiberius Gracchus was the first to enter the stormy arena of Roman politics. He attached himself to no particular party, but attempted, single-handed, to accomplish the reforms that seemed to him most important. He saw that the enormous estates, owned by single proprietors and worked by gangs of slaves, were doing irreparable damage to the commonwealth; that the free laborers were being driven from the country, and were fast gathering into the city of Rome, already sufficiently congested. He also perceived that the ranks of the unemployed and of the homeless were ever becoming greater. To him, therefore, the only feasible remedy that presented itself was to distribute more of the public land among the poor classes. The remedy was by no means new. Already by the Licinian laws it had been declared that no one should hold more than five hundred *jugera* of public land; but the law had been disregarded, and what he proposed was to enforce it anew.

He therefore tried to introduce a law that all the land held by private owners, above the legal amount, should be divided among the people. The proposal was just and reasonable, and was drawn up by persons eminent for wisdom and authority.

Unfortunately, however, something more was needed than a sense of justice and legal fitness. Both the Patricians and Knights were alike injured and offended. They were the organized parties in society. Unity, past experience, possession, both of office and of wealth, were at their command. They saw that their interests were vitally threatened. At once they joined their forces and proposed to crush the measures, and to defeat the intruder upon their long-established rights of prescription. To them, all that Tiberius Gracchus could oppose was the fickle allegiance of a short-sighted populace.

Gracchus, himself, lent them an instrument with which to accomplish his overthrow. This he did by trying to obtain the object by unconstitutional means. Octavius, his colleague in the tribunate, had thwarted the proposed reform by an obstinate veto. Tiberius, accordingly, proposed to the people that Octavius should be deposed from office. Such a proposal was distinctly revolutionary, for, according to Roman usage, no magistrate could be molested during his year of office. Octavius, however, was dragged from the rostra, the bill was passed, and thus, in addition to the Senators and Knights, a third party was organized in opposition to Tiberius, namely, the party of the Constitutionalists.

Tiberius then named a commission for the purpose of carrying out the distribution of land. Besides himself, the other two persons appointed were Caius Gracchus, his brother, and Appius Claudius, his father-in-law. Such a partial nomination was, under the circumstances, scarcely prudent. It gave to his reform the appearance of a movement dictated by motives of personal aggrandizement. The opposition gathered strength and became more and more turbulent. It was by violence that Tiberius had tried to accomplish his purpose, and, by a fitting retribution, it was by violence that he was defeated. On the day that he presented himself for re-election for the tribunate, a riot took place, in the course of which he lost his life.

Thus perished Tiberius. His unconstitutional behavior had had the effect of uniting still further the two orders of the Senators and of the *Equites,* and of making still more difficult the task of carrying out the law that had been passed by violent and illegal means.

But it was not likely that Caius Gracchus would submit tamely to the violent extinction of plans that were so dearly cherished, both by his brother and by himself. By a rapid series of movements, he soon displayed his real intentions. Violating established usage, he returned to Rome, although his term of questorship had not yet expired. He then struck at the opponents of the reform by proposing two laws, one which disqualified degraded magistrates from holding any magistracy—a law which was clearly aimed at Octavius—and the second law, which denounced the banishment of a citizen without trial, was aimed at Popilius, the pretor who had banished the friends of Tiberius. The first law failed to pass, but the second succeeded, with the result that Popilius thought it prudent to retire from Italy.

Having thus cleared the ground for action, Caius now brought forward a series of proposals. Some of these were economic in their nature, others were directly political. The economic reforms were of such a nature as to secure the popularity of the people, and of the *Equites* who, by means of them, would acquire great political as well as financial power.

The economic proposals were: (*a*) that the public land should be divided among the citizens; (*b*) that the citizens, every month, should receive a measure of corn for a sum of money below the market price; (*c*) that the soldiers should be clothed at the public expense, and that none should be forced to serve in the army who had not attained the full age of eighteen.

Evidently these proposals were likely to conciliate the good-will of the masses, and, what is especially to be noted, of the military element of the population.

It now remains to consider the clauses that were political in their nature. They were: (*a*) that the Knights only should sit as judges; (*b*) that all the Italians should share with the citizens of Rome in the right of voting.

If we compare carefully the economic with the political clauses, we shall find that both concurred to the same effect, namely, the alteration of the balance of power in the State. The practical power of the Senate would be reduced to a nullity, and the *Equites* would become supreme. Moreover, the interests of the Knights, as well as of the lower classes and of the Italians, would have been united against the Senate. Naturally, for the time being, Caius Gracchus became the most powerful man in Italy.

His economic administration was certainly most beneficial. In addition to the more equitable division of the land, he was also extremely anxious to find means that might lessen the congestion in the city and raise the economic condition of the people. Thus, amongst other things, he proposed that colonies should be established and that granaries should be built. He was also deeply interested in the construction of good roads. Indeed, the way in which the roads were paved, and, as far as possible, made level by bridges, and in which hollows were filled up, does great credit to the engineering skill of those times.

His political measures were not so uniformly worthy of praise. The clause that made the Knights holders of judicial power was especially disastrous. Hitherto, there had been, indeed, great abuses resulting from the partiality of the Senators as judges. Bribery or, as Cicero called it, "the itching palm," was only too frequent. In fact, collusion between the Senators and Knights enabled the latter to perpetrate almost any act of extortion. But matters became ten times worse when the Knights themselves became judges, and had the power to try accusations brought against members of their own order. True it is that Cicero commended this as working well, but we must also bear in mind his partiality to the *Equites,* of which he himself was a leader, while not overmuch confidence can be placed in the genuineness of the utterances of an advocate while arguing in a court of justice.

The clause that related to the Italian allies was certainly just and reasonable. So far, they, the Italian allies, had been in subjection to Rome, and had experienced all the burdens without the corresponding advantages of such subjection. As for the Latin allies, they were, as Appian remarks, blood relations of the Romans themselves, and as for the others, if they were called upon to pay taxes and to help fight the battles of Rome, it was only fair that they should also participate in some of the privileges of citizenship, especially that of voting.

The claim was certainly just when looked at from a general and far-reaching point of view, but its immediate effect was calculated to weaken and to irritate still further the Senate. It was inevitable that the allies should vote for whatever measures were proposed by Caius, and thus the Senate would have been placed still more helplessly under the heels of a man who was already their avowed enemy.

And there was also another element in the plans of Gracchus that had been either overlooked, or had been disregarded as not provocative of serious results. This was the natural hostility of the Roman citizens to the extension of the franchise. Nor was this hostility without some justification, when we remember that the enfranchisement of the Italian allies would have meant the undoing of the very nature of the Roman government, which was that of a City-State—especially as at that time there seemed to be no means of substituting anything in its place. For the allies could scarcely travel all the way to Rome from the distant parts of Italy in order to record their vote, and, on the other hand, representative government was then unknown.

A coalition between the Senate and the Roman citizens was speedily effected. The violence of the partizans of Gracchus hastened the reaction, and the result was a sanguinary riot in which Caius Gracchus was killed.

The attempted revolution of the Gracchi was, indeed, a failure from nearly all points of view. The enfranchisement of the Italian allies was still delayed. The Knights so grievously abused their new power that it had to be taken away from them, or at least partially reduced. Even the economic reforms also failed of their full effect. The great landed estates continually increased, the poor became poorer, and even more turbulent and seditious.

At the same time the revolution reveals like a powerful flash of light some of the many complex problems that were now facing Rome. It showed the presence of unseen forces that were gradually and completely altering the whole body politic of Rome, forces that in their very nature were economic, and were the very forces that had brought about the abolition of the distinction between Patrician and Plebeian, and which were now preparing the way for the closing act of the drama of the great Roman Republic.

We perceive more than ever that it was such burning questions as the division of land and the poverty of the masses that were continually shaping the destinies of the Roman people.   Alterations in the balance of political power, the rise and fall of political heroes, were but evanescent bubbles revealing the strong and ever-flowing current beneath.

CHAPTER VII

CONSPIRACY OF CATILINE, ASCENDENCY OF JULIUS CÆSAR, AND THE DOWNFALL OF THE REPUBLIC

THE failure of the reforms of the Gracchi allowed an unimpeded progress to the material forces that were fast undermining the whole structure of the Republican form of government. The people were still restless, owing to want of land and to their continual poverty; the vast estates still further increased, and, with the almost exclusive employment of slave labor, continued to drive away the free laborers, who added to the already congested population in the capital.

At the same time, in the political sphere, the evil results of what the Gracchi had succeeded in doing, and had failed to do, quickly became apparent. To the *Equites*, or Knights, had been confided the reins of judicial power, and this power they had grossly abused. So great was this abuse that Livius Drusus tried to apply a remedy by adding three hundred *Equites* to the Senate of three hundred, and by giving to the combined six hundred all judicial powers. The remedy, however, failed. Corruption still remained rampant. Then, what Gracchus had failed to do was also a festering worm in the commonwealth. The allies still clamored for the franchise, while many in Rome were in favor of it, but their demand was refused by the now powerful senatorial party. From this sprang the Marsic or Social War. Like all civil wars, the fight was extremely desperate, and at one time threatened the entire destruction of Rome, but in 89 B.C. the Italians were defeated by C. Pompeius Strabo. They were compelled to submit, but the object of the rebellion was gained, and the great majority of the Italians received the franchise and became full Roman citizens.

It was during the Social War that the power of Sulla began. His successes brought him to the front. Marius, his rival, was for a time successful, but was removed from the way by a natural death.

Then began the dictatorship of Sulla. He attempted to patch up the worn-out constitution of Rome. This he did by endeavoring to restore to the Senate its old prestige and important powers. He sought to infuse fresh blood into the Senate by the creation of three hundred new members, while he restored its dignity and prestige by transferring to it again its old judicial powers. On the other hand, he reduced the power of the rival elements of the Senate by the decree that the tribunes should not be eligible for any higher office, by the practical abolition of the censorship, and still more by the enactment that no man could be a magistrate and hold military office at the same time.

The general purport of all these legislative changes is perfectly clear, nor was he unmindful of the material means necessary for enforcing his ideas. The enfranchisement of ten thousand slaves gave him the use of a corresponding standing army that was always at his disposal, while throughout Italy the colonies that he assigned to his veterans were likely to crush any opposition coming from that quarter.

All the reforms of Sulla, however, were framed in perfect disregard of the important economic issues that were at stake. His constitutional fabric soon melted away like a castle of snow under the rays of the sun. Only the clauses of Sulla that effected the reforms of the law courts, and that rearranged certain magisterial functions, were allowed to remain.

By the time we come to the consulship of Cicero and the appearance of Julius Cæsar, we find ourselves face to face with a more definitely organized party in the State. This was the party of the Democrats. At first, their presence in the State was extremely shadowy and indefinite. It took time before they could assume a definite organization with a defined program and policy of action.

It contained, moreover, very heterogeneous elements. While on the one hand there were those who were content to wait until the expansion of ideas and force of circumstances should enforce the claims of the people, there was already a section of extremists who wanted a revolution immediately. Most of them were men of bankrupt means who had everything to gain and nothing to lose by a course of precipitate action.

This is curiously brought out by the Conspiracy of Catiline. This conspiracy, as Cicero clearly points out in his speeches, was concocted among fugitive rascals from different parts of the world, ruined spendthrifts and gamblers who marked out the citizens for slaughter, and the city itself for fire and pillage, while at the head of these was Catiline, who himself belonged to the Patrician order, but, owing to the persecution to which he had been subjected, was driven into the mistake of placing himself at the head of what was sure to turn out an abortive revolution.

Cæsar, on the other hand, was of quite a different temperament from that of Catiline. He was cautious and moderate. In the early stages of his career, he kept himself carefully in the background, and only by slow degrees engaged as the champion and leader of the

Democratic party. And yet Cæsar himself was implicated in the early proceedings of the Conspiracy of Catiline. The evidence given by Suetonius on this point seems fairly clear. Amongst other things, he quotes a fragment of one of Cicero's last letters which points to Cæsar as being implicated in the conspiracy, and it is also a very incriminating circumstance that, at the trial of the conspirators, it was Cæsar who proposed to substitute for capital punishment the milder punishment of imprisonment in the cities of Italy, from which, of course, they could be freed either by force or stratagem.

There is no doubt that Cæsar himself was at first cognizant of the desperate designs of Catiline, but the temporary coalition of the two men clearly indicates the temporary fusion of the moderate and the extreme revolutionary parties. It also incidentally shows how the policy of these two sections in the early stages considerably differed. Catiline's policy of force, at so early a stage, would have failed in one of the essential elements of the far-seeing policy of Cæsar—namely, the separation of the two orders of the Patricians and Plebeians. For any scheme of unusual confiscation would have menaced alike the interests of both Plebeian and Patrician.

Hence came the intense eagerness on the part of Cæsar to disassociate himself from such extreme partizans as the Catilinarian conspirators. Possibly he also saw already the importance of previously building up an organized military power with which to subject the military forces that were at the disposal of the Senate.

Anyhow it is interesting to notice how one of the factors of the revolution that was to terminate in the ascendency of Julius Cæsar was the economic element. The congested state of the city, the vast, unwieldy, and badly managed estates of rural Italy, the desperation of the poor free laborer, the recklessness of the debtors, ever increasing in number—it was these things that were gradually dissolving the old organism of oligarchic government in Italy. In all great revolutions, the driving force which hastens on events appears to reside chiefly in the turbulent discontent of the lower classes. Party leaders often tend to advance cautiously, but they are swept ahead by the blind, impassioned forces behind them.

Cæsar, however, did not, at the beginning of his career, rely upon the undisciplined masses of the people. He tried to gain time, and especially did he seek to isolate the Senate, that would have been the greatest obstacle to his plans. First he tried to isolate it from the Knights, who, as the capitalists, represented the financial power of the State. Their leader was the wealthy Crassus. Then, there was the army headed by the victorious general, Pompey, and finally there was the party of those who hoped to reorganize the State on constitutional lines.

Cæsar zealously made overtures to the leaders of these respective parties. The result was the formation of the celebrated triumvirate, consisting of Cæsar, Crassus, and Pompey.

By means of the triumvirate, Cæsar obtained what he wanted, namely, the consulship, while later on, by means of the same alliance, Cæsar also secured the extension of his proconsulship in Gaul for another five years. Such an extension of service was all-important. It enabled him to complete the conquest of Gaul, and to organize that military power which was to enable him finally to seize the reins of power.

At length, toward the end of the second term of Cæsar's proconsulship, the true natures of the forces that had been at work for years openly revealed themselves. Pompey, the old ally of Cæsar, became estranged from him; the senatorial and reactionist party looked to Pompey to prepare for a final struggle in order to retain their power, while Cæsar was now forced by the violence of his enemies at Rome to make the final bid for the supreme power, the possession of which, according to Mommsen, had been the object of his policy for years. At the head of his well-trained legions, Cæsar crossed the Rubicon, and with this act began the civil war which ended in making him supreme head of the State.

If we examine carefully the nature of Cæsar's work, we shall find that it was the final consummation of tendencies that had been working their way for generations. Poverty, discontent, bad distribution of wealth, hopeless misery, and a cry for a new system of government—all these had been inarticulate, or but feebly expressed, by such movements as those of the Gracchi. But now there had arrived the man for the epoch, the man who could make articulate the cry of centuries and could focus and guide all these material forces ever moving, but vainly groping their way.

We have already seen the nature of some of these forces. The early agitations of the poor Plebeians, the efforts of such reformers as Cassius, the Gracchi, and of Livius Drusus, revealed that the lower classes were suffering from a chronic condition of land hunger. We have also seen how industry had been depressed by the severe laws of debt and the want of any adequate bankruptcy law.

But there was another cause of disruption, one that, especially during the later years of the Roman Republic, had become prevalent. This cause was the alteration in the size and material structure of the Roman State.

From being a City-State, Rome had gradually developed into an empire. Her sway extended from Spain in the West to the rich lands of Asia Minor in the East. For weal or woe these possessions now formed her very self. And yet there was no form of government yet devised which could deal adequately with the needs of such widely distant lands. They were all practically at the mercy of the governors and tax-gatherers. The loss of their political independence might probably have been endured. Indeed, as a matter of fact, the local units of administration in the provinces enjoyed a great deal of local authority, some more, some less. What, perhaps, was the greatest cause of complaint was the lack of general uniformity, and the want of continuity of policy. The Roman governor administered the province very much according to his own fancy. There was no tradition of government in the province itself to bind him, and, if there had been such tradition in Rome, the distance was too great from the mother city to allow it to exercise any influence over him.

These complaints, however, were not of a very serious nature. But, when we come to the economic condition of the provinces, we find the case very different. The taxes which Rome levied on the provinces were not collected directly, but were farmed out to the publicans. These publicans, or tax-gatherers, were too often guilty of the greatest extortion. Possibly it is for this reason that in the New Testament the publicans are mentioned together with the sinners. How evil must have been their practices we can partly gather from a letter which Cicero wrote to his brother, who was governor of Asia. In this communication Cicero tells his brother that if he yields to the publicans, the consequence will be the utter ruin of those whose safety and interests it is his duty to guard. Cicero's own experience, when governor of Cilicia, confirms the same thing. Thus, he found that certain communities were in arrears with the tax-gatherers. A delay had been granted, but only on condition of the payment of exorbitant interest. It is no wonder that the tax-gatherer became an object of scorn and irritant hatred.

Besides the exactions of the publicans, there were also the financial burdens imposed upon the provinces by the Roman governor. This official had almost unlimited chances of gratifying his rapacity. As in the case of Appius, he could force the provincials to pay large sums of money under threat of quartering his troops upon them. But even leaving aside these violent means of extracting money, the ordinary legal allowances were a considerable drain upon the resources of the provincials. For example, there was the considerable quantity of corn that the Roman governor might requisition every year for his own consumption. Generally, this far exceeded the required amount, and the governor would then make profit by commuting the supply of corn for a sum of money.

Altogether the provinces, what between the exactions of the publicans and those of the bad governors, of whom there were plenty, were in a chronic state of economic discontent, nor did there seem to be any redress for their grievances. The governor, during his term, was in practical possession of unchecked jurisdiction, and at the end of his term of office it was rarely, indeed, that he could be brought to account for his evil doings.

When Cæsar, therefore, crossed the Rubicon, he found his presence demanded not only in Italy itself, but also in the provinces. To the lamentations of the poorer Romans was also added a yet inarticulate claim of the oppressed provincials.

Such was the condition of Italy and of the provinces, and Cæsar himself had already recognized that condition. During his sojourn in Gaul he had been able to take a calm and collected view of the condition of the empire as a whole. It was thus that he succeeded in drawing to a focus all the burning questions of the time, and that in his policy he showed wideness and thoroughness of view.

He saw that the old elements of the political constitution of Rome were beyond repair, and he saw that the only available substitute was a strong central government. He did, indeed, make use of the old Republican institutions, but he subordinated them all to his own authority. By altering the oligarchic tone of the Senate and by concentrating within himself the powers of the highest Roman magistracies he sought to introduce his own supreme rule under the veil of old forms and names. Greater success might have attended his efforts had the veil been less transparent. His assumption of the outward signs of royalty, such as the statue that he had erected to himself among the seven kings, and the head stamped on the new coinage, completely alienated from his side all who were in any way attached to the old traditions.

Far greater success attended his economic reforms. While his successors were obliged to go back to some extent upon his political ideas, they found that their main chance of keeping themselves in power and giving continuance to the empire was to carry out his various economic reforms.

Cæsar had already perceived that the greatest evils

under which Rome was groaning were the old harshness
of the laws of debt, the bad distribution of land, and the
ascendency of the capitalist class that was draining all
the resources of the land. To these evils he now tried
to apply a remedy.

With regard to the question of debt, he brought in
for the first time a law of bankruptcy. All liability to
personal bondage was removed, and the debtor was allowed a discharge on condition of his making over to
his creditor his property assessed at a reasonable valuation. Also, the interest that had been paid was to be
deducted from the capital sum. This compromise was
intended to give a chance to the debtor of rising from
poverty and desperation, and to the creditor a satisfaction of his claims, which, though perhaps not fully adequate, was better than none at all.

He then grappled with the agrarian problem. The
great landed estates had been in the possession of a few,
and these estates had been worked principally by slaves
to the great detriment of free labor. It was to Rome
that flocked all the flotsam and jetsam of humanity unable to get honest work in the country, and they were
now loafing about the streets of the city. It was, therefore, Cæsar's intention to place the land once more within the reach of the lower classes. In pursuance of this
he distributed large allotments of land, insisted that all
estates must employ a certain number of free laborers,
and passed a law that the capitalist should invest part
of his capital in agricultural industries.

This last provision also gives us a clue to Cæsar's
policy in respect to the capitalist. Congestion of capital
in a few hands is one of the worst possible evils. It
means that labor and productiveness are brought to a
standstill. Legislation, however, was necessary in order

to release some of the capital that lay in the hands of the capitalists. The discouragement of usury, the imposition of customs duties on foreign-made goods, thereby compelling the wealthy to pay to the State part of this wealth, and the necessity of paying wages to the free laborers on the landed estates were the means he adopted for this purpose.

While Cæsar thus tried to reduce the condition of the capitalist, he tried to relieve the squalid misery of the poor. Direct relief was still resorted to, but in a more sagacious way than before. The method of the Gracchi had been distribution without any discrimination. The result had been disastrous. Many thousands of idle and shiftless persons preferred to feed on the State rather than to work. Cæsar now established investigators, or inspectors, who were to inquire into the real condition of the applicants. So successful was this measure that the number of applicants for relief dwindled from three hundred thousand to one hundred and fifty thousand. This reduction meant that one hundred and fifty thousand idle persons now began to work and to contribute to the general wealth.

At the same time, Cæsar tried to lessen the congested population by transplanting eighty thousand citizens into the provinces, and founding such colonies as Corinth and Carthage. Unfortunately, however, his untimely death prevented him from witnessing the completion of this part of his reforms.

For those who remained at home, employment was found of such a nature as to contribute to the commercial prosperity and the magnificence of the State. One great barrier to internal communication had been the bad condition of the main crossroads leading north and south. This was remedied by repairing the old roads and constructing a new thoroughfare over the Apennines. Other important undertakings were the widening of the streets of Rome, and the construction of such buildings as the Basilica Julia in the Forum, and certain reconstructions in the Forum itself.

We must now consider the way in which Cæsar dealt with the urgent problem of provincial administration. It must be remembered that by curtailing the wealth of the capitalists he had already accomplished a great deal. It was chiefly the capitalists, who, like vampires, had fed on the wealth and the very life-blood of the provincials. It was they who had greedily gathered up all that had been produced by the hard labor of the provincials; and so, by curtailing their ill-gathered gains, by preventing them from having anything to do with the colonies except by themselves becoming permanent settlers, Cæsar struck at the very root of the evil of provincial administration.

From henceforth there were to be no more tyrannical, independent governors, no more rapacious tax-collectors. A new system was now inaugurated by which the taxes were gradually adapted to the relative financial strength of the provincials, and were no longer diverted from their proper channels.

It was this wholesome policy that, perhaps even more than anything else, contributed to the durability of the empire founded by Cæsar. The provinces were under the immediate control and supervision of the emperor. Whatever governors were sent out were mostly his legatees, absolutely responsible to the emperor. Indeed the government of the provinces had now become almost paternal. Of this we find ample proof in the correspondence in after years between the Emperor Trajan and Pliny, who was his legate in Bithynia.

Such, then, was the nature of the work accomplished by Julius Cæsar. Under him were redressed the economic troubles of ages, under him was remodeled the whole material structure of the empire, and under him was inaugurated that material prosperity upon which was founded that political empire that was destined to last for five centuries.

Future emperors only carried on and still further developed the structure, whose cornerstone had been laid by Cæsar. And even the crimes and misgovernment of such men as Nero and Caligula were more than balanced by the material prosperity of the empire as a whole, and by the affection of the distant provinces.

The downfall of the Roman Empire in the fourth and fifth centuries was mainly owing to the intervention of another element, namely, the element of religion, which is sometimes stronger than that of economics.

PART II
MEDIEVAL PERIOD

INTRODUCTION

UNDER the sway of the Roman emperors, the empire had been growing rapidly, both in extension and also in unity and strength. From the white shores of Britain to the sands of Sahara, the Roman flag floated peacefully and powerfully. Everywhere, throughout the empire, there flourished the old municipal institutions of ancient Rome; everywhere could be seen broad and well-constructed roads that, like arteries, connected the most distant parts of the empire.

Even more conspicuous was the internal unity that was imparted by the common diffusion of all that went to make up the religious, the intellectual, and the social life of man. The Roman religion had penetrated into all parts, and in every town the altar to the divine Cæsar had become an active symbol of unity. Even in remote provinces, the little children in the elementary schools were trained to the use of the Latin tongue, and in all the cities the public baths, the theaters, and other buildings of a like character, everything testified to the common social life and common tastes of a now united people.

By the third century Europe had been brought together in a way which had never been seen before nor has it been seen since. But almost as soon as she had attained to the very fulness of her development the empire began to show signs of disruption. Certain signs made it only too evident that the emperor was no longer able to maintain his supreme authority over such wide dominions. In fact, they were fast slipping from his grasp. Vainly did Diocletian and Constantine try to maintain the unity of the empire by instituting a hierarchy of officials amongst whom they distributed the administration of different departments and provinces. Such remedies only had the effect of hastening the end that they were intended to prevent.

Nor was this all. The very same economic disruptive tendencies that had continually menaced the Roman Republic now began to threaten the later empire. Old problems, such as the agrarian problem, the destruction of the fairly well-to-do middle class, and the burdens of onerous taxes, badly collected, again made their appearance.

It was this that caused the big estates gradually to absorb the smaller ones. In order to escape the burdens of taxation many of the small peasant holders gladly sold their holdings to some richer neighbors, still, however, retaining their possession but tilling the land for the benefit of the new owner.

We find, also, that the fairly well-to-do middle class was also fast decaying. This was partly owing to the heavy taxes which fell chiefly upon the middle class and partly owing to the abolition of freedom of trade and industry. Members of such trade associations as those of bakers, builders, and plumbers were forced to remain in their associations so that they should not evade taxation. Even the unskilled forms of labor were subject to the same treatment, with the result that all productive enterprises were suppressed and the very arms and sinews of industry were literally manacled in the fetters of slavery.

Besides these economic causes of decay, there must also be taken into account the disruptive nature of such agents as immorality and irreligion. Luxury and debauchery became rampant and slew their hecatombs of victims. The very life-blood of the nation was gradually oozing away, not in the field of battle, but in the pleasures that destroy nations. Even the faith in their own gods had decayed. To believe in something above this material world is better than to believe in nothing at all. With the spread of absolute infidelity, all moral checks were removed, while with the decay of the worship paid to the emperor there was also severed one of the ties that had bound together the scattered parts of the empire.

The empire thus, already on the verge of decay, quickly fell before the myriads of the barbarians in the fifth century. The different tribes of the Visigoths, Ostrogoths, Franks, and Burgundians, like some great wave, swept upon them.

The political structure of the empire in Western Europe was indeed undone and dismantled, but it was not altogether destroyed. Roman law still remained and was respected in all its majesty. Roman traditions also still lingered, especially the tradition of municipal institutions, a most valuable legacy, which was to prepare the way for the prosperous towns of the Middle Ages. Yet another fragment of the Roman Empire survived in the person of the Eastern emperor at Constantinople. For, even legally, he was emperor of the West as well as of the East. The division made between the Western and the Eastern empire by Diocletian was not intended to divide the *imperium,* and so, in reality, the emperor of Constantinople was the outward symbol of the unity of the whole empire, while, as we shall afterwards see, Byzantine influences had a great share in determining the political and economic destinies of Europe.

The process, however, of the blending of the Teutonic and Roman elements was long and much entangled.

While it is quite certain that both of these elements are to be found in after-European civilization, it is uncertain which of the two elements predominates, and in many cases, owing to the elemental discord and confusion of the early Middle Ages, it is exceedingly difficult to trace the different steps of the process.

While, however, objects begin to appear with distinct shape, one can clearly discern certain influences at work, some of them making for centralization, others tending toward decentralization.

The memory of the Roman Empire, the influence of the Papacy and of the Christian Church, and the foundation of the great Frankish monarchy, covering France and Germany, tended to bring Europe together. In fact, the Carolingian Empire seemed, at one time, to be acquiring almost the same extension as that which had been enjoyed by the empire of the pagan Cæsars. In the Holy Roman Empire the unitive force of the temporal ruler was joined to that of the spiritual ruler, and these different centralizing influences, being fused into one, were thus rendered powerful with a double force.

On the other hand, there were forces of a more decentralizing character, forces whose activity exercised itself rather in small local units of area. These influences were mainly economic. The relations between the serf and his master, and the industrial and municipal activities of the towns, tended rather in the direction of decentralization.

And yet, there was harmony between the centripetal and centrifugal tendencies. They were both necessary from the development of modern Europe. If we wish to illustrate by way of comparison we might think of the construction of a living body in which the different cells and tissues come into existence one by one, each gradually receiving its own shape and function, while at the same time all are gradually acted upon and endowed with one common purpose of action by the ruling principle of life.

Such then is the relation between the economic and the political element in the early formation of Europe. We must now consider a little more closely the different economic activities that especially distinguish the early Middle Ages. These may be distinguished under the following headings: (*a*) the feudal system; (*b*) the towns; (*c*) the guilds and crafts; (*d*) the industries and general production of wealth; (*e*) the distribution of wealth.

After these have been studied in detail, it will be easier to see how the economic element molded the political destinies of Europe during the Middle Ages.

CHAPTER I

THE FEUDAL SYSTEM

FEUDALISM is a system in which political power is connected with the holding of land. A man, that is to say, enjoys so much administrative and political power because he happens to have just so much land, and the more extensive the land he holds, so much more extensive becomes his political jurisdiction.

It will be helpful to our present purpose if we analyze feudalism into its essential elements. These are: (*a*) the real element; (*b*) the personal element; (*c*) immunity, which is the result of the combination of the real and personal elements.

a. The real element. This is sometimes called the benefice, and consisted of a piece of land rented by one man to another in return for the fulfilment of certain conditions. The most common and the most essential condition was the granting of military service, or the agreement to accompany the landlord to the field of battle for a certain definite time. Military service, however, was not the only condition. It often existed in combination with others of a financial nature. Thus, the tenant had to pay a sum of money when his eldest son was going to be knighted and his eldest daughter married. Other financial burdens laid upon the tenant were the relief, or a sum of money paid by the heir coming into possession of the estate, and the fine upon alienation, which was the sum of money that had to be paid if the tenant sold or gave his fief to another.

So far, the land contract between the landlord and tenant seems to be of the same essence as in our modern

system. Certainly, the rent was of a more varied nature, and could be discharged in kind as well as in money,
but that does not affect the nature of the contract between
the landlord and tenant. There were, however, two other
conditions annexed to the renting of the land that show
we are no longer dealing with a mere contract of rent.
These conditions were that the landlord had the guar-
dianship of a minor heir of his tenant, and that he had
the right to dispose of his female ward in marriage.

Evidently these two powers of the feudal landlord
show that he was something else besides a mere landlord, and this brings us to the second element.

b. The personal element, or fealty. In feudalism the
tenant became the vassal of his landlord. He became
bound to his landlord by peculiar personal obligations,
and, as the outward sign of this, the would-be tenant
had to swear fealty to his future lord, who in his turn
formally invested his tenant with his fief. Personal ties
were thus created between the lord and his tenant such
as are to be found nowhere in our modern times. Such
ties remind one of the connection between the old
Roman Patrician and his client. They were, however,
of a somewhat different nature and were much more
definite. The lord had to protect his vassal on all occasions, and, as times went on, this protection was carefully explained and set forth in detail. The tenant, on
his part, had to be faithful to his lord, especially in time
of war.

It was not long after that there sprang, from the
union of the real and personal elements, a third element.

c. Immunity. By immunity is meant that the landlord enjoyed political and judicial jurisdiction over his
tenant. In other words, the benefice was immune from
any jurisdiction outside that of the lord. The lord, ex-

cept in England, could frame laws and statutes for his tenants, and could give or refuse consent to the promulgation within his domain of the king's law. He also enjoyed civil and criminal jurisdiction, and in this court could even pass sentence of death. It is important to note, however, that in practice this power was protected from arbitrary misuse by certain well-defined forms of procedure to which the lord was supposed to adhere faithfully.

Having considered very briefly the nature of feudalism, and its constitutional elements, we must now consider feudalism more closely in its economic bearings. We shall thus see more in detail the importance of the economic element in medieval history.

The feudal system, both in its nature and in its origin, was economic. The very keystone was the possession of wealth in the form of land. As in Solon's time the possession of so many measures of wheat meant precisely so much social and political status, so in feudal times it was the land that conferred position and dignity.

Also the origin of feudalism was economic. It was to safeguard whatever wealth they had that the holders of small property commended themselves as vassals to the protection of some one more powerful than themselves. When the Danes were sweeping over the whole of Europe, the poor villagers were only too glad to huddle for protection around the walls of the medieval castle of their overlord. And, conversely, it was the financial necessities of the lord that made him only too glad to accept the services of his vassal, who would pay rent and work his land for him.

And this system, so essentially economic, affected the very heart of medieval society. It affected the whole condition of Europe from the administrative, political, financial, and military side; it also affected the social element by creating the classes and the caste systems of medieval society, and finally, even from the ecclesiastical point of view, it had, as we shall see, an enormous influence, both for good and evil.

From the administrative point of view, feudalism tended to diminish the central authority of the king, and substitute for it the local authority of the magistrate and powerful baron. According to the old law, neither the king could put a bar on the baron's land, nor could the baron put a bar on the king's land. It seemed as though government were being carried on by the different powerful vassals on some cooperative scheme. For, as we have already said, the king could not promulgate any law within his vassal's domain without the vassal's consent.

This tendency to independence on the part of the political element, so intimately bound up with the local territorial units, resulted in greatly retarding the growth of royal power in France and Germany. In France, it was only by the time of Louis XI that the authority of the Crown began really to assert itself over that of the nobles, while in Germany, feudalism put off the unification of the country until the time of Bismarck.

In England, however, we find an exception. William the Conqueror saw how detrimental to the Crown had been the decentralizing forces of the Continental feudalism. He was determined, therefore, from the very beginning to curb by constitutional means this dangerous power and to crush the rivalry on the part of the feudal barons. This he did most effectually by insisting that all, even the smallest landowners, should take an oath of allegiance and fealty directly to himself. This was in striking contrast to the prevailing practice on the Continent, where the minor vassals took the oath only to their immediate lord.   Hence the king could only call on the lesser vassals indirectly through the willing cooperation of the greater barons, while in England the lesser vassals were placed in direct subordination to the king, and thus the power of the barons was checked, even from the very beginning.

On the Continent, however, were certain forces that were opposed to the decentralizing tendencies of the forceful vassals, and first among them was the overshadowing authority of the king as such.   This authority was different from that which he exercised in his own domain.   It extended over the whole kingdom, though its precise nature would be hard to determine.   Then there were held certain congresses and especially the councils of the Church.   In these meetings a common plan of action was often determined upon, which saved the country from foreign invasion and from constant internal anarchy.

On the whole, however, the great tendency of feudalism was toward decentralizing all political activity and to delaying the formation of centralized monarchies.

Judicially, also, the feudal element exercised a very decentralizing influence.   Thus, in France, as late as 1363, we find the king admitting that his own court, namely, the court at Paris, had jurisdiction only over four kinds of cases, namely, those involving the peers of France, prelates, chapters of the royal domain, and appeals from royal officials.   Outside these four classes, the lord had, over his own domain, jurisdiction, both civil and criminal.

Only in England did this decentralizing influence of feudalism have no effect on the political system.   William the Conqueror, in order to lessen the power of the feudal barons, took away from them nearly all political power.

This he still left in the possession of such local courts as the shire and hundred, while in after years the circuit courts and the king's supreme courts monopolized all the important powers.

Feudalism, however, affected law in other ways, besides tending to decentralize its administration. The principle of primogeniture, by which the oldest son succeeded to the estate, and the principle of entail, by which an estate is tied down in perpetuity only to a certain class of heirs, are the result of feudalism. Moreover, the fundamental distinction between real and personal property, and the peculiar legal treatment of the former, are owing to the same feudal influence. Even the peculiar condition of our modern will may be traced to the same cause. For it was feudal primogeniture that first did away with the notion that the property of the deceased had to be distributed according to the shares prescribed by Roman law.

We must now consider the influence of feudalism on its financial side.

The different financial burdens incurred by the feudal tenant have already been enumerated. Taken altogether, they must have amounted to a considerable sum, especially on the larger estates. Now, the king was the largest landowner in the kingdom, and the feudal revenues that he derived from it must have been correspondingly great. In fact, they constituted both the king's own private fortune, and also the fund with which he was enabled to carry on the work of administration.

In early medieval times, therefore, the feudal revenues of the king took the place of any general system of taxation. Indeed, it was only after a long struggle that monarchical taxation succeeded in supplanting the feudal revenues. Only about the time of the twelfth century, chiefly on account of the needs of the Crusades, did the king succeed in levying any general tax extending outside his own domain. In France, the struggle was exceptionally severe. Only indirectly did the king succeed in establishing a central system of taxation, acquiring one by one the outlying provinces, and then disposing of them as his own personal estates.

Yet here, also, we find an exceptional anomaly in England. Besides the ordinary aids for marrying the king's oldest daughter, knighting his oldest son, and ransoming the king's person when taken prisoner, there were also extraordinary aids, which were levied only for extraordinary purposes. It was these extraordinary aids that developed in the course of time into a system of regular taxation. Thus, so far from there being a continued conflict in England between the feudal financial system and a uniform system of taxation, we find that the former gradually and harmoniously led up to the latter.

THE MILITARY ELEMENT OF SOCIETY

This also was profoundly affected by feudalism. There were no professional standing armies. Instead, there were the feudal levies. Each baron had around him his own personal retainers sworn to do him feudal service, while the king also could command the military service of the vassals on his own domain. But on the Continent the king could call upon the subjects of his barons only indirectly, by appealing to the barons. Naturally this was often disastrous for the welfare of the nation, and it opposed a strong material obstacle to the extension of the royal authority.

On the Continent this lasted for ages, but in England the strong policy of the kings quickly put down the military power of the barons. During the dispute between Stephen and Matilda for the possession of the throne, the castles of the barons were, it is true, a source of oppression, cruelty, and anarchy. But under King Henry II, many of the strong castles were razed to the ground, and for many years after his time the barons, so far from being centers of discord, rather posed as the champions of the people's rights, and of a system of well organized government.

In Europe, however, the military power of the nobles ever exercised a strong decentralizing influence. In Germany and Italy they postponed the unification of the State until the nineteenth century, while in France it took the king many years of patient toil and diplomacy in order to subdue the turbulent barons of the South.

Socially, the influence of feudalism was all-powerful. It caused the division of society into castes, one rising above the other. There were the upper classes and the lower classes, the former consisting of the nobility and clergy, and the latter consisting of the serfs and *villeins.** Even this distinction was thoroughly economic. It rose entirely from the land. Thus, the possession of certain estates gave to the owners certain distinct privileges, the possession of certain portions of land would render their owners villeins, while again other portions of land would reduce their owners to the condition of serfs.

Continental Europe was thus divided by feudalism into horizontal sections. The main divisions were between the upper and lower strata of society, not between nations. Indeed, there was far more intercourse and

*A villein was just one step above a serf. Though he was not bound to perform certain services, such as plowing and harvesting, yet he was tied down to the soil.

good fellowship between an English knight and a French knight than between an English knight and an English peasant. Hence, it is easy to see how this influence of feudalism must also have affected the main currents of European politics. It tended to broaden the area of the different struggles and agitations, and thus we are enabled better to understand how such movements as the struggle between the empire and the Papacy, and the Crusades, were able to draw into their vortex such enormous areas of territory.

Finally, the influence of feudalism made itself felt also in the Church. When Europe was threatened both by the Danes and by internal anarchy, many of the prelates, following the general example, commended themselves and their possessions to the protection of some powerful lord. Relations, essentially feudal, were established between them, only that the conditions of tenure were different. Yet, even by ecclesiastics, military service was often granted in spite of the prohibitions of Popes, many of the bishops insisting on putting on armor and appearing on the field of battle.

The Church thereby gained the advantage of protection, but it lost in other ways. Bishops and prelates often became mere feudal magnates. While holding the spiritual care of souls, they were also in possession of land with certain obligations attached, and with the necessity of performing certain personal obligations toward their lay lords.

It was this economic element entering into the Church that caused so many abuses in the time of Hildebrand. Many of the clergy married in order to perpetuate the estates in their families, and only too frequently, as we have already said, they sank into the position of purely feudal magistrates. Indeed, centuries elapsed before the

Church could entirely free herself from the worldly element that had then entered into her constitution.

It was the same cause that brought about the investiture contest between empire and Papacy. While the temporal ruler maintained that the prelate was a feudal magistrate, and, therefore, should be invested by him with the ring and crozier, the Pope, on the other hand, maintained that this was his right, since the prelate, having the care of souls, was subordinate to his jurisdiction.

Such were the main influences of feudalism on medieval society. Almost every single branch of human activity was dominated by the feudal element, and it seems almost incredible that such a simple thing as the holding of land should have had such an abiding influence on society and on the welfare of each and every individual.

CHAPTER II

THE TOWNS

In the history of ancient Greece and Rome the town or city had ever played a most important part. In fact, the men of those times could not conceive a State that was not identical with the city. Hence, the whole political interest of the ancient and classic periods of history centers around what is significantly called the City-State.

Also in medieval times the city or town was destined to play a very important part. No longer, however, did the towns, like isolated cells, live apart from one another, each revolving in the sphere of its own activity. They now began to form the tissue of a greater whole. Nor on this account was their importance diminished. For the medieval towns were a most essential factor in the formation of modern Europe, and it was through them that the economic influence of trade and commerce exerted itself on the power of monarchs and nobles, and in the direction of a limited and constitutional central government.

The word "town" means a wall, and the medieval meaning attached to the word is that of a group of persons who live together and are surrounded, for the sake of protection, by a wall. Some of the medieval towns were formed by the spontaneous action of the townspeople themselves; others were formed by the deliberate will of powerful princes. Thus, for example, one of the devices of Henry the Fowler for settling a country and protecting it from foreign invasion was that of building walled towns.

Soon these towns began to thrive and grow prosperous. It was not possible for a number of people to live close together without some emulation, or rather, without some cooperation and division of labor. The results showed themselves in greater production, while the towns soon became centers of commercial activity. Hitherto the village community had been the center; now it was the larger area of the town; and this, again, was destined to lead up to the still wider area of the State.

The inhabitants of the towns, however, soon found themselves impeded in their commercial activities by their subjection to the lord or bishop under whose jurisdiction they happened to reside. Soon, therefore, an effort was made on the part of the town to obtain its release from arbitrary jurisdiction and arbitrary financial burdens. All over Europe, during the tenth, eleventh, and twelfth centuries, there was going on an increasing conflict on the part of the towns to obtain this recognition of their independence as separate communes. Partly by bargaining, partly by force, the towns slowly gained the victory. The freedom that they obtained might have been greater in some cases than in others, but the general effect was to emancipate the towns from the hampering fetters of feudalism.

In order to see more in detail the influence of the towns on the political destinies of Europe, it will be helpful to consider the rise of the towns in the different countries that were at that time of growing importance. Such a brief survey will show in clearer outline how the power of the economic element acted on politics through the leverage of the towns.

In France, by the time of Louis VI, many towns had already obtained their charter of independence, and already it came to be seen that the towns were centers of refuge against the oppression of feudal magnates. Conspicuous among these towns were Noyon, Laon, and Amiens; while, besides these, must also be reckoned the towns on the royal domain.

All during the reigns of Louis VI, Louis VII, and Philip Augustus, the process of emancipation continued. The movement began in the northern parts of France, and from there spread also to the villages and towns under ecclesiastical control. The kings themselves found it useful to form an alliance with the towns as a counterpoise to the power of the feudal barons. It was the king who gave them protection against any oppression, each town obtaining a royal officer for that purpose; and already by the time of Louis VI we find the French king so far asserting his influence as to claim suzerainty over all the chartered towns. Philip Augustus, while repressing the revolutionary tendencies of the communes, boldly proclaimed himself their patron and champion. By superintending their material means of defense, and by encouraging their industries, he considerably hastened the communal movement. Most significant is a certain clause in one of the charters which declares that, "if any stranger commits a wrong on the inhabitants of the towns, the majority of the people shall destroy the house of the offender, but if the offender shall be a king's vassal, then he shall not be allowed to enter the town until he has done amends."

Such towns had great privileges. They were allowed to hold common property, to use the common seal of the corporation, and to let their children marry without the payment of any fine for obtaining the lord's permission. With the exception of the payment of a definite and limited rent, they were no longer bound down to their

lord, and were not even obliged to help him in times of
war. Internal freedom was also secured to them by
their exemption from the jurisdiction of royal and
territorial judges, and freedom to elect their own
magistrates.

The French towns were thus pledged to the support
of the throne by the strongest of ties, namely, that of
self-interest. While the king, on his side, lent them the
aid of his central authority against the aggressions of
the barons, the towns, on their side, became so many
different centers for expanding the royal influence
throughout the kingdom.

In Germany, the growth of towns began early but
was not so rapid as that of the French towns. Some of
them originally depended upon the emperor, others
were in the hands of the dukes, counts, and other members
of the German aristocracy. Worms and Cologne
were the first to receive recognition by the imperial enfranchisement
of the inferior artisans. Under Frederick,
there were elected councils of citizens who, at
first, were merely the assistants to the imperial vicar or
bailiff. But during the period of the decline of the
House of Hohenstauffen not only did the townsmen
frequently succeed in expelling the bailiff, but they also
set up an autonomous government of their own. Finally
by the time of Rudolf of Hapsburg, in 1291, the towns
had secured a place in the Imperial Diet, and were thus
placed on a footing superior even to that of the knights.

The power and opulence of many of the German
towns became afterwards closely connected with the rise
of Venice and the great trade routes from the East.
Venice was the converging center of the trade routes
from the East, and it was from Venice that the merchandise
was carried up the waters of the Rhine, enriching

the towns upon its banks.   In fact, in the political disintegration of Germany, the towns occupied as strong a
position as that of the bishops or barons.   Frederick II
saw in this a danger to his own authority.   He endeavored to check the rising tide by curtailing their jurisdiction, and taking away from the towns the power of har-
boring fugitives.   Such petty enactments, however, were
fruitless, and the towns grew more and more in
importance.

They also showed their development by drawing up
their own local codes of laws or customs.   Many of
these were of very ancient origin and were framed
chiefly with a view to the protection of commerce and
trade.

Individually the German towns were strong, but collectively they were still stronger.   For they formed
themselves into groups and thus became strong enough
to declare war and peace and to make separate treaties
with foreign States.   The two strongest of these leagues
were the League of the Rhine, which comprised most of
the towns in southern Germany, and the Hanseatic
League, containing most of the north German towns.
The League of the Rhine contained no fewer than sixty
cities, but the Hanseatic League was even still more
powerful.   The successful wars which it waged with
Sweden, Norway, and Denmark, and the treaties which
it concluded with England and Flanders sufficiently
demonstrate the importance of the League.   Nor was
this surprising when we take into account the extent and
complete solidarity of the League.

It not only comprised all the important cities in north
Germany and along the Baltic, but it even had factories
in such widely scattered places as London and Novgorod.   Lübeck was at the head of the League.   In this city

were kept the treasury and archives, and here also met both the regular and extraordinary assemblies. Some idea of the minuteness and rigor of its regulations may be gauged from the fact that its factors and clerks had to observe celibacy. Doubtless, such a regulation may seem to us extreme, but it serves to illustrate the power of the system that pervaded the shops and factories of the League.

The German towns were the most united and cohesive section of Germany. Their greatest wealth and political influence excited both the hopes and fears of German princes. And had it not been for the decline of the old trade routes in the sixteenth century, they might have hastened the process of the unification of Germany.

If we turn to Italy, especially to its northern provinces, we find similar evidence of the growth and political power of the towns.

Partly owing to the natural fertility of the soil, partly owing to their unrivaled manufactures, the towns of Lombardy soon became both numerous and thriving. Among them, Milan rapidly took the lead. Some idea of her size may be gathered from her population, which in 1288 amounted to two hundred thousand, while of these there were eight thousand gentlemen, six hundred notaries, two hundred doctors, and eighty schoolmasters. But other towns, like Pavia and Pisa, also grew in importance.

In 1051, the importance of Pisa may be judged from the fact that Emperor Henry IV promised, amongst its other privileges, not to nominate a new marquis over Tuscany without its consent.

The government of such towns was practically an oligarchy who ruled, however, in the name of the people. Their magistrates, called consuls, and varying in number, were elected by the people. Sometimes there were even as many as twenty consuls. Then, under the consuls were two councils. One of these, which was smaller in number, formed a kind of town-senate, and met in secret, while, on very important occasions, the general council of the whole people was assembled. Besides these units of government, there was also, after the time of Frederick Barbarossa, a *podesta,* or dictator, who acted as supreme judge and who was expected to restore order amid the furious factions and party strifes. A stranger was generally chosen for this, perhaps from some other town, as it was expected he would show greater impartiality.

It was not long before the towns had an opportunity of showing forth not only their individual love of freedom, and their material wealth and splendor, but also their collective strength.

The occasion was furnished by the war between the towns of Lombardy and the Emperor Frederick Barbarossa. Milan, in spite of the emperor's prohibition, continued to persecute its neighbors in the town of Lodi. Frederick employed force, and the result was a protracted siege of Milan which ended in the victory of the emperor and the sack of the towns.

After this, the emperor's officers in the different towns began to act with great severity. A strong feeling of resentment was thereby roused throughout the towns, and, in 1167, was formed the famous Lombard League, of which Pope Alexander III declared himself the patron and protector. About ten years afterwards, the battle of Legnano (1176) decided the fortune of war in favor of the towns, while the Treaty of Constance (1183), that followed, confirmed the towns in their practical independence. Not only were they allowed to retain their own internal administration, but they could also declare war and make peace, and even coin their own money—all rights that are commonly supposed to pertain to an independent sovereignty.

From henceforth the towns practically make the history of Italy. Not only did they take a very decisive part in the struggle between the empire and Papacy, but the history of Italy became afterwards nothing else than the history of separate independent City-States. Even to this day the stranger is impressed by the absolute difference between one Italian city and another. Each city has its own style of architecture, its own local traditions, and its own dialect. It is clear that the city life of Italy had deeply impressed itself even upon the social character of that country.

In Spain, the growth of towns also played a very important part in the history of the country. In this case, however, the starting point of its movement and its purpose considerably differed from those of the countries that we have been considering. The kings themselves were the first to inaugurate the independence of the towns. They voluntarily granted the towns such rights as the freedom to choose their own magistrates, but expected in return that the towns should help in defending the country from foreign invasion, and in forwarding the unity and consolidation of the kingdom. Also, as a guarantee for such services, a royal officer was appointed over each town with jurisdiction over such matters as military service and the payment of a common tax.

The towns soon fulfilled their purpose and, at the same time, worked out their own development. Like the towns in Germany, they managed to get a place in the national councils, or *cortes*. And it was their presence that gave to these assemblies such a democratic character.

If the towns in Spain differed in some respects from those on the Continent, the towns in England were even yet more different.

London may be considered a fair type of most of the English towns. Population may have been more numerous, the commodities and transactions more bulky and extensive, but the general resemblance may be considered sufficient to warrant the acceptance of London as a general type.

The charter of Henry I to the city of London clearly shows that its citizens had the same privileges as their patrons on the Continent—such privileges, for example, as magistrates elected by themselves, exemption from certain burdens, payment of a fixed rent, and full protection of trade and commerce.

But the English towns were unique in this, that they were never completely outside the royal authority. They always formed cooperating units in the national system. Not only the king, but Parliament as well, asserted over them authority and jurisdiction. Thus, in England the mutual relations between the towns and the central government were very different from what they would otherwise have been. From the very beginning, the towns, which, in the main, were almost exclusive centers of trade, industry, and commerce, were able to exercise an influence on the destinies of the country; and this influence was the more powerful and subtle since it was exercised not by a caste, but by a class of people that formed a vital part of the nation.

The growth of Parliament is intimately bound up with the growth of the towns. And the ultimate end of both was to throw the preponderance of political power into the hands of the middle class of English society.

Having thus taken a brief survey of the towns in some of the most important countries of Europe, we must now consider more minutely some of the characteristics of the English towns, not only because many of these characteristics are typical of what is to be found in other towns, but also because they partly explain many of the municipal institutions and customs of the towns of to-day.

The first prominent feature of town life in the Middle Ages is its exclusiveness. Very little was to be seen of that constant ebb and flow of outside life, such as we see at the present day. Only those who held land inside the town were considered to be truly citizens, and there were always evidences of an attempt to emphasize their peculiar prerogative.

In the same way as metic merchants in Greece were reminded of their inferior position by certain taxes, so the outsiders in the English towns were constantly reminded of their outside position by certain restrictions. Thus they were not permitted to buy and sell from other strangers, nor were they allowed to trade in retail. Another restriction was that every alien merchant should abide in the house of some citizen assigned him for that purpose. Already, by the Assize of Clarendon, it had been laid down that the stranger, visiting the town more than one night, should dwell in the house of one who should stand as security for his good behavior, and now this was further reinforced by the statute of Henry V, which required that every stranger should "go to his host."

All throughout the Middle Ages, great jealousy was shown toward the foreign merchants who often, under royal patronage, took up their residence in English cities, and during the Insurrection of Wat Tyler, one of the first objects of attack was the residences and factories of the wealthy Flemish weavers, who, in addition to their foreign extraction, had excited jealousy by their careful preservation of the secrets of their trade.

A second very conspicuous feature was the municipal control of trade. Trade, both in the market and in the public streets, was carefully regulated by the town authorities. Proper weights and measures were insisted upon; prices of such things as bread, ale, flesh, and fish were carefully regulated by ordinances. All unlawful gain was sternly prohibited, and a proper supply of corn had to be kept in store in order to meet seasons of scarcity.

Such strict control over the course of trade might seem at first arbitrary and somewhat detrimental even to the best interests of the whole community, but it must be remembered that, at that time, the area of trade was extremely narrow. It was comparatively easy to enforce wholesome legislation, and any abuses, such as too often occur in modern times, would have inflicted intolerable suffering in times and places where the opportunity and the market of buying were so few.

A third and important feature of the town was the fair. Not only in England, but also throughout Continental Europe, the fairs were the great centers of the distribution of wealth. They seem to have taken their origin from the great Church festivals, and at first were often connected with religious and monastic institutions. Later on, nearly all the important towns had fairs either within the walls or in close proximity. Some of these fairs, notably those of Novgorod in Russia, Leipzig in

Germany, and Stourbridge in England, were of world-wide importance.

It was at these places that the rarest merchandise could be found, and that goods could be obtained at the cheapest price. It was there, if anywhere, that buyer and seller could meet one another. Wines from France and Spain, silks and velvets from the East, furs and copper from the Hanse towns, all found their way to the walls of some of the great English fairs. Even rare books and precious stones were also displayed for sale. It was no wonder, then, that people traveled to the fairs even from the most distant parts, and that they found the expense of the journey amply defrayed by the cheapness of the goods that they bought.

Some idea of an English fair can be gained from Warton's description of the fair of St. Giles, near Winchester. We are told that the area of its jurisdiction was no less than seven miles, that it was frequented by several foreign merchants, and that entire streets were set apart for the sale of the different commodities, and that the duration of the fair was sixteen days.

Naturally, the organization of such fairs was highly complex. There were judges who had to settle any disputes that were bound to arise, and there was also a court, presided over, generally, by the mayor, that had jurisdiction over various causes; in fact, very often the fairs had mayors of their own elected by their own officers.

The fair during the Middle Ages was a matter of necessity. It was the one means by which distant parts of the market could be brought into contact one with another, and, more than anything else, it tended to divert trade to other than purely local channels. Nowadays, such means of communication and transit as are furnished by steam and electricity render the fair rather an antiquated, historical pageant than otherwise. But then it was the leading feature of medieval trade.

Just one more aspect of the medieval towns has to be noticed, and that is the government of the town by the members of the crafts, or guilds. From the political point of view, this feature is perhaps the most important of all. It meant the solidarity of the burgesses as a distinct order and gave to the middle classes that union and strength that reduced the power of the monarchy, and brought about the rise of democratic forms of government.

So important, however, was the function of the guilds and so complicated was their nature that a special section will be devoted to this subject.

CHAPTER III

THE GUILDS AND CRAFTS

CONFUSION has often been caused by taking the guilds to be the same as the crafts. It is true that the same society was often a guild and also a craft, but even in such cases the functions of each still remained different. The best way of arriving at a clear notion of the subject of this section will be to consider separately the definitions of the guild and of the craft.

By the thirteenth century, the guild was considered as an association primarily for some religious purpose. It was not necessarily connected with the practice of any trade, though frequently this was the case. Even in Anglo-Saxon times, there had been guilds formed for the purpose of self-defense and the preservation of peace; and in Norman times the guilds are mentioned in connection with industrial occupations. But after the thirteenth century the guild was always associated with some religious purpose.

On the other hand, a craft was an association that was always primarily of an industrial character. Unlike the word "guild," which somewhat fluctuated in the extension of its meaning, the word "craft" was constantly connected with some form of industry. At the same time, it frequently happened that the craft took upon itself the functions of a religious organization, but such functions were subordinated to the essential character of the craft, namely, an industrial society or organization.

Having thus far seen the precise meaning that is to be attached to the craft and the guild, we are now in a better position to understand their development and the character that they acquired by the later Middle Ages.

It has already been pointed out that in the economic development of ancient Rome there had gradually grown into existence an industrial and manufacturing system quite distinct from that of agriculture or of mere trade. The barbarian invasions, however, had swept away this system, and for some years medieval Europe reminds us of the condition of early Greece, when only agriculture and the hand-to-mouth industries were practised. But, by degrees, with the spread of peace and the consolidation of society, improvements began to appear. Men had the leisure to manufacture and to buy things that provided not only for the necessities, but also for the comforts of life.

Very soon we find trades and handicrafts appearing in a small way among the different towns. At first, these were carried on in the individualistic system, there being no organization and no cooperation. Such a system became quite antagonistic to the associative spirit of the Middle Ages, and thus these different industries and trades generally formed themselves into groups which entirely did away with individual effort and enterprise.

The first step in the movement was the municipal inspection and supervision of trade. Some need was felt of protecting the interests of the buyer and consumer, and of this need the members of the different trades showed themselves fully cognizant. It was they themselves who often took the initiative and prayed the authorities to appoint certain officials who should carefully inspect the quality of the goods they produced, the answer generally being that certain members should be chosen out of the crafts for this purpose. Such petitions clearly indicate that the need of supervision was the first thing that brought together the members of the same craft.

The second step in the development of the craft was the exclusiveness of its membership. Hitherto, everybody might practise any trade he chose. But it would manifestly be exceedingly difficult to secure efficient work and well-made goods if every individual were allowed to practise the trade and sell his wares. Hence, there began a movement on the part of the overseers, or wardens, in favor of a monopoly of trade. They begged that those only should practise the trade who had previously proved themselves good and efficient workmen. This previous proof, however, could not be given unless the newcomer had been working for some time under the actual supervision of other members of the trade. In other words, no person was considered fit to practise the trade unless he had gone through the preliminary and intermediate stages of apprenticeship and journeymanship.

With this exclusiveness on the part of the members of the different trades, there begins the true nature of the craft, or an industrial organization having a definite sphere of action, carried on according to certain rules and regulations, having special officers of its own, a peculiar hierarchy of grades, and often, though not always, having a charter of a corporation and a common seal and the power to purchase and to possess land.

Each one of these elements will be now considered separately. And although what is said applies mainly to the English crafts, it must be kept in mind that substantially the same was to be found, at one time or another, also, in the Continental countries.

First, there was a definite sphere of action laid down in certain rules. A part of this sphere of action has already been indicated, namely, the inspection of work and goods, but there were also, as well, other departments of work. The methods of performing the work, the hours of work, the amount of wages, the relations between employers and the employed—all these were minutely prescribed. Even the collection of debts was also one of their functions. In the town itself, the ordinary town court was the usual means of enforcing the payment of debt, but when the debtor lived in some other town, then the guild itself would intervene. The guild, by its powerful influence, ramifying into every part of the country, and by the wealth at its disposal with which it could prosecute almost any suit, enabled the creditor to collect his debt far more easily than would otherwise have been the case.

Certain other functions of a beneficiary character were undertaken by the crafts. In many cases they acted as insurance societies. When the member fell into poverty or fell under such misfortune as imprisonment, then he was frequently entitled to relief from the common fund. This was mostly the case with the religious guilds. Sometimes a weekly pittance was allowed, sometimes a small loan was granted in order to meet some urgent necessity. Such favors, however, were not of the character of a formal, binding contract, but rather the result of the spontaneous benevolence of the society or its officials. In later years, this charity assumed a more tangible shape. Hospitals were often erected for the reception of the poorer members of the fraternity, and in England, especially, there could be found a great number of such foundations in the times immediately preceding the Reformation.

Nor was the guild oblivious of the needs of its members in the other world. Foundations were left in order that Masses might be said for the souls of its deceased members, and charities were also established— that is to say, chapels were erected and endowed in order that one or more priests might say Mass for the defunct members of the guild.

From what has been said, it will be clearly seen how numerous and diversified were the functions of the medieval craft. Certainly, there must have been certain officials in the craft endowed with authority, who could regulate and enforce so many different kinds of activity. These officials were the wardens, who were usually elected every year. Judging from the statutes that mention these elections, the number of wardens seems to have varied; occasionally it was two, sometimes six.

Their authority was not autocratic. They were in office mainly for the purpose of carrying out the regulations of the guild and enforcing its decrees. Moreover, their power was generally expressly subordinated to that of the mayor of the town. It is also very probable that the police regulations of the guild were enforced by the town police, which thus extended even to such things as receiving of property and to the imposition of financial penalties by way of compensation for personal injuries.

Besides the wardens who enjoyed the limited jurisdiction already described, there were also other people in the craft, or guild, enjoying a limited local authority, and these were the masters who had under them apprentices and journeymen. And this brings us to the third element of the medieval guild, or craft, namely, *the hierarchy of grades.*

The lowest grade of all was that of the apprentice. We have already seen that one of the steps by which the craft became exclusive in its character was the regulation that none should practise the trade until he had given previous proof of his competency. This regulation necessitated some course of training which went by the name of apprenticeship.

Some idea of what this apprenticeship was may be gained from the following indenture of apprenticeship, drawn up in the fourteenth century, during the reign of King Edward III:

"This indenture made on the eighteenth day of September, the year of the reign of Edward III . between John Gare of St. Mary Cray, in the County of Kent, and Walter Bryce, son of J. Bryce of Wimelton of same County. Whereas, the said Walter Bryce hath covenanted with the said J. Gare for the time of seven years, and that the said J. Gare shall find the said Walter meat, drink and clothing during the said time. Also, the said J. Gare shall teach the said Walter his craft as he may and can, and also the said J. Gare shall give him the first year of said seven years IIId. in money, and the II year VId., and so after the sum of VIId. for each year of the said seven years, and the last year of the seven years the said J. Gare shall give the said Walter ten shillings of money. And the said Walter shall well and duly keep the occupation and do such things as the said J. Gare shall bid him to do as unto the said Walter shall be lawful. And the said Walter shall neither go to rebele or sport without the license of the said John. In witness thereof, the parties aforesaid have put their seals."

From this document can be roughly surmised the reciprocal relations between master and apprentice. The master was to board and clothe and pay the apprentice, as well as teach him the trade, while the apprentice was amenable to the general jurisdiction of the master and was tied down to the occupation of the trade for the period of seven years.

With regard, however, to the number of years' apprenticeship and the number of apprentices that might be employed by the same master, there does not seem to have been any general uniformity. In England and in France, longer terms of apprenticeship occur, sometimes amounting to the length of twelve years, though such cases were rare. In Germany, the time of apprenticeship was considerably shorter, amounting only to two or three years.

In regulating the number of apprentices, the general tendency was to restrict rather than increase. The reason for this was obvious. If an undue number of apprentices were employed, there would, in a few years' time, be an excessive number of masters practising the trade, which would then become overcrowded. Such restriction was brought about not only by directly limiting by statute the number of apprentices, sometimes only allowing a master to apprentice his own son, but also by exacting that journeymen should be appointed for every certain number of apprentices.

The apprentices in England speedily formed an association of their own, and became a very formidable body. Sometimes their disturbances and riots were a menace to the public peace, and during the troubles of the Stuart times they took a very active political part on the side of the Commonwealth, and were enrolled in the militia. Then afterwards, when the rebellion was over, they took a leading part in the Restoration.

One step above that of the apprentice was the journeyman. Even though the apprentice had gone through his seven or ten years' training, he was not yet considered sufficiently competent to set up as an independent master. He still had to serve a certain number of years as journeyman. While he was fully qualified to exercise his trade, yet he had to do so under the supervision of a master. Altogether the position of a journeyman was not unlucrative, or bereft of any kind of responsibility. His wages sometimes amounted to half the total income of the master himself, and he enjoyed authority and jurisdiction over the apprentice.

The custom of employing journeymen was prevalent, not only in England, but also on the Continent. In six of the great trading associations of Paris, it was distinctly laid down that the apprentice, after serving his term of apprenticeship, must also serve a certain number of years as companion, at the end of which time he must exhibit to the wardens of the company some masterpiece illustrating his skill in his art. In Germany, also, the same custom is found, though sometimes the aspirant might be admitted to the lower branches of the trade without going through the full course.

It is interesting to observe that the journeymen, like the apprentices, had a solidarity and an organization of their own. This was caused by their interests being opposed to those of their masters. Owing to the increase of population and keener competition for the rank of master, not all the journeymen could become masters. In addition to this, the selfishness of the masters attempted by artificial means to obstruct the increase in the number of journeymen.

It was not long before the journeymen associated themselves together for the protection of their rights. At first, they tried to disguise their real purpose under the cloak of religious worship. But the veil was transparent and the masters were frequently heard complaining that the journeymen formed conspiracies with the object of obtaining a rise in wages. For this purpose, strikes were sometimes resorted to, and the litigations between the journeymen and their masters began somewhat to resemble the modern antagonism between labor and capital.

We now come to the remaining feature of the medieval crafts, and that is their corporate functions. Many of the crafts had received royal charters, the first of the crafts to be thus honored being that of the weavers in London. As such they could use a common seal and were entitled to purchase and to possess land. Many of the crafts speedily acquired large amounts of land. Also they had large halls of their own, where they held their assemblies. These halls were often beautifully built and elaborately furnished and decorated. The Guildhall in London and in other old cities, both in England and on the Continent, testify to the wealth and taste of the craftsmen.

The guilds and crafts of the Middle Ages influenced to a very great extent the prosperity and power of the citizens, or middle class of the community. It was their associations that gave to the middle classes the political power which they wielded not only within the circumference of their own towns, but also in larger areas. The growth of Parliament in England, the crippling of the lawless feudal element in France and Germany, the overthrow of imperial despotism in Italy, are mainly to be attributed to the solidarity of the middle classes that had been accomplished mainly by the instrumentality of the guilds and crafts.

CHAPTER IV

COMMERCE AND INDUSTRY OF THE MIDDLE AGES

THE most important industry of the Middle Ages was that of agriculture. This resulted from the very nature of feudalism. Nearly everybody was a land-owner, and therefore all, from the highest to the lowest, were interested in the productiveness of land. And then, there was also the fundamental reason that of all other industries agriculture satisfies the necessities of life, producing at once all that is required for food and clothing.

Even the smallest peasant farmer indulged in all the various forms of the industry. He had his own little lot of ground, consisting of little strips scattered here and there in the different arable fields, and only separated from those belonging to other proprietors by lines of uncultivated ground. He would also have his oxen, sheep, and, especially, poultry. The keeping of pigs was also as common as it is in Ireland at the present day. In most of the villages, the swine of the different inhabitants were trusted to the vigilance of the common swineherd, much as in certain parts of Switzerland to-day the goats of different proprietors are under the watchful attention of a common official.

Agriculture also seems to have met with a great deal of scientific treatment. Books were written upon the subject, among them being twelve treatises composed by no less a person than Bishop Grosseteste of Lincoln, and another composition, written anonymously, called "Husbandry."

By the fourteenth century there seems to have been a

fairly general acquaintance with advanced methods of improving the soil by digging and trenching, and even of altering the condition of the poorer kind of soils. The methods practised for this purpose were marling and claying. The marl is a valuable fertilizing material, generally containing a varying quantity of lime, and quickly dissolving after being on the ground for some time. Claying the soil consists in artificially enriching its condition by mixing it with clay. Both these processes seem to have been known, and they considerably improved the soil as well as raised the price of the farm.

Of all the branches of agricultural industry, the most lucrative and the one that brought in most wealth to the nation was that of breeding sheep for the sake of the wool. This was the main source of extra profit. Amongst those who became famous for the quantity of wool that they produced were the Cistercian monks; indeed, the term *Cistercian wool* became quite common. Most of their estates seem to have been in the west of England, and the fleece that they exported added much both to their own wealth and that of the kingdom.

Up to about the thirteenth century, only the raw material was produced in England, and this was sent on to the Continent in order to be worked up into the finished material. Flanders was the country that did most of this trade, but Germany also received a considerable portion of the English wool for manufacture into cloth.

How enormous must have been the English trade in wool can be gathered from the celebrated statute of Edward I, dealing with the tax on wool, and the great importance attached to that tax. The extent of the trade can also be measured by its effects on Flanders, where the exportation of English wool was temporarily stopped in 1258. So great was the distress caused in

Flanders, that she was forced to accede to the political demands of England. Indeed, England, with regard to the production of wool, seems to have enjoyed quite a monopoly. Her insular position and comparative tranquillity allowed her opportunities that were denied to the often war-swept countries of the Continent. Also, the quality of English soil was such as to render the quality of the fleece both fine and substantial.

England, however, was not content to remain long in the mere position of an exporter of raw material. In a treatise called "The Golden Fleece," much praise is given to the English wool, and, after mentioning the enormous exportation of wool to Burgundy and the great advantage accruing therefrom to that country, the document goes on to say that the king had decided to look after the welfare of his own subjects in that respect, and, therefore, invited certain clothiers to convert the English wool into cloth. Shortly after this, appeared a statute in 1337 which offered protection to foreigners living in England, in order that they might inaugurate the woolen industry on English soil.

Between the years 1258 and 1340, there was a whole series of statutes and writs, all dealing in the same way with the promotion of the woolen industry in England. The Oxford Parliament in 1258 decreed that the wool should be worked up in England, and should not be sold to foreigners, and that every one should use woolen cloth made in the country. In 1271, a statute was passed prohibiting the importation of woolen cloth. Again in 1331, letters of protection were granted to John Kempe of Flanders, weaver of woolen cloth. In 1336, a similar letter was granted to two weavers from Brabant who had settled in York.

All these enactments illustrate very clearly the successive steps by which the woolen industry established itself in England. First, the exportation of wool was forbidden in order that the working of it up might be entrusted to home manufacture; then, upon this proving insufficient, the importation of foreign cloth was stopped, so as to prevent Englishmen from buying anything but the home-made material; finally, the inexperience of the English workmen entailed still further legislation, and foreign workmen were invited over to England under royal protection in order to start the industry on a proper footing.

By the year 1463, we find a still further change. Not only is the English-made cloth industry firmly established in England, but it is actually finding its way to the Continent, and competing there with the manufactures of Flanders and Germany. Even this is also illustrated by legislative enactments. For, in 1434, a statute was passed, forbidding the exportation of wool, in order to force Flanders into accepting the importation of English wool, while in 1496 the great commercial treaty called the *Intercursus Magnus* fully established the privilege of England to export her home-made cloth to Flanders. Naturally, this extension of trade in English manufactured goods added largely to the national wealth of England, while the counties of Norfolk and Suffolk, where these manufactures were the thickest, are shown, by the assessments of the period, to have been the wealthiest in England.

Another industry connected with the cloth manufacture was that of dyeing. The art of dyeing cloth was known even from the most ancient times. It was certainly practised during the Celtic occupation of Britain, and in the reign of King John considerable quantities of woad were imported for this purpose.

Altogether, the manufacturing and industrial system in England, though limited in variety, was extensive, its organization was complex, and its activities were subjected to much regulation on the part of the government. Thus, a special officer was sometimes appointed, called the *aulnager,* whose business it was to see that the cloth made was of the proper size and length, and what was still more important, certain towns were selected, called staple towns, and to these towns all goods of a certain class had to be sent before they could be exported abroad. Then, again, statutes were passed with the view of a constant provision of raw material for native manufacturers. Even the financial relations between the employers and their workmen were regulated. Thus, by the end of the fifteenth century, it was enacted that when the work was finished, the workmen should be paid in the coin of the realm and not in orders for provisions or other kind of goods. Such a statute as this would seem to show that the odious system of truck had already found its way into England, and that some necessity was felt of protecting the workman from his over-astute employer.

In general, the condition of the industrial classes seems to have been better than that on the Continent. In England, they were not regarded as something below the ordinary level, and such statutes as that of Magna Charta recognized them as a class with distinct rights and privileges of its own. We now turn to the distribution of wealth during the Middle Ages.

THE DISTRIBUTION OF WEALTH

Trade and commerce in Europe began to flourish at a very early period. By the eleventh century, we read of seaport towns on the east side of England doing a considerable trade with distant countries. In other parts could be found not only wines and vinegar from France, iron work from Belgium, and iron and steel from Scandinavia, but, later on, such commodities as soap, flax, and refined sugar from Italy, and even spices and cloves from the various countries of the Far East.

It was Italy, however, that led the way in commercial progress, and especially from the point of view of maritime commerce. Venice was the most important seaport town. Her fleet numbered no less than 3,000 merchant vessels, and was manned by 17,000 seamen, while the port of Venice was one of the first to compile a code of maritime laws which affected the construction, manning, and surveillance of ships. After Venice came Genoa. Already by 1088, the fleets of Genoa had obtained an important position on the list of maritime powers, and, in the thirteenth century, began to dispute with Venice the palm of supremacy. At Genoa, also, there was compiled a code of maritime laws, dealing chiefly with the dimensions of ships. And besides Venice and Genoa, other thriving seaport towns in Italy, though of less importance, were those of Ravenna, Ancona, and Amalfi.

In France and Spain there were also a number of trading centers. Lyons, in the south of France, became a very important emporium, and Marseilles did a very considerable trade with places even as far as Sicily. Also, in Marseilles we find the same combination of trade and aristocracy as at Venice, many of the merchants being also nobles. In Spain, Barcelona, even by the middle of the eleventh century, had become a very important commercial center, and from the time of Pedro III her merchants had enjoyed very great privileges.

Other countries that shared in the general circulation of commerce were the Netherlands and Germany. In the Netherlands, Bruges rapidly became an important commercial depot, and, perhaps even more than the other cities, profited by its position between the trading communities of the North and the South. Not only at one time was Bruges the principal emporium of Central Europe, but she was also the seat of a great woolen manufacturing industry. And it was in recognition of this that Philip the Good established there, in 1420, the celebrated Order of the Golden Fleece.

What has been said will easily show how extensive must have been the commercial activity of the Middle Ages. But it was after the Crusades that we find this activity at its highest. European merchants, especially the Italians from Venice, Genoa, and Pisa, held important trading quarters in Jerusalem, Jaffa, and Tripoli, while Venice after the Fourth Crusade had a considerable share in the division of the city of Constantinople. Such commercial colonies promoted rapid intercourse between the East and the West. New luxuries were introduced into Europe, new tastes and wants were developed, and, at the same time, the marvelous development of the shipping industry, owing to the requirements of the Crusaders, enabled these wants to be satisfied.

There were, however, certain other agencies at work, some of which had a great influence on the extent and direction of commerce. These agencies, which must be considered separately, were the banks, the Jews, the monasteries, and the influence of the State.

First of all, there were the banks. These, as in ancient Greece and Rome, played a great part in facilitating the movements of trade. Venice, which was fore-most in trade, was the first to develop the banking sys-tem. At first there were only private bankers, who, in addition to their ordinary business of money changers, found it convenient to accept deposits. Then the busi-ness assumed larger proportions, especially when, in 1171, a public debt was made transferable, and became thereby the nucleus of a great number of financial trans-actions.

The connection between the banking system and the State seems to have arisen from the fact that the Vene-tian government found it necessary to impose on private bankers certain regulations, in order to defend the in-terests of depositors. For example, greater amount of security was demanded, and bankers had to hold them-selves in readiness to pay their customers. The follow-ing three clauses will sufficiently indicate the stringency of government supervision:

"1. It shall be free for every one to accept, or not, a credit in a bank for contracts made heretofore, but this shall not be refused for those made hereafter, un-less by express agreement it shall have been declared that payment shall be made outside the bank.

"2. Credit in bank shall not be written off to any one for any amount in his absence, but credits shall be writ-ten with both parties present.

"3. Bankers, as aforesaid, must pay, to those who wish, in cash at once and in heavy gold and good money at the market rates, or rates current at our offices; and if any should refuse they shall be subject to the penalty of twenty-five ducats, and the provenditor, then present, shall none the less make them pay."

In course of time, the government began to lay down the nature of the different things in which banks might lawfully invest the money of their customers. Among such investments were the purchase of lands and houses, dealings in corn, and even loans to private individuals.

The next step after government supervision was that of forming a public State bank, which took place in 1587, and seems to have been the first example in medieval history of any kind of State bank. It was essentially a bank of deposit. It did not invest the money of its depositors, a practice which had been the ruin of many of the private banks. It only safeguarded absolutely the money of the depositors and either paid it out when required or made a transfer of the credit from one person to another.

The State bank did not mean the entire extinction of all other banking companies. In 1619 was created the celebrated *Banco del Giro*. The nature of this bank was interesting and somewhat reminds us of some of the features of the English consols. There were certain creditors of the republic and these were paid by being credited with a corresponding amount of deposit in the Banco del Giro. At the same time a large reserve was created in order to meet any possible immediate demands on the part of the creditors. Evidently the bank seems to have been founded upon a good and solid basis, for it had a long existence, enduring until the time of the occupation of Venice by Napoleon.

Another Italian bank, founded in 1407, was the Bank of Genoa. This, unlike the bank at Venice, was not merely a bank of deposit. It was more like the private Venetian banking concerns, and traded with the money that was left on deposit. Possibly, the modern system of checks drew its origin from this bank, since one of the functions of the bank was to issue and cash money orders. For a long time the Bank of Genoa had a prosperous existence, so much so that at one time it became, on account of its territorial possessions, almost a separate State. One of its clients, however, Philip II of Spain, brought it to ruin by the repudiation of the credit that he had opened with the bank.

A survey of the banking system of the Middle Ages would scarcely be complete, did we fail to mention the financial activity of the Templars. There must have been at least nine thousand of their houses scattered throughout Christendom. And at these houses deposits were received, advances made, and payments made in cash by important princes. Owing to the great number of the Templars' houses and to their scattered position, they often fulfilled the functions of the branches of one great bank, and were most useful intermediaries in the intercourse engendered by the Crusades between the East and the West.

The second agency which influenced commerce was the Jews. From the earliest times, the Jews have been an important factor in the movement and development of commerce. We gather from Cicero's oration, *Pro Flacco,* that even in his time the Jews had been instrumental in some very extensive transportations of bullion. Nor was their activity dormant during the empire, as is attested by the fact that many of them, owing to their great wealth, obtained the rank of Roman citizens, as well as exemption from military service.

During the Middle Ages the Jews became still more potent in the financial world. Their habits of saving and their trained experience in all sorts of business made them wealthier every day. Then the circumstances of the times tended to throw the employment of capital largely into their hands. Exclusion, almost entire, from the land system of feudalism directed their energies largely to the accumulation of floating capital, and the rigid laws against the various forms of money-lending practically gave them the monopoly of the money-lending business. What, perhaps, more than anything else, contributed to their success as capitalists, was the wonderful spirit of unity and solidarity that reigned amongst them. They had settlements all over Europe; they were constantly traveling, and these circumstances were sure to impart a thorough knowledge of the condition of the general market and the best ways of laying out their money.

It thus came about that the Jews, even more than the banks, were the means by which capital was brought into contact with labor. All important undertakings, including even the Crusades, were dependent upon money advanced by the Jews, and there is little doubt that many of the stately edifices of the Middle Ages owe their existence partly to the same source.

Nor did the storms of persecution succeed in extinguishing them or their financial activities. Legal disabilities, banishment from the soil, compulsion to wear a particular garb and to live in a particular quarter, and wholesale fines and even massacres, were of frequent occurrence. But, collectively, they still remained in existence. The persecutions were too intermittent, and too confined to local areas at any one particular time, to produce their full result.

Moreover, some of the kings found it convenient to take the Jews under their special protection. This was especially the case in France under Charlemagne, Louis le Débonnaire, and Charles the Bold, and in England under the first three Norman kings. In fact, up to the time of Edward I, they were considered as the special bondsmen of the king. He was the absolute lord of their persons and estates, and he allowed none to molest them but himself. So lucrative a source of wealth did they become, that for some time their wealth enabled the king to be independent of the national will, and under Henry II a special branch of the exchequer was devoted to the business with the Jews. This branch was called *Scaccarium Judaismi,* and its dealings entailed the employment of a small army of clerks and other officials.

The third agency was the monasteries. This, the third formative influence on European commerce and distribution of wealth, has been already mentioned. It has been pointed out that the monks spent most of their time in agricultural industry and especially in the breeding of large flocks of sheep. But they contributed also in other ways to the general wealth of the country in which they settled. Large tracts of land hitherto uncultivated were reclaimed, and what before were marshes and waste lands were made to produce wheat, barley, oats, beans, and other things sufficient not only for their own consumption but also for that of many other people.

The monasteries were also the direct cause of the great development of the building industry. At first, they had almost the monopoly, for it was only in the later Middle Ages that the laymen began to form themselves into guilds, or brotherhoods of masons, for the purpose of aiding one another in this industry. It is interesting to note, moreover, that the clergy themselves were mostly their own architects. A lay architect was quite the exception. Even as late as the times of Henry VII, the beautiful outlines of Magdalen College testify to the genius of an ecclesiastical architect.

Another very important function of the monasteries

of the Middle Ages was their care for the poor. At that time there was no poor-law system. The care of the poor and destitute was left almost entirely to private benevolence. In most religious orders a special rule prescribed the care and relief of the destitute. Some cases occur when even a specified amount of the monastic income had to be expended that way. Almost every monastery had its almoner, whose special duty it was to give alms to the poor, inquiring diligently, however, into the genuineness of their distress. Much has been said regarding the defects of this monastic relief, arising from a want of general system and the utter impossibility of ascertaining the truth of the narratives made by men who went roaming all over the country. But no other way of relief was possible, and the monastery in the earlier Middle Ages was the only organization that was able in any way to deal with the ever-present problems of poverty and starvation.

The fourth agency was government control. This, the fourth great influential factor in European commerce and distribution of wealth, acted in some ways for good, and in some ways for evil.

The activity of the government generally inclined to protect the purchaser and consumer from all forms of dishonesty. We have seen that the English Government required the crafts to elect certain officers to see that the work sold should be of a certain kind and quality. Also, we have seen that the prices of certain necessaries were carefully established by law.

Even the industries themselves were often fostered by government. This was especially the case in Italy when the great republics paid special attention to the development of their fleets, and to the improvement of agriculture on their domains. In England, also, the paternal care of the government was exercised in regard to all forms of industry. One notable illustration of this we have in the various statutes that were passed, allowing and encouraging foreign merchants and manufacturers to take up their residence in the country. While the local merchants were bitterly hostile to this apparent intrusion of the foreign element which seemed to threaten their monopoly, the kings, having at heart the general welfare of the country, insisted on the admission of the foreign trader. When, as in 1321, these aliens in London were threatened and molested, the king even sent special writs to the mayor and sheriffs, telling them to make proclamation that the king had taken the aliens under his special protection.

In other ways, however, government intervention tended to restrict somewhat the course of trade. This was done in two ways: first, by narrowing the activities of trade, and, secondly, by directly limiting the amount of merchandise that could be imported or exported. By the sixteenth century, certain towns were appointed where certain goods had to be sent before they could be exported. The purpose of these towns was partly to protect the producers and exporters, and partly to secure the more easy and rapid payments of the different towns that were due to the king. Such towns often had a special jurisdiction and organization of their own, and achieved considerable importance. Calais became one of the most important of the English staple towns, and the office of captain of the staple town of Calais was considered to be one of the most influential at the disposal of the Crown.

Besides determining the areas and channels of trade, governments also marked out in great measure its extent. It is interesting to observe that, theoretically, free trade was upheld during the Middle Ages. They held that the Creator purposely distributed His gifts among different countries in order that these countries might give and receive in exchange. In practice, however, a system of protection was very frequently adopted. Both Italy and France adopted a wholesale system of protection by means of heavy export duties and a most tyrannical customs system. Even Flanders endeavored to stamp out all competition, though free trade was allowed in the matter of cereals.

Altogether, the influence of the government was not disadvantageous. In an age when the individual was so weak, the assistance of the government was needed in order to protect him from fraud and oppression. What errors there were rose mainly from the unadvanced condition of the economic science of the times. It was not yet perceived that, very often, even local interests are better served by allowing trade to follow its natural channels, and that often the best means of procuring the welfare of all is to allow full scope to the laws of competition and of the relations between supply and demand.

CHAPTER V

INFLUENCE OF THE ECONOMIC ELEMENT ON
MEDIEVAL HISTORY

THE nature of medieval history and the relation between medieval times and the economic element differ considerably from those of ancient history. Medieval history is very much more complicated. It is a presentation of many different activities, going on at the same time in different areas, and of many currents of human activity, at times blended together into the same stream, and at other times pursuing their own course separately. If, however, we try to view medieval history as a whole, we shall find certain general movements that not only characterize the Middle Ages, but are also intimately connected with the development of the modern States. Such movements as the construction of Europe after the formation of the separate barbarian kingdoms, the conflict between empire and Papacy, the gradual acquisition of political power by the middle classes, as well as the political equilibrium of power when the separate nations had attained to a certain development —all these broad movements can be clearly discerned throughout the continual local agitations that were going on in different areas.

It is, therefore, to these broad, general movements that we shall chiefly direct our attention. Not only are they important in themselves, but they are also a general expression even of many of the lesser movements that make up the history of that time.

There is a great and fundamental difference between the formative influence of the economic element in ancient and medieval history. In the former, the economic activities are comparatively simple, their issues are clear, and their relations with the main movements of the times are sharply and clearly defined.

Thus, the economic distress of Athens at the time of Solon had only one kind of relation with the Solonian legislation, and in the history of Rome the agrarian and industrial problems all exercised the same constant and uniform kind of influence. There were scarcely ever economic activities pulling in different ways.

Far otherwise was it during the Middle Ages. There we find the economic elements both many and of a very diversified nature. Not only did some of these exercise an influence in entirely opposite directions, but occasionally the same economic element would exercise quite a different influence in different countries and times.

As one illustration among many, we might point out the divergent influences of the feudal element and of the towns. While feudalism generally tended in the direction of decentralization, namely, to make the local barons and magnates independent of the king, the towns, in some countries, tended to thwart this influence, and, as happened in France, they frequently became the most powerful agency in the spread of a strong and centralized government. Then, if we fix our attention even on the towns alone, we find that while in Italy they opposed, in France they upheld, the royal power.

Evidently the bearing of economics on medieval history cannot receive that simple treatment and presentation as is possible in ancient history. It would be impossible to label each political movement with its own economic label. And yet, economic causes are as equally powerful in medieval history as in the history of ancient Greece and Rome. Without the economic factor in medieval history, Europe would not have been what it was, nor would it present the same spectacle that it does to-day.

As the combined action of sea, sky, and air all concur in determining the shape and condition of any piece of land, so, in the Middle Ages, the combined and varied activity of diverse economic agencies all united in producing one definite result.

In the following pages, therefore, we shall show how the medieval political movements derived their initiation and peculiar character from economic factors, and at the same time we shall endeavor to show what was the precise part taken by each economic element in the construction of medieval Europe and in the guidance of its most important political movements. The first great movement, both in the chronological as well as in the logical order, is that of the

CONSTRUCTION OF EUROPE

By the end of the seventh century, the barbarian invasions of Europe had accomplished their purpose. The political power of ancient Rome had been swept away and all over Europe there had been set up Christianized Barbarian Kingdoms. In all these, there could be discerned some form of constitutional government, endowed with more or less strength. In Italy, we see Theodoric, the chief of the Ostrogoths, ruling both his own people and the Romans with a firm hand, advancing the national prosperity of the country and even dreaming of a pan-Germanic alliance. In France, we see established the Merovingian kingdom, extending its sway over both sides of the Rhine, and preserving law and order by the nominal power of the Diet and by the very real power of the Merovingian king. In England, the Anglo-Saxon settlement had been already an accomplished fact, and we behold the great struggle for supremacy between the Northern, Middle, and Southern Kingdoms.

And yet, the nations of Europe remained in a very fluid and helpless condition. They were, as yet, far from having reached a condition of solidarity and strength. A strong ruler like Theodoric, or Pepin, or Alfred, might indeed impart a temporary unity and strength, but in the nations themselves there was very little organic unity and independent vigor.

It was extreme pressure from without that hastened the process of growth and solidification. Toward the beginning of the tenth century, there took place the terrible invasions of the Northmen and Danes. From the recesses of Norway and Denmark, these fierce barbarians, whose breasts were steeled against every feeling of pity, dashed themselves against the still weak nations of Southern Europe. In their light craft they braved the perils of the sea, and ascending the rivers and streams, burned and pillaged without fear or discrimination.

Besides these Northern foes, there were also other barbarians appearing from the East and South. There were the Hungarians from the Danubian plains, the Wends from the banks of the Elbe and the shores of the Baltic, and, finally, the heathen Saracens, filled with hatred of Christianity and irresistible enthusiasm.

Europe seemed on the point of annihilation. The work of the last four centuries seemed on the point of completely collapsing, when suddenly the peril became the cause of its own antidote. Already we have pointed out that the small peasants of Europe, and all those who found themselves defenseless, huddled for protec-

tion around some powerful lord or magnate who, in return for the ownership of their land and enjoyment of
their services, undertook to give them protection and
government.

It was this system of feudalism, brought about mainly
by external pressure, that caused the rehabilitation of
Europe. Against the common enemy, Europe now
stood up, both united and armed. In every land there
were castles and strongly fortified places to which the
people could fly for refuge, and in every land there was
an army to beat off the invader. It is true that there was
no standing army in our modern sense of the word. But
there were the huge feudal levies all raised and com-
manded by a coordinated hierarchy of officials, and
never completely disbanded. It was an army that was
created by the necessities of the environment, and none
better could be found to ward off the spasmodic and
frequent attacks of the enemy.

Strength and swiftness were the two qualities most
essential for the medieval army, and these two qualities
were supplied by the typical institutions of feudalism,
namely, the castles and the knights, or mounted horse-
men. While the castles were nuclei of defense, the cav-
alry could attack and pursue the flying enemy. Europe
was thus saved from the invader. But she was saved
by feudalism from an even still greater danger, namely,
from internal anarchy and confusion. Oftentimes, when
societies have been on the verge of dissolution, the land
has formed a tie such as could not be supplied either by
family relationship, or race feeling, or past tribal traditions. Even such a prosaic economic factor as land
has often thus become the cradle of all the grand traditions of the Fatherland. This was the case in England
when the rapidly growing tribes of the Anglo-Saxons

exchanged the tie of family kinship for the wider and more enduring tie of land with all its associations, while in Switzerland and Germany we find examples still more conspicuous of this unifying power of land.

Under the peculiar influence of feudalism, the land in a new and special manner admirably fulfilled this important function of bringing together all the different individuals and sections of society. How this was done we have already explained in dealing with the nature of feudalism, but we still have to show, in greater detail, how this economic element of feudalism acted on the political fortunes of the European nations. In doing so, we shall find that the unifying influence of feudalism was not altogether constant—that while, in the early period of danger and invasions, it united Europe against the common invader, yet that, in many countries, it afterwards baffled and almost undid its own purpose by weakening, rather than by strengthening, the girdling ties of a centralized government.

From the very beginning of feudalism, two distinct principles of activity began to manifest themselves—these were the national principle and the separatist principle. Even the king of the nation embodied in himself these two principles. For he was chief feudal landowner and, at the same time, endowed with sovereignty over all the nation. In the former capacity, he was subject to all the limits imposed upon him by feudalism, while in the latter, his jurisdiction overleaped the boundaries that were set up by the feudal local areas of jurisdiction. Generally, it was as the chief feudal landowner that the man became king, and then, when he had once grasped the reins of power, we find the royal element conflicting with the feudal element, the king endeavoring to make his royal national jurisdiction assert itself over the system of which he himself had been and was still so prominent a member. Thus, in France, Hugh Capet, duke of the French, even during the weak reign of the last Merovingian kings, wielded the practical power. He, as chief feudal landowner, was more powerful than the puppet king, and it was his strong feudal position that enabled him to ascend the throne. But when his accession was accomplished, we behold the king reasserting in himself the national principle, and the monarchical influence gradually prevailing over that of the local baron. Similarly, in Germany, it was the strong local territorial position of Henry the Fowler that made him king, yet it was always the great problem of himself and his successors how to break down the isolation and independence of the other great German duchies.

It is this dual activity of feudalism that so complicates its action on the political history of medieval Europe. Feudalism seemed at the same time to unite and to tear asunder. And yet, the resultant action was harmonious and would have been the same in all the countries of Europe, had there not been present other elements that entered into the struggle and strengthened one or the other of these two conflicting tendencies. We can, however, see this clearly only by examining singly the most important nations, and tracing, step by step, the full working of the feudal element.

Powerful, indeed, had been the position of Hugh Capet as duke of the French. His domains included not only the Gaulish regions, north of the Seine, but also the district between the Seine and the Loire, even as far west as the county of Maine. His jurisdiction and wealth were also proportioned to his domains.

When he became king, considerable additions were

made, not, however, of a very tangible nature. In regard to financial power, he was, as king, almost entirely
indigent, being dependent mainly upon what could be
collected from such insignificant sources as tolls and
revenues derived from vacant ecclesiastical benefices.
But he had one great advantage in the prestige and in
the grand traditions that still hovered round the name
and office of king; and, above all, there was the influence of the Church.   Not only was the coronation of
the king regarded as a very sacred act, but everywhere
throughout France there were enormous ecclesiastical
temporalities which were never altogether feudal, and
these regarded the king as their special lord and protector.

The exact balance between the king's power and the
opposition of the independent feudal elements was always very hard to determine.   The land that was held
in feudal tenure was certainly a very strong disintegrating element.   The owner of such land derived from it,
and not from the king, any title of nobility and office
that he might possess.   He could in early years defy the
general ordinance of the king, and legislate for his own
domain; he could, on failure to obtain redress, even bid
mortal defiance to his sovereign; he enjoyed civil and
criminal jurisdiction in his territory, and in most cases
enjoyed the right of coining money without need, as in
England, of the king's stamp and supervision.

Evidently, these things, in the early years of French
history, must have been very serious obstacles to the
royal power.   But gradually there appeared fresh elements, whose collective weight was on the side of royal
authority and tended to neutralize to some extent the
decentralizing effects of the economic element of feudalism.

Even from the very beginning, the law of primogeniture was not so severe as in England. Thus, in the bigger fiefs, some provision had to be made in money for the benefit of the younger sons, while in the lesser fiefs even the land itself might be divided. Naturally, this tended to the gradual paring away of the big estates and the enrichment of the lesser holders. The result was that the Crown was placed in a position of great safety, for less danger was to be apprehended from the scattered, small units than from great, territorial estates, all united and wielded by one powerful lord.

Then, there were, also, certain councils, both summoned and controlled by the king, and their collective action tended to neutralize the insular activity of some of the powerful barons. Thus, there was the supreme judicial tribunal, over which the king was president, and in which alone could be tried the chief barons of the realm. By degrees the introduction into the court of councilors of lower rank, appointed by the king, insensibly diminished its exclusively baronial character, and caused it to assume the nature of a systematic tribunal.

There were also the meetings of the barons. Some of these meetings were general and accompanied with great pomp and solemnity, while others were only partial. It is true that the king's authority over these was at first very limited and that nothing could be done in the lord's own domain without his consent, yet these councils became convenient instruments in the hands of powerful kings. They prepared the way for the formation and development of councils of the realm, and of a ministry that would be perfectly dependent upon the king. Such submissive councils, for example, were the Great Administrative Council under St. Louis, and the *Parlement,* or king's judicial tribunal.

Another very important council which tended to undo the effects of the local land system was that of the townsmen or burgesses. It was the urgent need of money that impelled Philip the Fair, in 1302, to summon the representatives of the Third Estate, and the effect of this was almost as important as was that of the summoning of the citizens and burgesses in England under Simon de Montfort. It marked the rise of the Third Estate in France, whose power formed a counterbalance to the power of the nobles, whose feudal jurisdiction was already fast declining.

This summoning of the Third Estate combined with the other causes already mentioned to effect the overthrow of the feudal power. And it is thus interesting to observe that, while the economic element of feudalism tended to thwart the centralizing tendency of royal authority, the other economic element of the towns became a very powerful instrument in spreading the royal central authority.

Finally, the sagacious policy of the French kings themselves took advantage of the very nature of feudalism to effect its overthrow. The feudal estates were the personal appanages of the owners. They could, therefore, be made to coalesce by the marriage of the landowners. Both Louis VIII and Louis IX availed themselves of this, and, by effecting matrimonial alliances between members of the royal family and the owners of powerful dukedoms, managed to draw these possessions within the vortex of the royal jurisdiction. In this way, the lands of Auvergne, Toulouse, and Provence became part of the royal domain, and the skilful policy of kings, in organizing a centralized system of administrative, judicial, and financial administration, completely absorbed and consolidated what had been thus acquired.

By the end of the fifteenth century, therefore, the decentralizing influence of feudalism had ceased. The local areas of the land now formed part of one general system under royal control. Feudalism had accomplished its mission, and nothing of it remained save a few vestiges that were completely swept away by the French Revolution.

In Germany, we behold a process quite the reverse of that which was taking place in France. While, in the latter country, we find the feudal system opposing the central authority, and the towns upholding it, we see in Germany that the emperors regarded the feudal system rather as their most valuable ally, and that the towns were the main instrument in opposing the authority of the emperors.

Feudalism was of a much later growth in Germany than in France. What divisions there were ran chiefly on racial lines. The chief duchies were those of Saxony, Franconia, Suabia, and Bavaria, and these were grouped together so as to form one confederation. This confederation was of a very peculiar character. Owing to the absence of very strong racial differences, and to the fact that the racial element did not coincide with the demarcations of land, we find in the confederation a considerable amount of plasticity. Apparently, not much effort would have been required to weld the duchies into one united kingdom. Such, indeed, was the frequent aim of the German kings and emperors. But other elements fatally intervened. Family hatreds, divergences of language, the old traditional hostility between North and South, and the meddling interference of the emperors in Italy—all these conspired together to thwart any project of an immediate unification of Germany.

When, however, the Emperor Barbarossa seriously girded himself for the task of uniting Germany, he tried to make use of feudalism as his chief instrument. In the personal oath of allegiance to himself, and in all the financial and military ties of feudalism, he beheld immense possibilities. His first endeavor, therefore, was to hasten and spread everywhere throughout Germany the movement of feudalism. Hitherto, side by side with feudal territories, there had lain strips of allodial possessions. Barbarossa tried, as far as possible, to convert the allodial property into fiefs, and to bring the whole land under his sway by the feudal allegiance that would be due to him. He also insisted very strongly upon the exact fulfilment of all personal obligations owed to him by his feudal tenants. What more drastic proof of this could we find than his letter to the Count of Forcalquier that "he has contumaciously neglected to come to our court, and to receive his benefice from our hands. His country has, by a just sentence, been so adjudged to us that we may do with it what we will"?

To a certain extent, Barbarossa was successful. Unfortunately, however, the strands of feudalism were not strong enough to connect the violent German feuds with their liege sovereign. Only small provocation was needed to cause the duke or baron to throw off his promise of allegiance. Even during the strong reigns of Henry VI and Frederick II, the principalities of Germany remained wilful and turbulent.

While, however, feudalism, in the German possessions of the emperor, appears as an inefficient instrument for establishing the royal central authority, it appears in Italy under another aspect; namely, as the important obstacle to the royal jurisdiction. This was during the reign of Frederick II. This eccentric and, sometimes, inconsistent emperor seemed for a time to recognize the practical impossibility of establishing a royal bureaucracy in Germany, and sought compensation by setting up a despotic system of administration in Naples and Sicily. Here, he was opposed both by feudalism and by the great and opulent cities. But the skill and energy of Frederick triumphed over all. Feudal castles were either destroyed or occupied by royal garrisons; feudal tribunals of justice were replaced by the royal courts, and even the strong feudal prelates were compelled to content themselves with their spiritual functions, while the towns were too powerless to make any resistance.

Peculiar, indeed, was the part taken by the economic element in the empire. In Germany, we see feudalism apparently about to become an instrument in the consolidation of the kingdom, and then exercising an activity in the opposite direction, while, in Naples and Sicily, it was all along diametrically opposed to the formation of a centralized royal government.

Before leaving those countries that were more or less directly under imperial control, we must first consider what were the prospects of the consolidation of Italy. Of this, there could scarcely have been any hope. From the very first, Italy had become a prey to many different invaders, who successfully effected a settlement on Italian soil. The Greeks, the Lombards, the Normans, and the Saracens, all these contended for the mastery, and at the same time the emperor in Germany vainly strove to assert his authority, which, except in Rome, was practically only nominal.

The economic elements were also opposed to any form of centralized government. During the early period of the Middle Ages, the towns had been the in-

struments of organized government throughout Italy.
Ruled very often by the bishop, they asserted their jurisdiction and enforced law and order in the vast areas of
territory that lay outside the city walls. It is possible
that, had the rule of the bishops continued, the continuity of the ecclesiastical system might have welded together the towns in such a way as to bring about a general unity. But, before long, the reins of power slipped
from the hands of the bishops into the hands of the
townsmen themselves. Various causes contributed to
this. Among the most important was the fact that the
bishops were elected by the citizens, and that the very
nature of the episcopal office prevented the bishops from
continually exercising that hard and ruthless authority
which was so necessary in turbulent times. Then again,
the towns had been built for the purpose of warding
off barbarian invasions, and were therefore especially
able to fight against any outside power that should try
to force itself upon them.

By the middle of the twelfth century, the Lombard
cities had practically asserted their independence, and
were behaving as so many separate States. In vain did
the emperors seek to enforce their jurisdiction. Their
hands were too much tied by disputes in their own country, and such symbolic acts of sovereignty, as their names
appearing in the public acts and upon the coins, were
very little, in comparison with the active power enjoyed
by the towns to make war or declare peace.

The towns, as we shall see more fully in the next
section, succeeded in obtaining their full independence
to such an extent that the history of Italy down to the
nineteenth century is a history of separate City-States.

Nor did the economic element of feudalism act in a
different direction from that of the towns. For in Italy

feudalism was in a much looser condition than it was in France or even in Germany. Not only was the strife between the barons more rampant, but the lesser tenants more easily shook off their allegiance to their immediate superiors. Concerted action among the feudal landowners was, therefore, rendered extremely difficult. And in the course of long wars between the Papal and the imperial parties, feudalism became completely swept away by the overshadowing power of the towns.

In Italy, therefore, we see the economic element of the towns successfully exercising its disintegrating influence. Neither the centralizing influence of the Papacy, nor that of the imperial authority, succeeded in grasping and wielding that force which, in France, and partly in England, was the main instrument in the extension of unity and central power.

The only country where we see both feudalism and the towns working together for the consolidation of the kingdom and for a centralized authority is England.

This was mainly owing, as we have already suggested, to the vigorous policy of William of Normandy. He had seen too clearly the evils that had been wrought in France by the frequent insubordination of the vassals. He also perceived its remedy, and was quick to apply it. Instead of the inferior vassals and tenants taking the oath of allegiance directly to their immediate lord, they were required to take an oath of allegiance directly to the king. Thus, the bigger barons could no longer hurl the military forces of their tenants against the king. Feudalism, by this means, became no longer a decentralizing force, but rather one of the strongest bonds of unity.

During the reigns of William II and of Stephen,

the feudal barons did indeed seek to emancipate themselves from the national system, and to make themselves
so many independent sovereigns. This, however, was
rather in defiance of the feudal system, than by cooperation with its natural tendency. In any case, the king
threw himself upon the support of the great bulk of
his subjects, and with an iron hand crushed the conspiracy of the nobles.

During the reign of Stephen, they used the anarchy
of the times for their own advantage. Baronial castles
became centers of brigandage and oppression, and the
law for a time was dwarfed by individual tyranny.
When once, however, order was restored, the "unlawful" castles were razed to the ground, while the wisdom
of Henry I, by his celebrated Charter of Liberties, both
checked the abuses connected with the oppression of the
barons, and secured the good-will of the people by de-
tailed provisions of good government.

All through the pages of English history, we find that
the collective tendency of the English feudalism was in
the direction of centralization. It interfered in no way
with the local courts of the realm or with the general
system of administration and justice. On the other
hand, it served for a considerable time as one of the
most available means of procuring money for the royal
treasury, and of rallying around the throne the military
resources of the country.

The towns also played a very important part in the
central administration of the kingdom. They never
stood apart by themselves as did the towns in the Continental countries. Even from early times, they had
sent their representatives to the shire-mote, and had
taken part in its legislative and judicial business, and
from early times as well, the towns had also been con-

nected with the Crown, both by the patronage afforded them by the king, and by the money which they contributed to his coffers. When Simon de Montfort, holding for a time the direction of affairs, summoned to Parliament the representatives of the citizens and burgesses, he systematized still further the activities that connected the towns with the central system.

The towns in England became part of the one great national system. They were as so many healthy cells of the same organism, and never did they exercise that disintegrating influence, such as we too often find on the Continent.

Thus far, we have passed in brief review the process of the formation and solidification of the most important countries of medieval Europe. The result has been to demonstrate the tremendous importance of the economic factors of feudalism and of the towns. It was these elements that shaped the whole course of history in medieval Europe, and even to this day can be discerned certain vestiges of those forces that often, apparently acting at random, succeeded in producing very definite and far-reaching results.

CHAPTER VI

INFLUENCE OF THE ECONOMIC ELEMENT IN THE CONTEST BETWEEN THE EMPIRE AND THE PAPACY

THE struggle between the empire and the Papacy that convulsed Germany and Italy for nearly two hundred years, and made itself slightly felt even in England and France, began with the accession of Pope Gregory VII. The nature of the issues that were at stake demands careful consideration, and this will very soon reveal that while, on the one hand, rival jurisdictions were greatly responsible for the struggle, the economic element always played a very important part.

There was, indeed, the old question which even in our own times has hardly received a satisfactory solution, namely, "Is the Church in the State, or is the State in the Church?" Although the Church and the State are two distinct societies, having special ends of their own and special means for those ends, yet, in some respects, they touch and apparently overlap one another. For the State is always under the obligation of remembering that the temporal welfare of its members, and all its temporal regulations, must be subordinate to the law of God and to the spiritual welfare of mankind. Also, there are some things whose administration concerns both the Church and the State. Thus, the sacrament of Marriage is both a civil contract and also a sacrament. In this way, it is easy to see how opposite views and claims might very easily arise.

This was especially so in the Middle Ages. The Holy Roman Empire was supposed to be one society, governed both by the Pope and by the emperor. Important boundary lines between Church and State were most easily overlooked, and, therefore, there arose the quick and natural question as to who should be the supreme leader of this identical society. The views of the Sovereign Pontiff were clearly expressed in the words of Pope Gregory, who compared the emperor to the moon and himself to the sun, both shining in the same firmament. Nor, on the other hand, was it unnatural if the emperor held views of a somewhat opposite nature. Such a conflict of views was undoubtedly one of the main causes of the continued conflict between Pope and emperor. Such questions as that of investiture, as to who should invest a newly made prelate with the ring and crozier, did, indeed, involve questions of ephemeral and secondary import. But the question, who should be the supreme ruler in what was apparently one and the same society, could only be answered by a contest and a direct trial of strength.

The policy of the emperors tended greatly to secularize the Church. Obviously, the great bulk of the lay princes, uncultured and barbarous as they too often were, were not sufficiently competent to carry on the work of administration. It was therefore the policy of the emperors to draw their ministers and governors from the ranks of the clergy, to create a school of clerical statesmen and officials, who should help the emperor to carry on the task of government. Even in other countries, we behold very presentable types of such men. In England, for example, there were the Archbishops Lanfranc and Anselm of Canterbury; in France, the Abbot Suger; in Germany, such clerical statesmen as Bruno, brother of Otto I, were famed for efficiency. Whether as chancellors or legates, they often exercised jurisdiction in such a way as to enforce law and order, and spread culture and civilization. But as Pope Paschal complained to Henry V, the bishops and abbots were so occupied in secular causes that they were very often compelled to frequent the county courts or engage in military strife. And only too often the emperor's nomination of a bishop was decided by military considerations.

The performance of civil and judicial functions must have been exceedingly prejudicial to the spirit of the ministry, and they were certainly opposed to the precept of St. Paul, *Nemo se implicet negotiis secularibus* (Let none entangle himself in worldly affairs). It is no wonder, therefore, that Pope Gregory VII, a single-minded man who had at heart the true interests of the Church, perceived the need of reform, and, what was more, determined to effect its accomplishment.

To do this successfully involved two things: first, the active denial of the jurisdiction of the emperor to give away spiritual benefices; and, secondly, the liberation of the Church in Germany from the influences of feudalism. Both of these were drastic processes which were sure to displease both the emperor and a great part of the clergy, who would see their interests threatened and attacked.

When Pope Gregory VII proceeded to declare excommunication upon any emperor, king, duke, or count, or any other lay person presuming to give investiture of any ecclesiastical dignity, Henry IV regarded it as a personal challenge. At once, the question of investiture brought into the open the more general issues at stake. Both Pope and emperor make distinct statements as to what they conceived to be their powers of jurisdiction and coercion.

The conflict between Henry IV and Gregory VII ended in the apparent defeat of Gregory VII, who was driven into exile. But it was again renewed under Henry V and Pope Paschal II. A compromise was effected between the two, in which the Pope obtained recognition of the right of investiture, on condition of the cession to the emperor of all Church temporalities, excluding, however, the temporalities of the Holy See. Not until the Concordat of Worms (1177) between Henry V and Calixtus II was the dispute healed. And even this was only effected by concentrating the terms of the Concordat to one or two very narrow issues of the contest. It was stipulated that the Pope should invest with the spiritual symbols of the office, and that the emperor should invest with the symbols of the temporal jurisdiction annexed to the office.

Under Barbarossa, the contest between Pope and emperor came to be fought on the more general issues, and with far greater bitterness than before. This time, the main center of the struggle was in the north of Italy. Barbarossa gave the signal by his attempt to enforce certain vexatious feudal rights against the Italian towns. These rebelled, and were helped and patronized in their rebellion by Pope Alexander III. The power of the towns was more than a match for that of the emperor and his feudal nobles. At the battle of Legnano (1176), Barbarossa barely escaped with his life, and the result was the Treaty of Constance, which confirmed the towns in the possession of practical independence, and gave to the Pope a complete triumph over the imperial party in Italy.

It was the towns that had thus secured to the Pope his first great national victory over the emperor. With the natural strength of their walls and extent of their resources, they had occupied a position in the middle of the see-saw, and had decided the balance against the emperor.

The last phase of the great struggle between empire and Papacy took place under Frederick II. All over Italy and Germany the strife between the Ghibelline, or imperial party, and the Guelf, or Papal party, waxed strong. Brilliant, indeed, was the career of Frederick. In spite of the Pope's opposition, he proceeded on the Crusade to the Holy Land and, even while under excommunication, achieved more substantial results than had been gained in any other of the Crusades. In Naples and Sicily, he established a strong bureaucracy, put down the lawlessness of the barons, and established the foundation of a sound administrative, judicial, and financial system.

In Germany, however, he was less successful. He there gave full liberty, or rather license, to the feudal nobility. Abandoning what had been the consistent policy of previous emperors, he purposely increased the power of the independent units, and even forced his son, Henry VII, crowned king of the Romans, to recognize by edict the complete territorial supremacy of the nobles. To this measure, however, the towns in Germany were strongly opposed. The result was a struggle between the towns and the feudal barons, which ended in the extinction of neither. While the princes and nobles retained independent jurisdiction in their own domain, the cities and towns vindicated their own autonomy. Thus Germany passed completely beyond the control of any centralizing influence. The emperor practically abdicated all real authority, while Germany became a mere aggregate of rival units, some under clerical, others under lay jurisdiction.

In Italy, Frederick's success was but temporary. It is true that his party was successful in Lombardy, but just at this juncture he died, and with him perished the fortunes of the House of Hohenstauffen. The life-work of Frederick was practically a failure. The powerful aristocracy in Germany now divided amongst themselves the last vestiges of imperial power and administration, while the people in Northern Italy achieved their final independence. Even the kingdom of Naples and Sicily slipped from the control of the Hohenstauffen dynasty, and became ruled alternately by the Frenchmen and Spaniards.

Such was the struggle between the empire and Papacy. The whole struggle reveals the all-important part that was played in it by the economic elements of feudalism and the towns.

We might summarize this aspect of the struggle by remarking that it was the feudal element in the Church in Germany that brought about the collision between the Pope and the emperor. If the prelates had been merely spiritual officers, there would have been no reason or incentive for the emperor to claim the right of investiture. When, however, the bishop or abbot held not only a spiritual but also a temporal office; when, as sometimes happened, he had under him hundreds of knights and military retainers and sometimes even powerful fleets, then it was all-important that the emperor should have a large share in the choice of the candidate, and that, as far as possible, he himself should confer all the symbols of jurisdiction.

Then, again, it was the same powerful secular element in the Church in Germany that occasioned so keen a struggle between Pope and emperor for the mastery of the Church. German emperors regarded and used the Church not only as an important agent of administration, but also as an instrument for settling newly obtained provinces, and of diffusing German unity. When, however, the Papal jurisdiction began to assert itself, then the Church in Germany was in danger of becoming an *imperium in imperio.*

The feudal element, again, was the cause of many of the most grievous abuses in the Church in Germany. But when the Pope in the exercise of his own lawful jurisdiction attempted to bring about a reform he was resisted by the emperor. Thus the Pope also had reason to complain of an *imperium in imperio.* The feudal element, therefore, had the effect of causing both Church and State to infringe on each other's jurisdiction, and the result was a long and terrible struggle for the mastery.

During the course of the struggle it is somewhat hard to analyze all the subsidiary causes and minor issues. But one thing is certain, namely, that the feudal system and towns together effected the eventual overthrow of the imperial power, the temporary triumph of the Papacy, and the establishment for a long time of decentralized government both in Germany and in Italy. The two economic units of the land and of the town succeeded in neutralizing the unifying tendency of the shadowy Holy Roman Empire, and in considerably weakening the temporal jurisdiction even of the Popes.

But, even down to the fourteenth century, some vestiges could still be seen of the long conflict between the centralizing forces of feudalism and the towns. In Dante's time, the fierce feuds between Guelf and Ghibelline still continued, though the significance attached to these party names must have dwindled down almost to the vanishing point. Dante, in his *Monarchia,* dreams of the world-wide sovereignty of the Roman Empire, and believes that if the emperor would only once again visit Italy, and assert his power, discord would vanish and its place would be taken by universal peace and prosperity.

To Henry VII, of the House of Luxemburg, Dante addressed the touching and well-known words, "Come to see your Rome, which weeps, widowed and alone, and calls out day and night, 'My Cæsar, wherefore does he not attend to me!'" Henry VII listened to the request. In 1310 he crossed the Alps. But his arrival acted only as a torch to the combustible material. When the Ghibellines granted him a guard of honor, the Guelfs suspected force and treachery toward themselves. Many of the Guelfic cities like Florence shut their gates against him, and one-half of Rome rose up in arms against one whom it regarded as merely the champion of the Ghibelline party. Slowly he retreated northward, and only the hand of death prevented him from witnessing the utter failure of his expedition.

Still more humiliating, and even ridiculous, was the visit of Charles IV, the originator of the celebrated Golden Bull, and so successful in extending his own hereditary dominions. Not only did he fail to rally Italy around the imperial standard, but the very person of the emperor suffered the degradation of being locked up in the palace of Siena, and nearly dying from hunger.

The emperors ceased from attempting any longer to make a reality of the German Italian Empire. The old factions of the Guelfs and Ghibellines begin to die out, and both barons and towns live their own individual existence in an atmosphere of local quarrels and jealousies.

CHAPTER VII

INFLUENCE OF THE ECONOMIC ELEMENT IN RAISING THE MIDDLE CLASS TO THE POSSESSION OF POLITICAL POWER

DURING the early Middle Ages, the towns and the industrial classes enjoyed very little political power. Living in close subjection to their immediate lord they found themselves entirely cut off from any participation in the administration of the country, and were frequently humiliated by signs of servitude as well as galled by heavy money exactions. As yet, indeed, there was no middle class forming a recognized part of the social machinery, but gradually the principle of association, so dominant in the Middle Ages, began to assert itself among the industrial classes. In the cities, in the towns, and even in the country, associations were formed which gradually acquired a formal and legal standing, as well as a real share of political power. These associations were the communes.

What was the exact origin of the communes is hard to determine. Some writers, building an hypothesis on the analogy of such words as *civis, quæstores, forum, senatus,* maintain that the commune is of Roman origin, probably connected with the ancient *collegia,* or trade guilds. Others, again, think that the commune is of Teutonic origin. Both views, however, are destitute of any positive evidence. The probable explanation is that the commune of the Middle Ages rose into existence by the pressure of certain forces that were more or less prevailing throughout Europe. Need of protection from a foreign enemy or from the tyranny of their own lord, the desirability of promoting trade interests and maintaining internal order, forced many of the inhabitants of the towns to associate together.

Such associations when once formed speedily obtained much more than the original purpose for which they had previously united. Jurisdiction, both of an administrative and of a judicial nature, fell into their hands; and if the communes did not at first take an active part in the centralized system of government, they at least enjoyed a large share of local self-government.

Perhaps, if we examine deeply into the general aspects of communism, we shall find that it was but a reaction against the personal rule of the feudalistic régime. Prince and bishop could no longer be allowed to have the monopoly of prestige and power. The many began to assert their claim. Moreover, the writings of that age show clearly that the artisans in the towns and the peasants in the country banded themselves together, not merely under the lash of necessity, but also under the impulse of such high ideals as the rights of man and the claims of universal brotherhood. And it was probably from a recognition of this loftier element of communism that some of the prelates warmly espoused its cause and, like the Bishop of Noyon, even positively helped to its establishment.

From the very beginning of their formation, the communes began to enjoy some of the jurisdiction that had hitherto been the monopoly of feudalism. In some cases, it is true, they seem to have so far entered the precincts of feudalism as to assume the position of vassals toward the prince who gave them their communistic charter. For while, on their part, they swore to be faithful to their lord, he took upon himself the obligation to defend them as though they were his own men. The communes exercised legislative and judicial power that was confined only by the limits of the city. They could also build fortifications and impose taxes. Such powers may have varied greatly in the cities of different countries, and sometimes even in cities of the same country, but, whether many or few, these powers attest to the true nature of the communistic jurisdiction.

In the Middle Ages much importance was attached to symbols. One of the great symbols of administrative and judicial power was the seal. Emperors and kings possessed their own peculiar seal, and so, also, did the Popes, of whom there were some whose documents were called "bulls" from the peculiar *bolla,* or seal, attached to them. So, also, throughout every European country, the communes had the right of using their own seal, the seal of the corporation.

Another symbol of their power was the building where the administrative organ of the commune met and carried on its deliberations. Whether under the name of "guild hall" in England, *hôtel de ville* in France and Belgium, or *rathaus* in Germany, it was always an outward sign that the commune had power to perform some very important functions.

But one of the most precious of the outward signs of their jurisdiction and power was the charter. Unlike the power of the feudal baron, which was indefinite as to time, place, and limit, the power of the commune was absolutely definite as to the time of its origin, circumstances of its formation, and precise limits of its jurisdiction. Cases may have occurred of the commune having an actual existence before the charter was granted, but while in that embryonic condition it had no legal and formal existence.

The clauses of these charters varied considerably, both in quantity and quality. They generally touched upon the following points: namely, the organization of the commune, the appointment of a certain definite place where it could meet and carry on its functions, the definition of the limits of its administrative and judicial power, and, very often, the enumeration of certain powers still reserved to the feudal jurisdiction of the grantor of the charter. These are only examples of some of the clauses which were found in many of the charters. It must be remembered that scarcely two charters are found identically alike.

One of the extracts from charters still extant will serve as an illustration. In the charter given to the city of Beauvais, we read the following:

"The peers of the commune shall swear to favor no one for friendship sake, to injure no one on the ground of private enmity; they shall in every case give, according to their power, an equitable decision. All others shall swear to obey the decisions of the peers, and try to assist in seeing that they are carried out. Whenever any man has done an injury to a person who has sworn the commune, on a complaint of the same being made, the peers of the commune shall punish the delinquent either in his person or in his goods, deliberation having been held on the subject.

"If the culprit takes refuge in some castle, the peers of the commune shall refer to the lord of the castle or his representative, and if, according to their opinion, satisfaction is done them against the enemy of the commune, it will be enough; but if the lord refuses satisfaction, they shall do justice to themselves on the lord's property or on his retainers. If some foreign merchant comes to Beauvais for trading purposes, and if any one

does wrong or injury to him within the municipal precincts, if a complaint is entered before the peers, and if
the merchant can discover the malefactor in the town,
the peers shall punish him, unless the merchant should
be an enemy of the commune. If it happened that the
whole commune marched out of town against its enemies, no one shall hold parley with the enemies except
by leave of its peers."

Such are the most significant clauses of the charter.
They point to the peculiar circumstances under which
the charter was given, and they indicate that the main
object of the charter was defense against wrong-doing
from within or without. Protection from violence and
fraud seems to have been the dominant feature of the
charter. On the other hand, the clauses from the charter of Henry I to the city of London are of quite a different character and intent. Though not giving to the
citizens of London the legal status of a commune, they
distinctly lay down the framework of its future existence. Its main points are the following: namely, an
autonomous judicial administration of their own, freedom from the obligation to accept trial by battle, and
from the payment of various imposts, the right to elect
their own sheriff, and to have their own political meetings. Nothing is said about means of self-defense, and
the main purpose of the charter appears to be the
definite organization of municipal administration, and
a certain freedom from the control of the central
administration.

Evidently such charters were extremely valued and
kept with jealous care. Occasionally they met with mis-
hap, and then the first care of the burghers was to get
them replaced. Thus, for example, during the Hundred
Years' War, the charter of the commune of Polk was

destroyed, but the townsmen, after furnishing their lord with written proofs of the legitimacy of their demand, obtained from him the renewal of the original charter.

Besides the possession of a charter and a definite organization, the communes also enjoyed an organized military force of their own. In England this was used mainly for the purpose of keeping order within the limits of the town. Patrols of townsmen paraded the walls and streets and stood on guard at the gates. It is true that this police system in England was prescribed and regulated by royal ordinance, but that does not take away from the fact that the town military organization was a function of the commune as such.

Similarly on the Continent, we find that the communes had also a military organization of their own. In many cases, such organization formed a direct part of the defensive forces of the country, and the inhabitants of the towns, like the feudal knight, might be called upon by the lord to wage war against the common enemy. This was the case with some of the exposed towns in Germany, and it was so in many parts of France. In these places we find clauses in the charters, stating in minute terms the exact conditions and limits of the military service that had to be given by the towns.

Besides having a military organization of its own, the commune also possessed control over its own finances. In some cases these must have been very considerable. Besides certain lands and forests that were the common property of the town, a considerable income was derived from judicial fines, market tolls, and even the imposition of local taxes. Many charters contain special mention of these financial privileges. Even the privilege of coining their own money is sometimes allowed to the members of the commune. In England, however, this privilege was very much restricted. In France it was quietly removed altogether by the policy of the kings, and only in Germany and Italy did local coinage hold its ground for a long time, a fact which testifies to the strong decentralizing tendencies of those countries.

Before concluding our general description of the communes, just one word must be said regarding their methods of government. Naturally, these differed very widely in different countries. Magistrates and councils seem to have been the usual nominal governing body. Then, as the guilds and crafts gradually became more and more important, they managed to usurp, in many cases, the entire municipal control. For a long time there was a fierce and widespread contest between the members of the upper and lower guilds for the posses-sion of the municipal authority. The lower guilds were, in the main, successful, and the basis of the government of the town grew more and more democratic. In Italy, however, each of the important towns had a special, typical form of government of its own, incapable of being included in any ordinary classified group. Thus, Venice furnishes us with an oligarchic type of government, Florence with a despotic. Rome, on the other hand, has the unique privilege of possessing a theocratic form of government, while Naples continued for many years the feudal system, which in other parts of Italy had long become obsolete.

We must now consider in detail the different countries of Europe, for the purpose of discovering how far, in each of them, the towns became the instruments for placing a large share of political power in the hands of the middle class. We shall thus see more clearly how the economic element of the town became the lever by which political power became transferred from the hands of feudal magnates into the hands of the people.

In France, the relations between the towns and the monarchy were of a varied nature. Sometimes, the kings favored the communes, and made use of them for extending the royal power; at other times, they acted toward the communes with the greatest hostility.

On the king's own personal domain, the communes were generally discouraged. Nor was this a matter of wonder. The autonomous jurisdiction of the communes meant a corresponding deprivation of royal power. When, therefore, such towns as Orleans, Poitiers, and Paris tried to form themselves into communes, they were prevented from doing so by main force.

When, however, it was a question of establishing communes on the domain of other feudal lords, then the royal policy was generally in their favor. For the communes, by being placed under royal protection, became so many expansive nuclei of royal influence, and, at the same time, tended to diminish the formidable power of the great feudatories. It was, however, on the domains of the great bishops and abbots that such communes were first established, and only by slow degrees did the movement also spread to the domains of the feudal lords. At first, the kings only confirmed the charters that had been given by the immediate lord. Such a confirmation, at first quite voluntary, became changed by custom into a necessity, until eventually no charter was considered valid without the royal signature. In fact, by the middle of the fourteenth century, it was definitely proclaimed by the king that to him alone belonged the right to establish the commune.

Under Philip Augustus and Louis XIII, the communes became the most powerful agents of the royal power. They not only diminished the formidable power of the great feudatories, but were most useful instruments in the centralized system of government. In certain parts of the kingdom that were exposed to hostile invasion, they fulfilled the same purpose as the walled towns built by Henry the Fowler. They served as fortresses against the enemy.

From the financial point of view, the communes were extremely useful to the king. It was mainly the desire of getting more money from them that induced the kings of England and France to allow the communes to send representatives to the great national assembly, and it was thus, through these, that the great wealth accumulated by the middle classes was diverted to the needs of the treasury of the nation.

By degrees, however, the power of the communes began to menace the interests of the Crown. After the time of Philip Augustus, we find the royal authority coming into frequent collision with the communes. Sometimes there was open violence, but usually the kings tried to obtain their end by more pacific means. They began to assume to themselves the prerogative of choosing the magistrates, and availing themselves of the plea of financial mismanagement, they placed the administration of the funds under royal control.

It was not long before the communes began to lose their independent existence. In spite of the revolutionary movement of 1382, when the important cities of Paris, Rouen, and Orleans flew to arms and resisted the aggressions of the French king, they were gradually brought into submission. After all, the communes were only one section of the community. Against them were the king and the barons, and, more powerful still, the wonderful administrative systems that enveloped, like a network, the whole kingdom.

The communes, in spite of their temporary extinction, had done an important and lasting work. When the French king allowed them to send representatives to the national council, he little dreamed that he was putting into the hands of the middle class what would become, in the future, a most formidable power. It is true that with the growth of the French monarchy the Third Estate was rarely assembled, and that between the year 1616 and the beginning of the French Revolution it met only once. Yet the power of the people had a legal instrument with which to act on the destinies of the nation. And when, in the year 1789, the Third Estate met together and gradually took over all the political power, it was only continuing the work that was done by the early communes—a work that was interrupted by centuries of royal despotism.

In Germany, the towns, by means of the communes, also became, in great measure, the instrument by which the middle class asserted its weight and influence.

At first, the towns in Germany had very little government of their own. Most of them were placed under the control of counts. By degrees, many of these cities became released from this subjection. The tyranny and rapacity of the overlords were so intolerable, and the injury done to the interests of trade and commerce was so great, that the emperors interfered and, as in France, began to take the market towns under their protection. Thus, none were permitted to interfere with the markets of such towns; their functions were protected from all interference and hindrance, and all unjust charges were sternly prohibited. Jurisdiction over offenses committed during the market was also frequently removed from the hands of the local courts and referred to the judge of the province.

Their military strength became almost of as much benefit to the emperor as his protection was to them. Their forces became part of the military strength of the empire, and were often more to be depended upon than those of the feudal barons. Naturally, the alliance between the emperor and the cities that was thus based on mutual interests was bound to increase. Cities frequently rebelled against their overlord, and placed themselves under the protection of the emperor. Sometimes, as in the case of the city of Speyer in 1707, they would even shake off the jurisdiction of a spiritual overlord.

Such cities occupied the feudal position of a vassal-in-chief, and thus enjoyed a distinct right to send representatives to the Imperial Diet, where, together with the elector and princes, they took part in the gravest affairs of State. Thus, in 1338, a summons was sent to the imperial city of Lübeck, and the wording of it was, that it should send two representatives to Frankfort in order to confer with the princes, courts, and other cities.

Together with this political power which they enjoyed by sharing in the deliberations of the Diet, the German towns were able to exercise political power in another and very unique way. The leagues of the towns which we have already mentioned gave to the middle class some of the rights and prerogatives of sovereign powers. Not only did they declare war and make treaties, but they formulated a code of maritime laws and made themselves responsible for the general preservation of order. The following passage, taken from the Agreement of the Rhine League, will show how the middle class asserted for themselves an equality of power and of rights with the princes of the empire:

"We, the judges, consuls (aldermen), and all the citizens of Mainz, Cologne, Worms, Speyer, Strassburg, Basel, and other cities which are bound together in the league of the holy peace. We have mutually bound ourselves by oath to observe a general peace for ten years from St. Margaret's day. The venerable archbishops, Gerhard of Mainz, Conrad of Cologne, Arnold of Trier, and the bishops, Richard of Worms, Henry of Strassburg, Jacob of Metz, Berthold of Basel, and many counts and nobles of this land have joined us in this oath, and they, as well as we, have all surrendered the unjust tolls which we have been collecting, both by land and water   not only the greater areas among us shall have the advantage of the common protection."

In another document, issued by the Rhine League, we read:

"If any knight, in trying to aid his lord, who is at war with us, attacks us or molests us anywhere outside of the walled towns of his lord, he is breaking the peace and we will inflict due punishment on him and his possessions. We wish to be protectors of the peasants, and we will protect them against all violence if they will observe the peace with us."

Such clauses clearly show that the middle class in Germany enjoyed, by means of the towns, an almost separate *imperium,* or political jurisdiction. It is no wonder that Frederick II did all in his power to encourage the feudal element at the expense of the towns. The fruitlessness of his efforts testifies to their strength. When single towns, like Cologne, were able to put into the field an armed force of thirty thousand men, it is evident that in their collective capacity they could not do otherwise than shake off the yoke of the feudal magnates. Even to this day the fact that the three towns of Hamburg, Bremen, and Lübeck entered the German Imperial Confederation as separate States amply sets forth the sovereignty of the middle class in later medieval Germany.

When we come to the towns in Italy, we find a remarkably rapid development of the middle class. Already, by the ninth century, there began to appear independent communes. This is mainly accounted for by the fact that the towns, in the earliest phase of their existence, were under the jurisdiction of the bishops. It was, therefore, much easier for the townsmen to assert their independence than if they had to struggle against some powerful and unscrupulous lay ruler. Moreover, the people themselves took part in the election of their bishop, and this share, however nominal, in the making of their own government, was already one step forward in the direction of democratic government.

In the twelfth century we behold throughout Italy a glorious constellation of happy and thriving republic towns: Amalfi, with its fifty thousand inhabitants, trading with the farthest regions of the East; Salerno, with its medical school, its gorgeous palaces and enchanting gardens; Pisa, with ten thousand towers within its city walls, and already by 1114 enjoying full self-government; Genoa, with its spacious harbor, green-clad hills, and trading settlements all over the Mediterranean; while, above all, towering in natural strength and mercantile splendor, was Venice with its seven fleets, its supremacy in trade and commerce, and in full enjoyment of its republican constitution. Similarly, the Lombard towns, at the same time that they grew commercially, developed constitutions that were essentially democratic.

The conflict between Frederick Barbarossa and the

towns only hastened the commercial movement.   His arrogant claim to feudal rights and personal jurisdiction over the towns only welded together still more strongly the democratic forces.   One conspicuous feature about this movement was that even many of the aristocracy shared in it, and thus contributed their aid to the over-throw of the feudal system of government.

Unfortunately, the relaxation of imperial aggressive-ness became the accidental cause of disunion, both among the cities and even inside the cities themselves. The nobles and the merchant classes strove to monop-olize government to the exclusion of the lower classes. In other words, the towns remained infected by the bad feudal element of clique and class.   Bitterness and strife resulted, and things were made worse by the angry quarrels between the Papal and imperial party, which penetrated into almost every town of Italy.

Instead of democratic institutions, anarchy and con-fusion reigned supreme, until gradually there crystal-lized into shape almost every conceivable form of gov-ernment.   In Milan, for example, the Sforzas, military adventurers, seized the occasion to establish a despotism whose odious character was mitigated, however, by the paternal and beneficial character of their personal rule. In Florence, we behold likewise a despotism ingrafting itself upon what was nominally a republic; in Venice, the republic gradually transforms itself into an oligarchy of the most powerful kind that the world has ever seen.

The reign of the middle class in Italy was, therefore, short-lived.   Owing to bad conditions, the democracy only prepared the way for other and various forms of government.   But if these abnormal conditions had not been present, the people would have enjoyed as much political power as they did in other countries.

We now come to England, in which the towns, more than elsewhere, prepared the way for placing the preponderance of power in the hands of the middle class.

Even from Anglo-Saxon times, the towns had sent representatives to the shire court, and had thus taken part in the government of a larger area than their own. In 1265, Simon de Montfort gave to the towns even wider activity, and empowered them to send representatives to Parliament. Although, at first, the representation was not regular or complete, yet, by the Parliament of 1295, it had become so, and the Third Estate took part in the deliberations of Parliament, as permanent and essential members. It is true that for some considerable time their influence was in the background. They were timid and were inexperienced. But the advance of time overcame both these obstacles. Moreover, the important fact, that the knights of the shire sat side by side with citizens and burgesses in the town-house, gave to the Third Estate a power and a prestige that it could not enjoy in the assemblies on the Continent.

By the time of Richard III, in the fourteenth century, we find that preponderance of power already lodged in the hands of the representatives of the Third Estate. For they had by then acquired the all-important control of the purse. All money bills had to originate in the house of the representatives of the middle class; they, alone, could appropriate sums of money, and could examine into the financial accounts. They alone had the right of impeachment, and used that right for the purpose of getting rid of powerful and obnoxious ministers. And they also took an active part in matters dealing with domestic and foreign policy.

At first, the middle class took the side of the king against the all-powerful barons, but as the king's power became stronger and more centralized, their interests became affected in another way, and their policy underwent a corresponding change. By the time of the Tudor kings there had crystallized into definite shape that tremendous struggle between the monarchy and the representatives of the middle class that culminated in the civil war between Charles I and his Parliament, the execution of the king, and the revolution of 1688, when James II was driven from the throne, and William III of Orange was called over from Holland to take his place.

The main part in this contest was taken by the representatives of the middle class sitting in the House of Commons. Using their power of the purse, it was they who dared to question the will even of Henry VIII and Elizabeth, and continually brought their remonstrances to the notice of James I. It was the Commons again who, by silent and patient waiting, brought about the psychological moment when Charles I was forced to summon the representatives to ask them for supplies to carry on the Scotch war, and it was they again who, goaded into desperation by the violation of their rights and privileges, summoned around them the armed force of the greater part of the nation, beat the king into submission, and took him prisoner. When, on the 19th of January, 1649, the king's head rolled on the block, we behold the apotheosis of the power of the people and the downfall of its rival, the power of the Crown.

Even the reaction, which followed in the restoration of Charles II, did not end the onward march of the middle class. Under James II, they asserted law-making powers of the Parliament, and when, in defiance of their opposition, he still insisted on his royal prerogative of dispensing with the laws which they had made and promulgated, then they rose up a second time and invited William III to take the throne and govern conjointly with them, as a limited constitutional monarch.

From henceforth, there was only one obstacle to the political power of the people, and that was the limitation of the franchise. Only persons of considerable property enjoyed the right of voting. Small and decayed towns still sent up representatives, while large and growing towns were still deprived of all representation, and there were even rotten boroughs, merely nominal boroughs, who sent up representatives that were not the people's representatives, but only the paid hirelings of some aristocratic or wealthy individual. By this means, the middle class were practically shut out from their real share of political power; only in some wave of popular agitation could their voice make itself heard.

All this, however, was remedied by the Reform Bill of 1832. Rotten boroughs were swept away, the franchise widened, and the big towns allowed their proper share of representation. From henceforth, the towns resumed their old functions as the levers by which the middle class controls the destinies of the nation. Even at the present day, at a general election, the returns from the large towns are a subject of vital interest, because the will of the nation makes itself known through candidates of the large towns.

If we glance at the condition of things on the other side of the Atlantic, we shall find ourselves face to face with the same facts. The American is derived mainly from the English constitution. In nearly all the American colonies, there was a Popular Assembly, consisting of representatives from the towns or boroughs. And the power of such assemblies was the imitation, and counterpart, and continuation of the very same power that was enjoyed by the English House of Commons. Control of the purse, exclusive right to initiate money bills, power to legislate, were privileges that were claimed and exercised by the colonial Popular Assemblies. The governor might, indeed, refuse his consent, and no bill in that case could become law, but the Assembly had the power to deprive the governor of his salary, and thus the governor, like the English king, was compelled to comply with the popular wish under pain of financial embarrassments.

When, later on, the American nation became an accomplished fact, its constitution was modeled upon the best and most democratic elements in the English constitution. Altered circumstances rendered necessary a corresponding alteration in the method of representation. It is the States and congressional districts that send representatives to the Houses of Congress, while in the separate States it is the county that, singly or collectively, forms the nominal unit of representation. But no one doubts that, even to this day, the big towns and cities are the real centers of the political life and activity of the country. It is there that the conventions, caucuses, and political committees exercise their sovereignty; and the more important the city, so much the more weight is attached to its political verdict.

The town, therefore, even in our modern times, still remains the fulcrum through which, and in which, the great middle class choose their real rulers, and shape the destinies of nations. And this important function began, as we have shown, during the turbulent times of the Middle Ages. Then was laid the foundation of the democratic structure of to-day. The struggles between the communes and the royal power in England and on the Continent, their gradual emancipation from outside control, and development of local autonomy were all steps in this important process. Still more eventful was the time when the Third Estate came into control of the purse. For it was by this means that the Third Estate was able to handle that which is now far more powerful than the sword was in the Middle Ages, namely, the power of money. The victory of the early commune spelled the rule of the middle class throughout the world of the twentieth century.

PART III
MODERN PERIOD

INTRODUCTION

THE Modern Period is often said to begin about the sixteenth century, just at the time of the fall of Constantinople. Although it is impossible to divide history into absolutely watertight compartments, rigidly divided from one another, yet, roughly speaking, there are certain times when the human race seems to make a distinct step forward. New ideals come to the foreground, new subjects of interest are cultivated, and the whole mental horizon becomes widened and enlarged.

Such was the case in the sixteenth century. The religious reformation, the revival of the classics, the rise of diplomacy—these mark, all over Europe, an entirely new condition of intellectual activity.

The political condition of Europe was also undergoing important alterations. Empire and Papacy were ceasing to be dominant factors in politics. Strong monarchical nations were rising up with national characteristics, aspirations, and ambitions. While, in previous times, Europe had been divided vertically into the class distinction of noble, burgher, and peasant, it was now divided by horizontal lines of division. Each nation was now beginning to have a separate characteristic activity of its own, endowed with all the more dramatic intensity on account of the greater narrowness of space.

Diplomacy had also become a new factor in politics. Ambassadors could be found in nearly all the important countries of Europe, and alliances and treaties occupied a larger share of attention. Also, diplomatic correspondence and interviews now counted for much among the political forces of Europe. Venice was the first, and, for a long time, the main center of all this activity. Her ambassadors could be found in every court, and their despatches, still preserved in the archives, show the minuteness of their observation, their agility in acquiring information, and their sagacious acquaintance with human nature.

But the activity which more than ever begins to dominate Europe is the economic activity. It is this which makes friends and enemies of nations. If wars break out, their fundamental origin is some rivalry in trade or commerce that causes the dispute. Alliances between nations are determined by economic considerations, and details regarding the state of the market, and the amount of bullion, occupy the minds of the greatest statesmen. Still more influential becomes the power of money, which exalts and depresses nations, and which becomes now the real test of a nation's power, according to the words of Louis XIV, "It is the last louis d'or that wins."

But the economic activity of the Modern Period of history is intensely complicated and varied. It has a great number of different ramifications, and at least the chief of these must be considered in order that we may obtain some idea of the economic position of Europe in modern times. They may be classified as follows: (1) economic theories, (2) geographical discoveries and their immediate results, (3) altered methods in the production of wealth, (4) distribution of wealth, (5) relations between governments, and also the various ways in which government acts on the industrial life of nations.

CHAPTER I

ECONOMIC THEORIES DURING THE MODERN PERIOD OF HISTORY

DURING the Modern Period of history, there gradually grew up a formidable collection of views regarding economic subjects. These views were not advanced in a loose and spasmodic order, as had been the case in ancient times. So closely connected were they, and so coordinated, that they began to form a complete system of economic doctrine. Thus, there appears for the first time the science of economics.

This science, however, had its beginnings quite early in the Middle Ages. In fact, the main lines of economic thought can, many of them, be traced back to the writings of the Schoolmen. Considerable advantage will, therefore, be gained if we consider, first, all of the economic theories broached during the Middle Ages.

Aristotle's views were at first the source of much of the early medieval opinion on economic subjects. This was especially so with regard to trade, the employment of money, and the exaction of interest. St. Thomas Aquinas held that trade was lawful, but only in strict moderation, only in so far as it contributed to the support of oneself and family and the general well-being of the commonwealth. Other writers adopted the same view. Where they seem to differ is in naming the precise limits that constitute the lawfulness of trade. When, for example, labor had been expended in order to improve the quality of goods, some held that it was lawful to sell the goods at a higher price than when they were originally purchased.

Medieval writers also entertained views regarding such things as capital and partnership. Capital was defined by St. Bernardino as money considered as an agent of producing gain. Such a definition, though too partial, certainly expressed a portion of the truth. If he had defined capital as a good, considered as an agent of procuring some form of gain, then the definition would have coincided with the view still held by most modern economists. Partnership, again, was the subject of much discussion and legislation. The earliest form of partnership was that called the *commenda*. The *commenda* was an arrangement between a certain party who engaged in some business enterprise, and contributed the necessary capital, and some other party who acted as an agent or helper, and received, not only wages, but also a share of the profits. The person who contributed the capital was called *commendator,* and the agent was called *commendatarius.* Often, however, the *commendatarius* would himself contribute a share of the capital, and would thus originate something very closely resembling our modern partnership.

In Germany, there was another kind of partnership which was still more interesting, as being the parent of our modern partnership. This was a business society, either between members of the same family still continuing to live together, or between members of the same craft.

With regard to these different forms of partnership, questions were frequently raised as to the lawfulness of gain that might be derived. According to St. Thomas Aquinas, such gain was lawful only on condition that the investor actually shared in the risk of the enterprise.

What, however, raised most discussion during the Middle Ages was the question of interest on money. Following the lead of Aristotle, many writers of that time condemned interest as absolutely unlawful. At a very early period even, the practice on this point was very severe. Not only were the clergy themselves prohibited to lend money at interest, but the civil legislation also endeavored to stop the practice of lending at interest. Such severity was occasioned by not seeing clearly the distinction between the exchange value of a thing and its value in use, and that money has a peculiar producing power of its own, which should be taken into account.

Also, they did not see clearly the distinction between the *jus in re* and the *jus ad rem.* They imagined that the money of the lender had passed altogether out of his possession, and that, therefore, he was not entitled to any compensation for its use.

By degrees, however, the writers of that time came to moderate their opinions and to make the practice easier by the introduction of many distinctions and exceptions. While still maintaining that it was wrong to demand interest for the loan of the money itself, they held that there might be claims to compensation on other grounds. When the lender parted with his money, even for a time, he was deprived of the opportunity of using it as capital; in other words, the gain from its use began to cease. Such a loss was termed *lucrum cessans* and justified a demand for compensation. Sometimes the creditor was subjected to a positive loss on account of the loan. This loss, also, received a technical name, *damnum emergens,* and might constitute another claim to compensation. Finally, there was a danger, more or less remote, of losing the money that had been lent, and this danger, called *periculum sortis,* became the immediate cause of the justification of the practice of interest.

Oftentimes, the debtor failed to pay at the time that

had been stipulated, and he was, therefore, punished by being called upon to pay not only the sum borrowed but also another sum, in order to compensate for the delay. Nothing could be easier after this than to lend money for a short time gratuitously, and, after the period had elapsed, to pay interest under the name and pretext of a fine.

In practice, therefore, the payment of interest became general. And even the theory of interest very soon underwent modifications. The chief writers on such economic subjects were the canonists, that is, men who made a study of sacred and ecclesiastical law. Such persons as St. Bernardino of Siena and St. Antonius of Florence wrote long treatises on the subject, all tending to extenuate and justify, in various ways, the giving and receiving of interest. And these opinions were drawn up in manuals destined for the practical use of confessors. In fact, even at the present day, the books of Catholic moral theology still make use of the medieval terms, *damnum emergens, lucrum cessans, periculum sortis,* as justifying the payment of interest.

Closely connected with the discussions on the lawfulness of interest in general was the question that was raised regarding loans made to the State. Was it lawful in such cases to pay and receive interest? Some of the Italian cities, reduced to the need of demanding forced loans from their citizen subjects, had allowed a small annual interest in order to prevent dangerous discontent. It soon became clear that such interest was justified by the reasons already alleged. For, very often, there was *lucrum cessans* or *damnum emergens.* But apart from such considerations, the loans were compulsory, and were not made for the sake of gain. St. Thomas had allowed the grateful debtor to make a present to his creditor, in return for the favor he had received. What, however, met with more strenuous opposition was the charitable loan societies, called *montes pietatis*. These were started and managed by the Franciscans, and they conferred great benefit upon the poorer classes. But the Dominicans strongly objected to such institutions. Among their main contentions were the absence of the ordinary conditions justifying the payment of interest, and also the poverty of the borrower. Eventually, however, the Church, recognizing the real benefit to the borrower, sanctioned the *montes*. And, at the present day, on the Continent they are ranked among the most useful of charitable institutions; for the small interest demanded not only maintains the institution, but takes away from the loan its pauperizing effects.

There is no question but that the medieval discussions on interest had a great bearing on the whole course of economics. Not only do they still leave important traces in the teaching of the Church, but they influenced, as well, even secular legislation and largely affected the economics even of the Modern Period.

We must now consider some other economic theories, which, though not formally expanded into a system, yet were tacitly acted upon during the Middle Ages, but during the Modern Period were fully taught and developed. The most important of these theories are those of the Mercantilists and Physiocrats. Ever since the sixteenth century, governments have been actually and avowedly influenced by one of these two schools of economic thought.

The fundamental principle of the Mercantile school was that money is the same as wealth. Modern economics have shown this principle to be false. But the mistake was natural. People's wealth is generally estimated in money, business men only accumulate material goods with the intention of converting them into hard cash, and, above all, money has a value in exchange, for with it can be purchased an indefinite variety of commodities.

This principle, when once adopted by the State, led to very practical consequences. Legislators thought they must regulate trade and industry with a view to enriching the national treasury. They, therefore, sought to make exports exceed imports so as to secure the balance in the precious metals. They paid great attention to the shipping industry, and encouraged home manufactures by such artificial means as bounties and monopolies, and attached much importance to increase of population.

Even in the Middle Ages some of the methods of the Mercantile system were practised. Venice, for example, had sought by heavy duties to reserve for herself the monopoly of commerce and trade under the idea that by so doing she would enrich her own treasury at the expense of that of other nations. In France, we find that for the same purpose many of the provinces inaugurated a severe customs system, while in England, as early as the reign of Edward III, there were laws passed for the express purpose of multiplying the precious metals inside the country. Under Edward III, again, it was forbidden to export gold and silver without a license, while under Richard II, another law was passed, that in any foreign transaction the exports must exceed the imports.

It was not, however, until the Tudor and Stuart times that Mercantilism received its fullest development. Not only were laws passed of the same character as those mentioned in the previous paragraph, but attempts were made to confine by statute the carrying trade of goods, to and from the country, only to English ships. It was even sought to force the English to wear none other than English-made goods. Thus, under Elizabeth, all had to wear English-made caps on Sundays and holydays, and, under Charles II, all had to be buried in woolen shrouds of native manufacture.

Perhaps the greatest financier and administrator connected with the Mercantile system was Colbert, who flourished in France during the reign of Louis XIV. His economic reforms were many and varied, but they all tended to this one end, namely, to enhance the national treasury. Nor can it be denied that he met with a great deal of partial success. French industries of all kinds prospered, and by means of the wealth thus accumulated in the treasury Louis XIV was able to fight a long series of exhausting wars. Indeed, the success of Louis XIV, during the early part of his reign, is the best defense of Mercantilism.

Some of the reforms were of a general nature. Amongst these, the most important were his reduction of the interest on public loans to five per cent., the reduction of the *taille,* and the construction of roads and canals. But other reforms of his were closely connected with the principles of the Mercantile system. He dealt lavishly in such things as privileges, patents, monopolies, and honors, hoping thus to benefit the industries of France. While heavy duties were imposed on all foreign-made goods, native manufactures were encouraged by bounties and rewards. The French fleet was raised to a high state of perfection, and companies for trading and settling in foreign parts received elaborate patronage from the government.

Only one industry seems to have received very little attention, and that was agriculture. But all other departments of economic activity received a wonderful impetus. And the French treasury during the earlier parts of Louis XIV's reign was well equipped to meet all emergencies.

In the meantime, a new school of economic thinkers had arisen, who held tenets directly opposite to those of the Mercantilists. The writers of this school advocated as their three fundamental principles that money was not wealth, but only a part of wealth, that the government should not interfere with business and trade, and that agriculture is the chief source of true wealth. In strict accordance with these fundamental principles, the Physiocrats protested against all such things as patents, bounties, and monopolies; also against heavy customs duties and other restrictions to the course of free trade.

The motto of the Physiocrats was *laissez faire.* They maintained that if trade were left to its own natural laws, all nations would become more wealthy and prosperous. Quesnay, one of the great French Physiocratic writers, was constantly reminding the French king that "he should do nothing but let the laws rule." Such advice was no doubt closely connected with the rising democratic spirit of the times, and especially with the philosophical doctrines broached by Rousseau. In the opinion of Rousseau, all evils resulted from a bad condition of society, which was something artificial and frequently quite opposed to the best natural tendencies of humanity. Remove such artificial obstacles to the general well-being, and at once the *jus naturæ,* the law of nature—in other words, the natural tendencies of things—would immediately assert themselves with the best results.

It was not long before there appeared many ardent advocates of the new system, not only in England, but also on the Continent.   In France, Quesnay, the court physician of Louis XV, was the first who disputed the statement of Colbert, that money was wealth, and was the first to enunciate the doctrine that if the lands were cultivated, then manufacturing industries would take care of themselves.   In Italy, among many other distinguished writers, was Cesare Beccaria, whose work on this subject was translated into twenty-two languages. He agrees with the other Physiocrats in denouncing monopolies and privileges, but slightly differs from them in the less extension that he gives to the doctrine of Free Trade.   Even in Germany, many writers advocated the system, but they did not go to the same length as writers in other countries, and the general tendency of Germany always seems to have been in the opposite direction.

It was in England that the doctrine of the Physiocrats received fullest acceptance and development.   Adam Smith in his "Wealth of Nations" exposes, with great exactness and subtlety, the main principles of the new system.   Occasionally, he even goes to extremes, as when he declares that the value of money is purely conventional.   But, in the main, his principles were exceedingly sound, and none knew better than he how to bring economic principles into contact with the events of every-day life.   His book soon acquired great influence. It not only actuated to a great extent the commercial policy of Pitt, but it opened the way for the formation of the Free Trade School in England, whose tenets have dominated England's commercial policy up to this present day.

The two schools of the Mercantilists and Physiocrats still survive, and, under various names, dominate com-

mercial policies of modern governments. All interference of government with trade, the imposition of tariff
duties, the adoption of a protective system, the regulation of such things as railways and telegraph communication, and the supervision of trusts, labor-unions, and
the like—all these are part of the system of Mercantilism. On the other hand, there is the system of natural
liberty, advocated by the Physiocrats. These uphold the
doctrine of Free Trade, the abolition of restrictive duties,
and unlimited powers of self-activity to all trade-unions
of whatever description. It is true that we no longer
hear of Mercantilists and Physiocrats. These now obsolete labels are replaced by those of Protectionists and
Free-traders. But the opposing parties and principles
remain the same. And even at the present day, they
form distinct political badges. Some nations, like Germany and the United States, are distinctly Protectionist
in their policy; England, on the other hand, is still a
perspicuous example of a Free-trading country. Even in
the same State, they set off opposite political parties.
Thus, in America, the Republicans are Protectionists,
while the Democrats clamor for a reduction of the tariff;
and in England, it was the tariff question that threatened
to create a serious division in the Unionist-Conservative
Party.

CHAPTER II

GEOGRAPHICAL DISCOVERIES

FROM the fifteenth century and onward there took place the remarkable geographical discoveries that revolutionized trade and commerce, altered the political balance of power in Europe, and gradually brought about the formation of a greater Europe.

In these discoveries, the Portuguese played an early and important part. Through the enterprise of Prince Henry, they discovered the Azores and the Madeiras in the Atlantic. This discovery, however, was of minor importance, in comparison with the navigation round the Cape of Good Hope, made for the first time by Bartolomeo Diaz. Already, the old trade routes from the East, which ran through the Mediterranean, converged in Venice, and then went northward up by the Rhine and the Danube, were seriously threatened by the Turks, and the larger ocean routes opened by Diaz enabled the traders to reach India by a safer way. The first successful accomplishment of the entire route is to be attributed to Vasco da Gama, who, in 1498, arrived at the Malabar coast in India. A few years afterwards, the Portuguese were successful in another direction. In 1500, Brazil was discovered by the Portuguese sailor Cabral, and this country formed one of the most powerful of the Portuguese dependencies.

Spain also took a leading part in geographical research. To Spain, indeed, belongs the honor of the discovery of America. It is true that Columbus was a Genoese by birth, but Spain, alone, of the maritime nations, gave him the necessary encouragement and means for his famous voyages. In 1492 took place his eventful discovery, which had the result of placing within Spanish jurisdiction most of the central and eastern portions of the great continent.

France had also taken a share, though a minor one, in the rage for exploration. As early as the reign of Louis XII, French seamen had discovered Cape Breton and Newfoundland, together with the Gulf of St. Lawrence. Under Francis I, this discovery was followed by the exertions of Jacques Cartier, who sailed up the gulf as far south as Montreal.

Holland, also, came in for a considerable amount of jealousy, on account of her keenness for exploration. The Dutch navy began during the revolt of the Netherlands against Philip II. Brill was captured by the recalcitrant Dutch ships, and this circumstance became the first sign of the strength and expansiveness of the Dutch navy. In 1598 their ships succeeded in reaching India by the Cape route, and this was now followed by important Dutch settlements in Africa itself. In 1609 New York began to grow under the industrious hands of the Dutch, who had settled there, while certain names still testify to the fact that a considerable portion of the Hudson River district was inhabited by the same enterprising people.

But the nation that was eventually destined to carry off the palm for maritime discovery was England. At first, she was behind in the race. She had been anticipated by other nations, such as Spain and Portugal. Where, however, they had gone, she also followed, and with more permanent success, while in later times, she achieved most important discoveries on her own account. By the year 1553, the Englishman, Chancellor, successfully reached the White Sea, and began trading negotiations with Russia, and between 1532 and 1595 successful voyages were made to the Guinea coast of Africa, and to Brazil and Mexico. More independent voyages of discovery were made under Queen Elizabeth by Frobisher and Drake; the former attempted, though without any practical result, to find out a northwest passage to China, by cruising round the top of the American continent, while the latter successfully accomplished a voyage round the world. What made Drake's voyage the more remarkable, was the fact that he traveled in a westerly direction, and with his small craft had to encounter the furious storms that prevail from the west. Nor was attention paid merely to sea voyages. Under Queen Elizabeth, Raleigh had made himself famous for his attempt to explore the valley of the Orinoco, and by his foundation of the Virginia colony.

It was, however, during the eighteenth century that England began to take the decided lead in maritime enterprise. Captain Cook then discovered the eastern coast of Australia, and also New Zealand. His work was afterwards completed by others who surveyed these lands, and revealed their true position, nature, and powers of production. In the central parts of South Africa, important journeys of exploration were made by such men as James Bruce, Mungo Park, and David Livingstone. It is mainly owing to the exertions of these men that at the present day we know so much of interior Africa, and that very soon a complete communication between North and South Africa will have become an accomplished fact.

Such, in rough outline, were the main geographical discoveries of the Modern Period, and with just such indications as are sufficient for our purpose. We must

now consider some of the more important results of
these discoveries, both upon the commerce and upon
the political condition of Europe.

The immediate result was to widen the whole market.
All sorts of hitherto unknown commodities were now
imported from far-off, distant lands. New comforts
and luxuries created new wants, and these, again, necessitated a continued series of relations with the uttermost
countries of the earth. From the mines of Spanish
America came gold and silver in great abundance.
Spain, therefore, became for a time the richest country
in Europe. Unfortunately, however, she neglected the
true wealth, which consists in native industry and manufactures. Though possessed of more gold and silver
than any other nation, her decline became portentously
rapid. Indeed, she was but the channel through which
the precious metals were distributed throughout the
other countries. By degrees, the average supply of gold
and silver increased all round. Of this, the general results were, in the main, beneficial. It is true that prices
suddenly rose, and that wages did not rise with the same
rapidity, thereby causing temporary distress to the
working classes. But, gradually, things adjusted themselves to the altered condition of the currency. In any
case, capital became more abundant, and became more
easy of transfer from one form of employment to another.

This widening of the market also affected the condition, even, of local markets and industries. They no
longer catered for narrow areas. The commercial
world, like the intellectual world of the Renaissance, had
sprung suddenly upon the view of men. And, for the
first time, business men and manufacturers became acquainted with the more general and universal laws that

regulated the market and the connections between supply and demand.

Another effect was the abandonment of the old trade routes. Already, these had been seriously threatened by the Turk. Under the influence of the Sultan Selim, the Turks had done their best to ruin the Eastern trade. Alexandria ceased to be the great emporium that it once had been; the Nile valley became a valley of desolation, and soon it was only too evident that all communication between Europe and India would be completely cut off.

It was just at this time that the discoveries were made which enabled men to get what they wanted from other countries, or through other ways of communication. The route to India, by way of the Cape of Good Hope, still kept up part of the old trade communication, and the discovery of the western lands opened up an entirely new market.

The political results of these changes were also incalculable. Among them was the rapid decline of Venice. It was at Venice that converged the old, important trading routes from the East, and from Venice the merchandise was carried up the waters of the Danube and the Rhine. Naturally, the cities along the banks of these rivers shared in the commercial and consequent political greatness. Such towns as Worms, Mainz, Speyer, Bingen, and Hamburg owed their importance mainly to their situation along these trade routes. Even the greatness of the Hanseatic League was to be partly attributed to the same cause. But now, with the extinction of the old trade routes, these German cities and the League alike began to languish, and for a time suffered an eclipse.

Disastrous results from the destruction of the old

trade routes appeared also in Germany. As we have already said, the towns along the Rhine underwent a period of decline, though it proved but temporary. Moreover, there is little doubt but that the peasant risings in Germany, in the sixteenth century, were partly owing to the distress occasioned by the loss of what had been to them a source of living in previous times.

Political events followed fast and thick. In the sixteenth century, we find Venice almost on the verge of extinction. Her commerce was crippled, part of her colonial possessions were taken away, and even her own autonomy was threatened. Only her own native strength and the force of circumstances enabled her to survive—the energy of the Republic, the ability of the military commander, Petigliano, combined with the strong natural position of Venice to ward off the invader. Also, discord and strife divided the members of the league that had been formed against her. Venice, therefore, still remained a factor in Italian politics, but her supremacy became impaired, and her trade passed into other hands.

Perhaps of still greater dramatic significance was the abandonment of the Mediterranean as a center of commerce and human interest, a circumstance also brought about by the destruction of the old trade routes. From most ancient times, the Mediterranean had been the center of all that was grandest in human activity. Phenicians, Greeks, and Romans plowed their barks across its waters. Also, in medieval times, the greatest merchant fleets of civilized countries still continued to make it the center of many human hopes and fears. Now, all this was changed. The ocean, and no longer the inland sea, was to become the center of commerce and political activity. Civilization, in its course from East to West, now lingered over the waters of the Atlantic, until, by the twentieth century, it gradually finds its way even to the waters of the Pacific.

Such a change was not without profound significance for the future of the nations whose shores were washed by the great Atlantic. An extraordinary stimulus was given to the shipbuilding industry, and to the formation of the important seaport towns and harbors. What Venice had been, that England, France, Holland, now strove to be. And thus, an intense rivalry, and often bitter strife, was created between these nations.

We now come to the last important consequence of the great geographical discoveries of the sixteenth century, and that is the formation of important colonies all over the world.

In America, there were the Spanish colonies in the south, central, and eastern portions; the Portuguese in the southwest; the English colonies on what is now the Atlantic seaboard of the United States; and the French colonies in Canada. In Africa, were Dutch, English, Portuguese, and French colonies. And, later on, there were the important English colonies in Australia and New Zealand.

There was thus given an impetus to the colonizing movement, which has never since died out. Even at the present day, almost every European nation, and even America itself, has a colonial policy which is fraught with great importance. Even Germany, whose comparatively inland position would little mark her out for a colonizing nation, has aspirations in this direction, which may possibly bring her into collision with some of the other powers.

The colonizing movements, even during the sixteenth and seventeenth centuries, became a source of emulation and strife. Each country was desirous of retaining for itself the exclusive possession of the commerce of its own colony. Many wars were the result of this policy, and much loss of mutual profit. Rulers, at that time, did not perceive that the exclusive confinement of trade between the mother country and the colony meant the deprivation to both of the profits that might have accrued from consulting the productive powers and the wants of other countries. But the most serious result of all was the unnecessary wars that were fought out, for the purpose of thus limiting the market. Such wars were waged not only for the obtainment of an end that was in itself fruitless, but they caused a great deal of useless taxation and consequent suffering to the persons that waged them.

CHAPTER III

PRODUCTION OF WEALTH

UP TO the sixteenth century, the main source of wealth in England had been the agricultural industry. Rough calculations have estimated that about nine-tenths of English industry was agricultural. Even in the Modern Period of history, agriculture also played a very important part. But in order to understand more clearly the relation between modern agriculture and modern wealth, it will be necessary to trace first the important revolutions that were slowly taking place in English agricultural industry from the fourteenth century and onward.

During feudal times, the land had been worked in the following way: In each separate manor, or district, presided over by the lord, the land was regularly laid out and divided, partly according to a basis of property, partly according to a basis of purpose or use. First of all, there was the land that was owned and worked directly by the lord of the manor himself, or by his bailiff; secondly, there was the land that belonged to the dependent villages, some of whom were freeholders, but the great majority were *villeins*. These *villeins* held their land in greater or less dependence upon their lord, and had to pay a rent which at first was discharged by personal service, but was afterwards commuted into a money payment. Besides these personal lands of the lord and the tenants, there were also the common waste, the common pasture, and the meadows. Though the land was thus divided up according to ownership, the several proprietors did not keep their respective lands together. There were no such boundaries as ditches, hedges, or stone walls. Oftentimes, some of the tenants' buildings would be interspersed in the lord's own demesne, and the invariable custom was for each tenant to have his land, not altogether in one place, but divided up into small strips, distributed here and there over a large area. The only sign of different ownership was the small fringes of border grass, some of which can be seen even at the present day.

Such a system may seem strange to our modern ideas, but it suited the needs of those times. The land could be more easily worked collectively, and the old feudal spirit of cooperation allowed greater freedom of action. Also, such an arrangement provided for greater equality in the distribution of land. No single individual could enjoy the monopoly of the richer portions of land.

Thus far, the land was divided on a basis of ownership. But the basis of purpose or use must also be taken into account. The land was partly pasture, that is, used for feeding cattle, and partly arable, used for the growing of crops. Then, the arable land itself was subdivided into three fields. One of these, during one season, was allowed to lie fallow; during the next season, the field that had been sown for wheat would be sown for barley, and the field that had been sown for barley would be fallow; while the field that had lain fallow would be sown for wheat. In this way each of the three fields would continually pass through the three stages of being sown for wheat, for barley, and then being allowed to lie fallow.

This system, even during the Middle Ages, gradually underwent certain alterations. Many of the landlords had found it convenient to accept money payment from their tenants, in place of personal service. Thus, by degrees, there grew up in England a class of freeholders, when, suddenly, the Black Plague depopulated the country, and the landlords, in search of laborers, by fair means or foul, tried to force the tenants back into their old position of holders of land on condition of payment of personal service. Thereupon followed, as a protest, the Peasants' Revolt. Opinions differ as to the tangible result of this outbreak, but, for some years afterwards, both kinds of rent seem to have been in vogue.

There were, however, other changes that were destined to revolutionize completely the whole aspect of English agricultural industry. The first of these was the system of enclosures. By this is meant that the land which had hitherto lain open was now divided off by railings, fences, and ditches. This change was brought about by the enormous growth of the weaker industry. It was found far more profitable to discard arable land and go in for pasture, so as to accommodate the great flocks of sheep. For, not only did such enclosed spaces mean great security for the sheep themselves, but the accumulation of manure on one spot was highly beneficial to the land.

Such enclosures took place on all the different kinds that we have mentioned. Naturally, there was very little difficulty in the way of the landlord and the freehold tenant enclosing their own lands. But, with regard to the waste lands and common pasturage, there was some difficulty. Enclosures of these lands, made by the lord of the manor, would have seemed in many cases an infringement of public right, especially if there was a tradition that such lands were originally the communal property of the whole village. The landlord, however, very likely adopted the view that such lands were originally the lord's own personal property, which, either

through beneficence or for the sake of personal convenience, he had allowed to be used by the village.
Whatever view may have been correct, the landlord
was in the stronger position, and better able to enforce
his claim.

In Germany, the lord's attempt to enforce his rights
over the common lands was partly the cause of the
Peasants' Revolt. We can gather this from some of
the demands of the peasants. They asked that the common fields and woods should be restored, that the fuel
in the woods should be free to all, and that they should
have access to the game, fowl, and fish. The lord had
evidently been attempting to encroach upon the traditional rights of the *villeins* to the common lands and
streams.

With regard to the enclosure of the property of the
customary tenants, there was a far more serious struggle, and much consequent distress. The tenants held
that they had a customary right to the perpetual ten-
ancy of the land, and that, so long as they paid the rent,
they could not be evicted. On the other hand, the landlord held that they were only tenants at will.

While usage and prescription were on the side of
the tenant, there was also strong evidence in support
of the contention of the landlord. Most of the leases
contained the expressions, "at the will of the lord," or
"for life," and these clearly pointed to a terminal ten-
ancy. Moreover, the old feudal custom by which a
fine, called "relief," had to be paid by the successor to an
estate, also implied that the land did not follow rigidly
the law of inheritance. In any case, the lord, whether
by force, or by use of legal technicalities, generally
managed to evict the tenant.

Such evictions caused at first a great amount of distress. The tenants were cut off from the soil which they had been cultivating for ages. The class of the small farmer began to decline rapidly. At the same time, there also arose the acute problem of finding work for the unemployed. The ejected tenants, who had been allowed to till their own soil, and also obtain additional revenue by sharing in the cultivation of the other unenclosed neighboring lands, now found themselves bereft alike of home and employment. Starvation and vagabondage became exceedingly prevalent, and were one of the chief causes of the introduction of the poor-laws under Henry VIII and Elizabeth.

At the same time, it must be admitted that the farming industry, as a whole, became more prosperous. Not only did the enclosed pasture lands favor the breeding of sheep, but even the arable land itself became more productive, since it now lay more together, and a more uniform system of cultivation now became possible.

Another important change in agriculture was the introduction of what is known as convertible husbandry. This meant that the same land would at one time be used for pasture and at another time for plowing. Much more was obtained from the soil in this way than when part of the land was allowed to lie fallow, as was the case in the three-field system.

This process underwent still further development in the eighteenth century, under Lord Townshend. When this nobleman had retired from the ministry, he devoted much of his attention and time to the agricultural industry, and, by borrowing a great deal from the methods employed by the Dutch, considerably forwarded the advance of this industry. It was he that gave to turnips and artificial grasses a definite place in the rotation of crops. At first, the experiment was conducted on a comparatively small scale on his little farm at Raynham in Norfolk, and its results were so successful that it was copied in other places as well, and became general all over England.

This marked the complete accomplishment of the agrarian revolution. Enclosures were carried out more vigorously than ever, no fewer than three thousand enclosure acts being passed under the reign of George III. The small farmer became still more scarce. His place was taken by the large capitalist farmer, constantly experimenting, working on scientific principles, and bringing the land up to the highest degree of cultivation.

Still one more change has to be noted, in connection with the agricultural industry, and that is the reclamation of waste lands. In the eastern counties of England, there had been large tracts of low-lying land, as yet unfit for cultivation, because they were so frequently flooded by the waters that drained them. Even in Elizabeth's time, there had been some thought of reclaiming these lands, and an act was passed for that purpose. Not, however, till the seventeenth century was the idea carried into execution. Dutchmen were then entrusted with the design, and also with the actual work of the undertaking. New channels were made, which completely carried off the surplus water into the sea, and enabled the land to be used for purposes of agriculture.

Even this apparently beneficent operation met with a great deal of discontent. A great number of persons had hitherto found a respectable living in hunting the fowl and fish that abounded in those regions. Moreover, the inhabitants had settled down to the peculiar condition of those places, and were by no means anxious for a change. Frequent collisions resulted between the Dutch workmen and the fensmen, in which the former, supported by the government, were completely victorious. The temporary sufferings of the local inhabitants were afterwards more than compensated by the richness of the soil reclaimed, and the abundant harvests that rejoiced the heart of the farmer.

On the whole, the agricultural industry made great strides during the Modern Period. The enclosure of lands, the use of convertible husbandry, the introduction of the growth of winter roots which, without exhausting the soil, provided winter food for cattle—all these added largely to the agricultural wealth of the country.

But even the advance in the agricultural industry can hardly be compared with the progress made in the manufacturing industries during the same period.

Hitherto, the domestic system had prevailed. This meant that there had been no large factories, such as we see in the present day, but that the cloth was spun and made up in the cottages of the workmen. And there is no doubt that this system had its advantages. It gave the workmen more liberty. They could work when they pleased and just as long as they pleased. Also, they could apply themselves more easily to other and subsidiary branches of industry. A great part of the work was done in the country, and, when times were slack and work scarce, it was easy for the family still to earn a livelihood by agricultural labor.

There was also a certain amount of economy in the direct communication between the producer and the consumer. There were no middlemen in those days who absorbed part of the profits, and although the market may have been narrow, yet there were no enormous fluctuations in the conditions of supply and demand. Employment, therefore, was fairly regular.

But the disadvantages of such a system were very great. There was no division of labor. One man had to do a great many things, and the result was that he had too little leisure in which to make himself an expert in any special department of the trade, while a considerable time was lost in passing from one occupation to another. Then, again, hand-made goods, put together in the laborer's cottage, were necessarily deficient in quantity, and very often in quality. It was also exceedingly hard for the master to exercise a proper supervision over his men. Accordingly, frequent complaint was made of dishonesty on the part of the man who embezzled the material.

However, this old system, with all its attendant advantages and disadvantages, was done away with by the wonderful mechanical inventions of the eighteenth century. In 1753 was invented the flying shuttle by Kay, and after him came Arkwright, who, in 1769, invented the water frame, and Crompton, who, in 1799, first introduced the mule.

The first results of these inventions were the decline of the woolen industry and the rise of the cotton manufacture, which has maintained its supremacy even to this day. Greater quantity and better quality of goods were produced at a lower price. A greater demand was created, and high wages and profits brought about a season of great prosperity.

It must not be supposed, however, that these inventions were adopted immediately all over the country. In some counties, machinery was not used until ten or fifteen years after it had been adopted.

What chiefly hastened the new movement and completely revolutionized the whole system of manufacturing was the discovery of new driving power, by which large pieces of machinery could be simultaneously set in motion. In the year 1785, the steam engine, which had already been invented by Watt, was introduced into the cotton factory. Up till then, water power had been used. Lancashire was singularly favored in this respect, and hence speedily became remarkable for its manufacturing growth. Even when steam was introduced, Lancashire still occupied a very favorable position, owing to its large stores of coal.

It was the discovery of coal that completed the industrial revolution, by bringing about the factory system. It was then that the mills, that had been scattered throughout the same district, now grouped themselves together, so as to form large towns, and that we now find huge buildings, employing thousands of operatives. The rate of production was multiplied indefinitely. Consumers benefited considerably, both as regards quality and cheapness of goods, and even during the terrible Napoleonic wars English manufactured goods found their way into the heart of the enemy's country. Indeed, it is said that the French soldiers marched to their Russian campaign clad in English-made coats and shoes.

It is true that there were frequent riots, owing to the fear that labor would be displaced by machinery. But the evils of the factory system did not lie here. For the invention and use of machinery only means that the coarser processes are done by bars and wheels and metal. Human intelligence and human hands will still be wanted to guide the machinery. Statistics also show that, whereas before the invention of machinery the number of the employed could be counted by hundreds, afterwards they amounted to thousands.

The real abuses connected with the factory system are of quite a different nature. One of these, which is rather sentimental, concerns the relations between the employer and employed. Heretofore, the master knew individually the few workmen under his control, but the workmen now are to him only a vast army of units. In the words of Carlyle, a cash nexus now takes the place of the living bond between the master and the workman.

This, however, is not in itself such a serious evil. But incidentally it might easily lead, and actually has led, to a great deal of seeming callousness on the part of masters toward their operatives. This was especially so during the early days of the factory system. Young children were often employed, and made to work several hours of the day, in a stuffy atmosphere, and deprived of all opportunities of schooling and physical development. Also, very little care was taken of the health and safety even of adults. Factories were often very badly ventilated, too little time allowed for meals, and no care taken to place fencing round dangerous machinery.

Such abuses, however, were greatly remedied by the factory legislation. Through the influence of such men as Sir Robert Peel, Lord Althorp, and the Earl of Shaftesbury, the great philanthropist, many acts were passed for the purpose of improving the material and even mental condition of the employed. By these acts, the employment of child labor was greatly curtailed, over-crowding and night work were forbidden, and proper ventilation and cleanliness were insisted upon. Regulations were also made for the proper fencing of dangerous machinery and for the protection of men engaged in particularly dangerous or unwholesome employments. Still more important, perhaps, was the appointment of factory inspectors whose duty it was to inspect the different factories, to report abuses, and make what further suggestions might be necessary.

Social improvements soon followed in the wake of legislative enactments. The number of churches and chapels began to increase, and the number of saloons to decrease. Schools were established and institutions set afoot for the purpose of encouraging thrift and providing harmless recreation for the evening hours. All this has combined to make the condition of the manufacturing class quite tolerable, if not comfortable. At the present day, even delicate girls labor in the factories, and find their employment both easy and sanitary. And there is no doubt that the middle class, as a whole, have derived great benefit from the increased quantity of goods and lowering of prices brought about by the manufacturing system.

Great, indeed, has been the influence of machinery on production and sale of wool and cotton goods, but the same influence must also be considered in relation to certain departments of commercial activity.

Among these was the smelting of iron. Hitherto, only wood had been used for this purpose. The southeastern counties of England had been well-nigh the exclusive seat of the industry, but operations there were gradually slackening, owing to the exhaustion of the forests. For a time, there was indeed a partial revival of industry, owing to the use of coal in place of wood, and this also had the effect of removing the locality of the industry from the southeastern to the northern counties of England, like Lancashire and Durham, where coal is more abundant. Even here the progress was slow, until the celebrated invention of Dr. Roebuck.

He conceived the idea of applying Watt's steam engine to effect more powerful blast in the furnaces. Success followed his efforts, and soon the metallurgical industries took deep root in the northern parts of England, among the most conspicuous of the cities owing their prosperity to this cause being Darlington, Middlesborough, and Hartlepool—all in the northern counties of England.

Very important too was the influence of machinery in facilitating the means for the freightage of goods from one town to another, and from one county to another. Already, before the invention of steam, it had been perceived that the development of manufactures was greatly dependent upon the rapidity and cheapness with which goods could be transported from place to place. At first, canals were chiefly relied upon. Most famous was the Bridgewater Canal, constructed by the Duke of Bridgewater, in 1761, in order to connect together the two cities of Manchester and Liverpool. Another important canal was the Grand Trunk Canal, connecting Gloucester with the river Severn, while, even in quite recent times, the Manchester Ship Canal is contributing largely to the shipping trade of Manchester.

It was the railway, however, that was destined in later years to perform the greater part of the inland carrying trade. Between 1821 and 1848, were constructed the earliest railways. At first, the rails were roughly laid, and the speed was extremely slow. But improvements were soon devised, and even in 1839 the train between London and Birmingham ran at the rate of twenty miles an hour.

These means of transit manifestly gave an extraordinary impetus to the manufacturing system—in fact, to industries of all descriptions. The markets became widened, and the increased demand necessitated also an increase in the quantity of production. At the same time, there was also created in the community the important class of wealthy manufacturers, which was to form such an influential middle section of society. This class was rising into existence even during the time of Pitt, and his policy deliberately inaugurated the movement by which political influence became gradually transferred from the hands of the rural magnates into the hands of the rising merchant aristocracy, with the result that the general policy of England became, more than ever, guided by economic principles.

So far we have been dealing exclusively with England, but it must not be forgotten that what took place in England was also repeated on the Continent. Indeed, one or two countries, like France, slightly anticipated the English manufacturing system. But some specific mention ought to be made regarding the production of wealth in the great continent on the other side of the Atlantic.

Up to the time of the American Revolution, the main industry of the Americans was agricultural, and even at the present day it still remains one of the chief sources of American wealth. Owing to the enormous territory comprised within the States, and the great variety of latitude, the agricultural products are perhaps more varied than in any other country of the world. Wheat, corn, and flax are grown in the temperate regions of the States, while, in the South, cotton, tobacco, and tropical fruits are to be met with in large quantities. One great difference between American agriculture and that in the old countries is the method of farming. In Europe, what is called the intensive method prevails. This means that the farmer, by means of rotation of crops, and the employment of the latest scientific expedients, gets as much as is absolutely possible from the same plot of ground. But, in America, in early times, the extensive system was followed—the farmer, after exhausting one plot of ground, going on to another. But, now, especially in the Eastern States, the farmer is beginning to follow the intensive system. Besides the surface products of the soil, there are also many valuable deposits of ores. During the first fifty years of the nineteenth century, were discovered extensive gold mines in the Carolinas, Georgia, and especially in California; and, later on, silver mines in Nevada. And what, perhaps, are of still more permanent value, there are the coal mines of Pennsylvania, while, lately, discoveries point to considerable quantities of the same ore in South Dakota.

The manufacturing system of America is also a great contributor to the national wealth. Even before the American Revolution, there had been some factories, and the iron trade had already made some progress. But England had always been jealously afraid of competition on the part of her colonies. She made illegal all manufactures, hoping that the colonists would thus be forced to import English-made goods. The result was to cripple American manufactures. But after the Revolution manufacturing spread all over America and prospered.

The same inventions that had achieved so much success in England were used also in America, and they brought about the same results in the creation of the factory system, and in the rearing of a very wealthy manufacturing class. It was also the invention of the cotton gin that had such tremendous political consequences in the southern section of America, on account of the great impetus that it gave to the slave trade, and the consequent collision between the slave States and the anti-slave States.

In America, also, the transport system played a very great part in the development of manufactures. These may be named in their order of development, as follows: trails, roads, canals, and railways. The first railway was the Baltimore and Ohio line, constructed in 1830. Between that date and 1870, there were constructed 68,484 miles of railroad. There are now trunk lines, connecting all the important towns of the States, and these lines have, perhaps, more than anything else, tended to break down the barriers between the different States. Besides facilitating the transport of freight and passengers, the railways also play a very important part even in opening up new centers of business and commerce.

Having now indicated the chief sources of wealth, both in the Old and New World, we must turn to consider the way in which this vast amount of wealth is distributed.

CHAPTER IV

DISTRIBUTION OF WEALTH

WHEN the wave of revolution had already affected so many departments of human activity, both political and economic, there is little matter for wonder if commerce also underwent some very drastic changes. Indeed, the altered cultivation of land, and the growth of the manufacturing system, not only entailed a greater accumulation of wealth, but also materially affected its distribution.

With regard to extent, trade and commerce advanced by leaps and bounds. By the fifteenth century commerce had considerably expanded. In return for her exports of wool, lead, and tin, England imported such commodities as glass, silks, and velvets from Italy; linens and fine cloths from the manufacturing towns of the Netherlands; wines and salt from Gascony and Guienne. Even with such distant countries as Russia, there was a certain amount of trade, though this was very irregular.

Naturally, the improvement of English shipping under the Tudors largely contributed to this result. A great deal of merchandise was now carried in English ships. Moreover, the English men-of-war now took a more active part in the abolition of piracy. The pirates of that time had been almost as audacious as the pirates that molested Rome in the days of Cicero, and almost every merchant vessel had to be accompanied by a protecting convoy. Under the early Stuarts, great attempts were made to remedy the evil, but it was not until the reign of Charles II, when the naval power of England had been established in the Mediterranean, that the scourge was at last substantially removed.

While the English navy was continually increasing, England also was fortunate with regard to the rivalry which she had to undergo from the commercial quarters of Antwerp. Owing to the hostility of Emperor Maximilian, the trade of Bruges had passed almost entirely into the hands of Antwerp. In the words of the contemporary Italian writer, Giucciardini, "Antwerp exported jewels, precious stones, silver bullion, quicksilver; wrought silks, gold and silver cloth and thread, spices, drugs, sugar, cotton, cinnamon, lemons, fine and coarse serges, tapestry, madder, hops in large quantities, glass, salt fish, and other merceries of all sorts, besides arms of all kinds, ammunition for war, and household furniture."

These goods clearly indicate, by the variety of their nature, the enormous extent of the trade between Antwerp and other countries. But Antwerp began to decline. Continual sackings and massacres, during the administration of Alva, and, later on, the closing of the Scheldt by the Treaty of Westphalia, had the effect of extinguishing for some considerable time her commercial activity and transferring it to England.

When, again, the colonial system was introduced, England was equally fortunate in the race for trade competition. When the Dutch became rivals to the English, hostile combinations of rival powers brought them to the ground. Not only in the Mediterranean did the Dutch begin to lose their trade, but also in the West Indies and in India, where they had been the foremost pioneers and discoverers.

What at first might have seemed an obstacle became a blessing in disguise, namely, the rising agricultural and manufacturing conditions in other countries. The silk industries in France, that were fostered and promoted by the wise Duke de Sully, and the great carpet manufactures, reestablished by Colbert, were the means of providing England with new business, and impelled her to produce still more of the goods that were required to pay for these luxuries. In Germany, the great linen manufactures; in Spain, the cultivation of the vine and the accumulation from her colonial possessions of such goods as spices and Peruvian bark; and, in Italy, the power to export oil, potash, cork, and marble—all this tended in the same way to supply England's demands, and at the same time to promote more and more the spirit of industry and enterprise. In spite of mutual jealousies and government restraints, the increase of wealth in one country is sure to bring about, indirectly, the increase of wealth in other countries. There are, of course, exceptions. But such only tend, if anything, to illustrate the general rule that under normal conditions wealth tends to diffuse, rather than to concentrate into one spot alone.

Besides this extensive European market, England also enjoyed the benefits that accrued from trade communication with her many colonies beyond the seas. From the American plantations came cotton, rice, and tobacco. Also, the extensive slave trade, carried on between Africa and the plantations, was indirectly a source of revenue to England, especially since, by the Assiento Treaty between England and Spain, the former country enjoyed the exclusive right of shipping the negroes from Africa into the plantations. Then, in much later years, there was a considerable amount of trade between England and her colonies in the far Western seas, in India, and in Australia. During the American wars, which stopped the supply of cotton from America, England was forced to depend for the supply mainly upon India. Amongst other goods that were imported into the mother country from India were tea, coffee, sugar, ivory, saltpeter, spices, and, what were very important, jute and indigo. From Australia came also kauri gum, the precious metals, timber, sperm oil, and, during the last century, great quantities of frozen meat.

Naturally, the trade between England and the colonies received a great deal of attention. Unfortunately, the mother country was dominated by a very selfish and short-sighted policy. She imagined that it would be to her advantage to prevent the colonies from trading in certain commodities with any other nation but herself. This was especially so in regard to the American colonies. A distinction was made between enumerated goods, which the colonists were allowed to export into England only, and unenumerated goods, which they were allowed to export to other European countries. The enumerated goods were practically all those that could not be produced on English soil, while among the unenumerated goods were salted provisions, corn, and timber. Sugar and rum were also permitted, but for special reasons, these commodities being manufactured by Englishmen who could use their influence in Parliament for their own interests.

Besides limiting the commerce of these colonies, England also attempted to stop their manufactures. In doing so she was actuated, partly by the fear of the importation of rival manufactured goods from the colonies, and partly by a desire to find in the colonies a constant market for the sale of English-made goods. The woolen and iron manufactures were especially prohibited, as these were most likely to be dangerous competitors.

In spite, however, of these difficulties, the net production of the world's wealth continually increased, and commerce continually widened its activity; nor was it long before a reaction began to appear. Artificial barriers were seen to be not only too weak to accomplish their purpose, but even positively injurious to the country from which they emanated, and when these barriers were swept away altogether, commercial prosperity made still more rapid strides, while wealth accumulated in still greater profusion.

In the organization, distribution, and application of such wealth, there were some very powerful agencies that must now be carefully considered in detail.

First, there were the merchant companies. The spirit of association, that was so strong in the Middle Ages, reappears also during the Modern Period, only in a different form. Individuals could not, and did not, carry on the greater part of the trade between the different countries. Danger from pirates and want of capital would alone have been sufficient deterrents. The only resource was to combine together and to trade in companies, and the trading companies that resulted had practically the entire enjoyment and control of commerce. Some of them were only what was called regulated companies. This means that the individual still retained the command and disposal of his capital. But, in the joint-stock companies, the capital invested by the individual was practically owned and controlled by the company. Evidently, the powers of operation in these companies were very much greater than in the others and, in fact, the great companies of the Modern Period were all joint-stock companies.

Among the earliest companies to be formed was the Russian Company, which made its appearance under

Edward VI. Although called the Russian Company, it did business with other countries besides Russia, even going as far as Persia. It was also greatly interested in whale fishing.

Under the reign of Elizabeth, there rose into importance the Merchant Adventurers' Company. This, in its origin, was not an English company, but had been formed in Antwerp, and from there spread throughout the empire. In England, it received a charter from Henry IV, and gradually acquired a great deal of English trade between England and the Netherlands. Perhaps owing to its being a regulated company, it acquired a more national character than some of the joint-stock companies. It seems to have been regarded as an institution that might be applied to any place and locality. Thus, we read of the Merchant Adventurers of Exeter and of the royal burghs of Scotland.

The policy of Elizabeth also favored the promotion of another company; namely, the Levant Company, chartered in 1581. Venetian trade in the Mediterranean, which had been so disorganized by the destruction of the old trade routes, now passed mainly into the hands of this company. It also did a considerable trade in spices with Persia, and it became for a time so influential as partly to damage the trade even of the famous East Indian Company. Not until 1875 did the privileges of the Levant Company altogether cease.

Unlike the two previous companies, which were regulated companies, the Royal African Company was a joint-stock company. It was granted a royal charter in 1672 by Charles II. But it had never received Parliamentary sanction, and therefore the only exclusiveness of trade that it was allowed to enjoy was the privilege of levying a duty of ten per cent. on the exports of those who did not belong to the company. Gold and negroes were the two chief commodities that it exported from Africa. The gold went to England, where it was coined into guineas, while the negroes were exported to the American plantations. Owing to new competition from outsiders, and the great expense of maintaining forts and factories, the company, in 1750, was reconstituted so as to include all the merchants then trading with Africa. But even this company failed, and by the nineteenth century it had died out altogether.

Of far greater political importance were the companies that were formed in the American plantations. The first of these companies to receive a charter was the Virginia Company, in 1587. Owing to a series of disasters, the charter proved abortive. In 1606, another attempt was made, and charters were granted to a London Company and a Plymouth or West of England Company, the latter operating in the northern, the former in the southern regions of the Atlantic seaboard. While the West of England Company failed, the London Company took root and flourished. Order was established, industry encouraged, churches built, and the whole work of colonization thoroughly carried out. Unfortunately, however, the affairs of the colony were badly administered by the management at home, and in 1674 the charter was taken away and the company dissolved. But in the meantime the seeds of democratic government had been sown, and the representative assembly of the Virginian Burgesses, for a long time, stood forth as the champions of liberty and popular government.

Of all the companies, however, none could compete in political importance with the East Indian Company, which received the first charter from Elizabeth in 1602.

From the very first, the company prospered. It speedily supplanted both the Portuguese and the Dutch. Important depots were established at Calicut and Delhi, while Calcutta, at first only a small trading station purchased by the company, afterwards became the seat of the English government in India. Its trade grew with equal rapidity. Tea, saltpeter, spices, and jewels were the chief commodities imported by its means from India to England.

Opposition, however, arose from various quarters. In a short time, there was formed the French East Indian Company, which proved a very formidable rival. Dupleix, the French governor, by his skilful administration, and by diplomatic use of the dissensions among the native princes, both strengthened and expanded French influence until at one time it seemed as though the English would be driven out of India. The situation, however, was saved by the skill and bravery of Lord Clive, who ended by completely overthrowing the power of the French, and preparing the way for the British Empire in India.

Opposition was also encountered from certain merchants who were jealous of the monopoly enjoyed by the company, and tried to break through that monopoly, both by force and by agitations in Parliament. This difficulty, however, was also solved by the reconstruction of the company in such a way as to admit these rival competitors.

By the second half of the eighteenth century, the East Indian Company began to assume quite a political aspect. The London directors of the company practically controlled and administered all the legislation and judicial business of the country. Great difficulty, it is true, was encountered in the administration of tropical countries by people living in temperate zones, and it was not to be wondered at if here, also, there should have been great disturbances and grave abuses.

The company's rule began to be subjected to severe discussions, and the result was the passing of Pitt's East India Bill, which established a Board of Control to watch over and correct the political activity of the company. This was the beginning of a succession of steps by which the reins of political power were transferred from the company into the hands of the government. And by 1858, at the time of the suppression of the terrible Indian Mutiny which broke out among the Sepoys, or native soldiers, the whole of the country was declared formally annexed to the British Crown.

What has been said will be quite sufficient to indicate the political as well as the commercial importance of the trading companies. In a future section, we shall also see how these companies affected the course of international politics.

Besides the companies, another great instrument in the development of commerce was the currency system, the changes that were made in the monetary systems of the different countries.

Between the reigns of William I and Edward I, the coins in use were the great or four pence, the silver penny and halfpenny and farthing. Between that time and the reign of Elizabeth, there were also introduced the gold nobles, the sovereign, the crown, the shilling, and the sixpenny and threepenny piece. During the reign of Elizabeth was also introduced the gold guinea, made at first equivalent to sixty-two shillings, but reduced during the reign of Charles II to twenty-one shillings. Great difficulties were constantly experienced in regulating the currency in such a way as to fit in with the requirements of commerce, and there were important fluctuations in the values of the precious metals. Then again, debasement of the coin was a constant source of difficulty. The odious practice first began on the Continent, and when debased foreign coins found their way into England the king thought there was no other alternative but to depreciate the English coinage as well; otherwise all the good coins would be picked out and hoarded, or exported abroad, according to the well-known formula of Gresham, that bad money drives out good. Already, on the Continent, various writers had pointed out the disastrous effects of such a practice.

In France, the learned bishop, Nicholas Oresme, and in Italy, Andreas de Pampinis, pointed out the great injury that resulted from it to the commonwealth. Few arguments, however, were so clear and scathing as those of Lowndes, who says: "Great contentions do daily rise among the king's subjects, in fairs, markets, shops, and other places throughout the kingdom, about the passing or refusing the same, to the disturbance of public peace; many bargains, doings, and dealings are totally prevented and laid aside which lessen trade in general; persons, before they conclude in any bargains, are necessitated first to settle the price or value of the very money they are to receive for their goods; and if it be in guineas at a high rate, or in clipt or bad money, they set the price of their goods accordingly, which, I think, has been one great cause of raising the price, not only of merchandise, but even of edibles, and other necessaries for the sustenance of the common people, to their great inconvenience. The receipts and collection of the public taxes, revenues, and debts are exceedingly retarded." These words touch upon the main evils that resulted from the debasement of the coin of the realm, and they go far to justify the assertion of the Italian, Musciati Guidi, who maintained that the debasement was more injurious to the country than an open war.

It was, however, one of the great merits of Elizabeth that she perceived this, and that she tried to apply an efficient remedy. The old coins that had become depreciated were either continued in circulation at their debased value, or presented at the mint for exchange, while new coins of the proper value were coined and issued. Great benefits resulted from this, both in regard to definiteness of contracts and the payment of taxes. It is true that prices did not fall, but this was owing to other causes, among them being the enormous quantity of bullion imported into Europe from the American mines.

Besides the debasement of the coin, yet another difficulty presented itself, and that was the natural fluctuation in the value of the precious metals and the relation between gold and silver. During the seventeenth century, the distinction was not clearly seen between the intrinsic and conventional value of money. It was believed that money could have whatever value might be legally attributed to it by the State. Hence, for purposes of fraud, the currency in various States was often artificially raised in value. Writers of those times proposed as a remedy an international agreement, but the age was not advanced enough for such a process.

Still more important and lasting was the relation between gold and silver. At first, only silver was the standard coin; that is to say, all bargains and contracts were expressed in terms of silver coinage. But afterwards gold also appeared as the standard coin, and by the fifteenth century great confusion resulted therefrom, for it was impossible to define the constant ratio between gold and silver. The difficulty was only removed when gold was accepted as the only standard, and silver assumed the position of token money, that is, money whose value depends not upon its intrinsic value, but upon the relation it conventionally bears to the standard coinage.

Whether it is better to adopt only one of them is still hotly disputed. It is called the battle of the standards. At the present day, the silver standard has been almost everywhere rejected, but the question still remains whether gold shall be adopted as the exclusive standard, or whether silver, also, shall be included. The disadvantages of the double standard are obvious, since silver beyond a certain quantity becomes exceedingly heavy and cumbersome. On the other hand, if gold were adopted as the exclusive standard, it would become largely enhanced in value, and silver would become correspondingly depreciated.

In the United States, the silver question figures very largely in politics. At the present time, silver is not entirely discarded. Silver certificates, or paper money, promising to pay in silver dollars, are issued and circulated. This, however, is only a compromise, and probably the question will again arise in a form still more acute.

Very closely connected with the currency system, both in the Old and New World, is the banking system. Already, as we have seen, there were banks in medieval Europe, such as the banks of Venice, Genoa, and Amsterdam. But, during the Modern Period, banks were destined to undergo far greater development, and to fulfil very important and manifold functions.

During the sixteenth century, the London goldsmiths seemed to have a great deal of banking business, although they had received no charter, and had not acquired the formal status of a bank. These goldsmiths frequently received money to keep on deposit, and they also advanced loans of money. Cromwell carried on extensive transactions with these private bankers, borrowing from them large sums of money. So also did James I and Charles II, the latter of whom proved a rather unsatisfactory customer.

When William III was seated on the throne, some more extensive system was required for borrowing money for the royal treasury. A new scheme, therefore, was originated by William Paterson, a Scotchman, and was carried into execution by Montague, chancellor of the exchequer. The scheme was to contract, not merely temporary, but permanent loans. A number of London merchants were allowed to form themselves into a bank with full charter and special privileges, on condition of their making a loan to the government of £1,200,000 at eight per cent. The bank proved a great success. By the beginning of the eighteenth century, it had quadrupled its capital, and whereas at first the Grocers' Hall was large enough for its operations, in later years the bank premises occupied the area of a whole parish, and gave employment to many hundreds of persons.

The Bank of England has always occupied a very important position, both in regard to the English Government, and to the world in general. It keeps an open account with the government, undertakes the management of the national debt, and is the medium through which the interest on the national debt is paid. It also advances money to the government. In regard to the commercial world in general, the issue department of the bank circulates bank notes which are of legal tender, and, what is of supreme importance, it is the great central banking reserve, both of the provincial banks in England, and also of the great Continental countries. The surplus money of the provincial banks of England—that is to say, such money as is not laid out in investments, or kept at hand, in order to discharge current accounts—is deposited with the Bank of England. The banks of the different European countries, in like manner, now deposit their reserve with the Bank of England. Hitherto, the Bank of France had shared this privilege together with the Bank of England. But after the Franco-German War, the Bank of England became the sole bank of deposit for the Continental countries also. How great, therefore, is the responsibility of the Bank of England entailed by this fact has been made pretty evident on various occasions. One instance alone, however, will suffice. A few years ago, the German Government wished to draw out, at an inopportune moment, an enormous sum of money, and was only prevented from thus causing a widespread disaster by the readiness with which it obeyed the warning to defer the demand until the reserve in the Bank had again become replenished.

Other banks besides the great national Bank of England are the joint-stock banks and the private banks. These also do a considerable amount of business, and are very useful for making loans and initiating enterprises throughout the local areas, while their current accounts are extremely useful for the swollen business transactions. And here again England leads the way, for in the Continental countries, partly owing to greater unwillingness to make deposits, partly owing to fear of foreign war, the amount of business done by the banks is comparatively small.

In America, there is, at the present day, no bank in

any way resembling the Bank of England, either in its nature, or in the importance of its functions. Under Hamilton's administration an attempt was indeed made to form a United States Bank, and in many ways this was made to resemble the Bank of England. Thus, in both cases it was forbidden to trade save in bills of exchange and gold and silver bullion, and in both cases the amount of issue was definitely limited.

Unfortunately, the first Bank of the United States, owing to the downfall of the Federal Party, with which it was connected, came to an end. A second Bank of the United States was formed in the year 1817. But this also failed, owing to the inveterate hostility of President Jackson, and after this no further attempt was made to organize a bank for all the States until 1907.

There were formed, however, banks of a different and more local nature which have fulfilled a very important function in the world of commerce. The national banks were constituted by the act of Congress of 1863. They receive money on deposit, make loans, collect bills of exchange, and have the peculiar privilege of issuing notes that are not of legal tender, but are used as money. Each national bank is closely under the control of the government. Its books are carefully inspected, and its general capital, as well as the amount of capital that it must have, are defined by Congress.

Besides the national, there are also the State and private banks. The State banks and private banks fulfil the same functions as the national banks, but do not issue notes.

The American banking system is very different from that in England. There is no one central reserve of capital, and it is, therefore, less easy to obtain, on the moment, a large amount of money. On the other hand, there is a greater amount of capital distributed throughout the country, and, if we take into account the special needs of the separate State systems, perhaps this is more convenient. This is also shown by the varying popularity of the national and State banks. In some States, the latter attain far greater success than the former. And there is no doubt but that this is mainly to be attributed to greater facility and greater opportunity of local inspection, and also to more intimate relations between the State banks and local needs.

In these days of wide markets and great enterprises, the banking system is essential for all parts of the world. By means of it capital is stored up and can be applied where needed, while it is also one of the most powerful buttresses of the whole system of credit. Without the banks, there would be a great deal of useless hoarding of wealth, while much time would also be lost in making the different payments connected with the transaction of business.

CHAPTER V

GOVERNMENT ADMINISTRATION OF FINANCES

OWING to the great complexity of modern industry and commerce, as well as to the increasing power and importance of wealth, the influence of government in economics became, during the Modern Period, even more powerful than during the Medieval Period. Each nation required more money for carrying on the expenses of government, and at the same time incurred greater responsibility for the way in which it controlled the whole course of industry and commerce in the general interests of all.

By the tenth century, the main source of revenue in each State was taxation. Sometimes the taxes were paid directly from the people to the officers of the Crown; at other times, as was the case in France before the time of Henry IV, they were sold for a net sum to certain officials who, in their turn, tried to get what they could out of the people. Some of the taxes, again, were levied directly on the people who were destined to bear the burden; while others, again, were levied only indirectly, as, for example, the tariff duties, the burden of which only ultimately fell upon the consumer.

In most of the European countries, the imposition of taxes led to serious conflicts, and often to much hardship and distress. This was especially the case in England, where the unjust taxation of the Stuart kings brought about the conflict between king and Parliament, a conflict that terminated in the civil war and the overthrow and destruction of Charles I. It was also the assumption of the principle that England could tax her colonies as she pleased, that was one of the causes of the American Revolution.

Even apart from the selfish greed of kings, there were certainly very great difficulties connected with taxation. Numerous wars and an extensive civil service had necessitated an enormous number of taxes, and of many different kinds. There were taxes levied on lands, houses, horses, and carriages, on windows, and, for some years, on the regular proceeds of a person's income; also, there were the indirect taxes of the excise and customs. By the year 1815, Sydney Smith, observing the extent and multiplicity of taxation, uses the following descriptive words: "The school boy whips his taxed top; the beardless youth manages his taxed horse with a taxed bridle on a taxed road; and the dying Englishman, pouring his medicine, which has paid seven per cent., in a spoon that has paid fifteen per cent., flings himself upon his chintz bed which has paid twenty per cent., makes his will on an eight-pound stamp, and expires in the arms of an apothecary, who has paid a license of one hundred pounds for the privilege of putting him to death. His whole property is then immediately taxed up ten per cent. Besides the probate, large fees are demanded for burying him in the chancel. His virtues are handed down to posterity on taxed marble, and he will then be gathered to his fathers to be taxed no more." Such was the bewildering multitude of taxes that had come into existence by the beginning of the nineteenth century! And yet, each one of these taxes involved a study of very abstruse problems. How to make sure that the people shall be taxed according to their means and that the rich shall bear their proper share of the burden; how to prevent taxation from impeding industry and trade, and avoid destroying the very sources of wealth, and how to prevent the tax from being rendered abortive by the incompetency and dishonesty of officials or taxpayers, are questions that have to be solved at the introduction of every new tax.

It is not surprising that, even before the evil reached its climax, there should have appeared certain theories regarding taxation, and among the first to elaborate any principles of taxation was Turgot. According to him, every tax, in order to be successful, must be equal, certain, and must be collected as conveniently, and as economically, as possible.

Every tax must make all bear the same proportionate amount of discomfort, and must be such that none can escape from its payment. Also, the tax must be collected just at the time that is most convenient for the payer, and must be collected with least possible expenditure. Adam Smith, in his "Wealth of Nations," elaborated these principles in his dissertation on taxation, and the great William Pitt strove to reduce them to practice. He mitigated the inequalities of the land tax, repealed certain taxes that had been levied on the necessities of life, imposed other taxes that bore more heavily on the richer classes, and tried to reform and economize the whole system of collecting the taxes. To a great extent he was successful. But although circumstances are constantly changing, the problem of taxation always remains, and frequently occasions dangerous friction between the rulers and the governed. In fact, only a few years after these reforms, the great Continental war brought about the disastrous state of affairs described by Sydney Smith, and everywhere throughout England starvation and ever-deepening discontent.

In France, as we shall see in a following chapter, the

burden of taxation was one of the contributory causes of
the French Revolution; not that the taxes themselves
were so enormous, but they violated the canons laid
down by Turgot. They bore unequally on different
classes of society, and were collected by inopportune
methods.

Besides taxation, another source of revenue to the
State was loans. Already in the twelfth and thirteenth
centuries, this method had been made use of by various
European States. In Venice a forced loan had been
made by the people, the amount collected varying
according to the income of the individual. A special
bank was created for this purpose, and annual interest
of four per cent. was paid. During the thirteenth century, Frederick borrowed money in order to carry on
his struggle with the Pope, while in France, also, St.
Louis had adopted the same expedient in order to find
means for carrying on the two Crusades that ended so
disastrously. Spain was exceptionally notorious for its
government loans. Philip II not only repudiated his
debts toward his own subjects on no fewer than three
distinct occasions, but his insolvency was the main cause
of the failure of the Bank of Genoa.

In England, the kings had frequent recourse to loans,
among the chief offenders in this particular being
Charles I. In order to force the merchants to make
the required loans, he would resort to such means as bil-
leting soldiers upon them, and even throwing them into
prison.

Although, however, forced loans were, and are, unconstitutional, yet *voluntary* and legal loans became of
frequent occurrence, and are now an admitted part of
the financial system of almost every modern nation. In
the reign of William III, Montagu, the same minister

that had established the Bank of England, also began the national debt. This differed from the previous loans, inasmuch as it was voluntary, permanent, and placed upon a sound financial basis. At first, the only security given by the government was the tonnage dues, but, in course of time, other securities were added, in order to procure further loans, while government annuities also became very common. In 1751, the whole system of the national debt was greatly simplified. All the public securities, including the annuities, were consolidated into one stock, the interest being fixed at the rate of three per cent.

In 1786, Pitt attempted to reduce the national debt by setting aside a sum of money every year, and using the interest of that money for the purpose of reducing the debt. A more permanent scheme was that of Mr. Goschen, who offered to the holders of consols either repayment of capital at its full value, or reduction of the interest from four per cent. to three per cent. up to the year 1903, and afterwards at two and one-half per cent. The second alternative was generally adopted with the result of saving to the country nearly two million pounds a year.

The same system of government loans has been also adopted in other countries. At the present day, almost every nation has its own debt consolidated into stock, the subscribers to which are found in all parts of the world. Variations are constantly taking place, both in the value of the shares and the rate of interest paid, and these variations constitute one of the best criteria of the condition of the nation.

Taxation and loans, therefore, are the usual sources of a State's revenue, and with these the government has to carry on the entire expenses of the administration.

Waging war, building fleets and fortifications, undertaking many works of public utility, establishing an efficient civil service, feeing public servants—all this is done with the public revenues.

Besides the administration by the State of its own finances, there are also other ways in which the State has a large share in determining the fortunes of the commercial world. Already it has been pointed out that both the Mercantile and Physiocratic schools of economists still exist, and that, both in theory and in practice, the government interference, inculcated by the former school, forms a marked feature of the Modern Period of history. Some of the ways in which government regulates trade and commerce will now be considered in detail. The first which will claim our attention is that of granting monopolies.

A monopoly takes place when one kind of trade or business is unlimited by competition. Some monopolies are natural, that is to say, are created by nature, as when a certain kind of cereal grows only in a certain country. Other monopolies are artificial, and these happen whenever government, by taxes or other restrictions, limits the power of manufacture or trade only to certain individuals. Even from medieval times, monopolies began to exist. Thus, in Venice, only certain fleets were allowed to convey commerce to certain countries; in France, certain trading companies, like the Jurandi of Bordeaux, had obtained from their lords the exclusive power of trading, and later on when the colonial system was established each country tried to enjoy the monopoly with its colony. England also was not behind in the system of monopolies. Queen Elizabeth, for example, gave to Lord Essex the monopoly of sweet wines; James granted a monopoly of licensing taverns and also houses, and of making gold and silver thread; while Charles gave to a particular company the monopoly of selling soap.

In addition to these monopolies granted to private persons or firms, the nation itself tried to establish its own monopolies, as against other countries. Perhaps the most famous example of this is the navigation acts. The first navigation act was passed under Richard II. It provided that no merchandise should enter or leave England except in English ships. Under Cromwell, Dutch vessels were forbidden to bring to England any goods save those produced in Holland. Evidently, this act was aimed at the rival Dutch carrying trade, and it was one of the main causes of the war between England and Holland. Further navigation acts had the effect of removing all danger to the supremacy of the English navy from Dutch rivalry. Navigation acts still continued until 1827, at which time they caused considerable friction between England and the United States. Owing to retaliation from other countries, England, for a time, abandoned her old policy and adopted the more liberal policy of reciprocity, allowing foreign ships to enter her harbors in return for similar privileges allowed to the English ships. The navigation acts, however, were not finally repealed until 1849.

At present, the States that in any way keep up the policy of the navigation acts are the United States and Russia. These reserve the coasting trade for their own ships. Nor does the United States interpret coasting trade to mean trade that is carried on merely between one part and another inside the area of its States; it implies that a foreign steamer cannot carry goods from the Atlantic coast to any port on the western coast via Cape Horn. Already this restriction has caused dissatisfaction. And it certainly seems hardly equitable that an American line should be able to compete with an English line along the English coast; while an English line could not do the same by competing on the American coast. It is highly probable that, in defense of the present declining British shipping industry, England will be forced to resort again to the policy of the navigation acts, in order to secure equitable treatment for herself.

Another way in which government tries to foster and regulate trade is by the system of bounties. A bounty is an encouragement given by the State to some particular enterprise. Very often, it takes the form of a sum of money, paid to the manufacturer, for every quantity of goods that he produces. Such stimulants to industry are sometimes highly beneficial, especially in the initial stages of an industry. But, if continued too long, they discourage invention and the spirit of enterprise, and thus have the effect of a deterrent, rather than of a stimulant.

In England, bounties seem to have been introduced about the year 1688. A bounty of five shillings per quarter was then granted on the export of English corn. At first, the effects were beneficial, for the farmers grew a greater quantity of corn, and thus prices were lowered. But, toward the end of the eighteenth century, it had a most mischievous effect, by encouraging the exportation of corn just at the time when it was most needed at home. Bounties were also granted to other industries; thus, in 1772, a bounty of eight shillings was granted on the exportation of every pound weight of silks. In 1789, a bounty was given to the manufacturers of linen.

In the Continental countries of Europe, the same system was adopted, in order to promote native industry and commerce. Colbert, in France, greatly promoted the growth of French manufactures by lavish use of bounties, while the present greatness of the German manufacturing industry was brought about by the same means.

Yet another way in which governments tried to foster industry was by the imposition of tariff duties. These are intended to have the effect of keeping out foreign competition and thus protecting the native manufacturers and trades. Much discussion is still raised regarding the merits or demerits of the system of Protection. Some maintain that it fosters the national spirit, makes a nation more independent, and gives the manufacturer a surer market. Others as hotly maintain that Protection interferes with the natural laws of trade, that it fosters monopolies and artificial combinations, and that it diverts labor to non-productive channels.

The system of Protection began exceedingly early. It was practised even by the Byzantine Empire, which raised a customs barrier that mercilessly barred out all foreign competition. In Italy, it was adopted by the lords of Lucca, in France by Colbert, while England, during the seventeenth century, became then as much protectionist as she now is in favor of Free Trade. About the same time that bounties were given for the exportation of corn, the importation of corn was practically prevented by highly protective duties. Also, in the seventeenth century, there were imposed many duties on foreign lace, embroidery, and wool cords.

At the present time, the countries that mostly adopt the protective system are Germany and the United States. In the latter country, the duties that were introduced after the War of 1812 have always been of a very protective character. After the Civil War, still heavier protective duties were imposed, and this time not only upon cotton and woolen goods, but upon almost every conceivable article that could be imported. The question as to whether the tariff shall be increased or decreased has become now a party question between the Republicans and Democrats, the former voting for a continuance of the tariff, and the latter for its abolition, or at least a considerable reduction.

Another field of commerce in which the benefits of government interference are very warmly discussed is the regulation of combinations, whether of laborers or of employers.

For the sake of bettering their material condition, as regards hours of work, wages, and conditions of employment, laboring men have frequently combined so as to form societies. In speaking of the journeymen of the Middle Ages, we have seen that among them there was some kind of combination that was peculiarly distasteful to the masters. Not, however, until the eighteenth century did these combinations begin to attract any particular attention. At first, they were recognized favorably by the law, but in 1800 they were declared by Act of Parliament illegal. The few years following this date may be considered as the criminal period of the history of trade-unions. A horror of plebeian associations of any kind, the dread of violence, and an ignorance of the rights of labor, were the root causes of a long series of persecutions.

In 1824, however, mainly owing to the assiduity of Francis Peace, the act was repealed. Labor-unions, by this repeal, acquired at least the right of existence. From this, to a definitely recognized legal status, was a comparatively easy step, and, in 1871, combinations of laborers were recognized actively by the law, while, in 1876, they even received a legal organization, to the extent of being able to hold property, and sue district treasurers or other officials. Something, however, still remains to their complete emancipation, for they are still under a cloud of legal disfavor, being regarded as associations for restraining trade, and they can not be prosecuted, no matter how harshly they may treat their members. A privilege of this kind is not likely to be felt very keenly by its absence.

Much good and much ill has been said of the trade-unions, and perhaps with equal truth. While, on the one hand, they are often guilty of injustice and violence in their intimidation of non-unionists, and in the perpetration of useless strikes, yet, if properly managed and conducted, they uphold the rights of labor and increase productiveness. They often become the means of protecting the laborers from the tyranny and dishonesty of their masters; they often become a means of educating the laborer in political and economic problems, and, when affairs of the union are regulated, as often happens, by a central board of prudent and self-restrained men, strikes will not be allowed through mere caprice or idle ill-will.

In America, the trade-unions are quite as powerful as in England. They are comprised under two distinct organizations, namely, the American Federation of Labor and the Knights of Labor. Strikes are far more numerous and not so well regulated as in England. Occasions have arisen, especially in Chicago, when the Federal troops have had to be called out, in order to suppress the lawlessness of the unionist strikers. But it is only fair to remember that many of these strikes are the work of recent immigrants, who have not become thoroughly naturalized, and who have not yet attained to that self-control and power of reflection that so characterize the American workman. So far, the government in the United States has adopted a policy of *laissez-faire* toward the trade-unions, except when they overstep the limits of the laws protecting person and property.

From what has been said in the last few pages, it will be seen that the attitude of government toward commercial questions still hovers between the Mercantilist and the Physiocratic systems, and that it is still often a matter of doubt as to whether government interference on this or that particular occasion is beneficial or injurious.

Before concluding this subject it would be desirable to consider, briefly, one important though indirect way in which government has an influence on the distribution of wealth, namely, the poor-law system of relief. During the Middle Ages, the State, as we have seen, made no provision for the poor. Such institutions as the monasteries and guilds combined with private munificence to relieve the condition of the suffering poor.

When society began to enter on the highly complex conditions of the Modern Period, this system proved insufficient. The conversion of arable into pasture land, which meant the deprivation of employment to thousands of agricultural laborers, the greater fluctuations in trade entailed by wider markets, and the shiftless condition of many soldiers, returning from almost chronic European wars, swelled enormously the ranks of the destitute.

Some new system of relief had to be devised which, owing to the greater means at its disposal, and to a more centralized organization than that of private institutions, might deal more efficiently with the ever-growing problem of poverty.

The result was a general movement, both in England and on the Continent, both in the Catholic Church and amongst the followers of Luther, in the devotion of State relief. In this movement, the Catholic town of Ypres took a very leading part; in fact, it was the first town to adopt anything like a system of poor-law relief. From Ypres the movement spread all over the Catholic world. And, what gave to it great impetus, was the decision of the theological faculty of the University of Paris, that a system of State relief was lawful and expedient. From the Continent, the movement spread to England, chiefly through the instrumentality of the great Catholic humanist, Vives, who lived for some time at the court of Henry VIII, and was very often consulted by his ministers. His influence could, indeed, be distinctly seen in various branches of the English-poor-laws, especially those regarding the classification of the poor.

In the reign of Elizabeth was formulated a poor-law which in many respects was remarkable for its practical wisdom, and which even at the present day forms the basis of the present poor-law system in England and especially in the United States. It says that two or three or four substantial householders shall, under the seal of two or more justices of the peace, be nominated yearly, in Easter week, and that these, with the church wardens, shall be overseers of the poor. These shall, with the consent of the justices, take order from time to time for carrying into effect the several provisions of the act and shall raise by taxation, weekly or otherwise, such sums of money as they think fit for the following purposes: (1) to set to work the children of the poor and the adult poor; (2) to furnish a convenient stock of hemp and of flax to provide work for the poor; (3) to relieve the sick, the blind, and the feeble. To effect these objects, the church wardens and overseers are to meet at least once a week after divine service. The act then provides for the mutual responsibility of relations, extending this even to the grandparents. It also provides that the overseers can, with the consent of two justices, apprentice out the poor children, males to the age of twenty-four, females to the age of twenty. Finally, the justices are empowered to commit to houses of correction persons refusing to work.

We may now consider the accidental and the permanent elements of this poor-law code. The repressive element of it has almost disappeared. Perhaps the only remnant of it still in existence in England is that begging, by the English law, is unlawful, and any person caught begging can be handed over to the police. But there is another defect in the Elizabethan code which ought not to be passed over. It leaves no room for private charity. It is perfectly true that there should be some general principle of legislation with inflexible rules which should apply to all general cases. But there are always exceptional cases, and it is precisely these with which private charities have to deal. Hence, in England, they have St. Vincent de Paul societies, Jewish lending societies and, finally, the "Charity Organization Society," which closely corresponds to the "Association of Charities," professing to supply information regarding applicants for relief. But we must now consider the permanent elements of the Elizabethan code.

The first permanent element is the distinctive treatment meted out to the impotent poor, and to those who are sturdy and able to work. For the blind, sick, and feeble, habitations had to be erected from which they were not to stray, and in which they had to do such work as they were able to do, while, for the unruly vagabond, there was the house of correction. Now it is this clause which gave rise, for the first time, to the poorhouse, which in England goes by the name of workhouse. The English poorhouse, however, is at the same time a house of correction. Into the English poorhouse are admitted the sick, the feeble, the impotent poor, and the able-bodied who are able to work. Any one, no matter who he is, can be admitted to the workhouse. As a matter of fact, however, the workhouse is quite a misnomer. It is a *lucus a non lucendo.* In most of the English workhouses only about twenty per cent. are able to work. In one of them only sixty out of two thousand are able to work. The rest are either morally or physically incapacitated. But the work test is still vigorously applied. Inmates are bound to do what work they can, and the vagrants who demand a night's lodging are required to perform in return two or three hours of hard work next morning. The Elizabethan legislators had great trust in this work test as a means for distinguishing between the genuine and fictitious poor. They said, "If a man is really in want, he will work for the relief that is given him." This principle was also the basis of the English Poor-Law Reform of 1834, when it was recognized that the main antidote against the evils of the times was to make the condition of the pauper worse than that of the lowest paid laborer. In the United States, in Minnesota, not only the spirit, but also the letter of the Elizabethan code is faithfully preserved, for there are the poorhouses, where the impotent poor are received, and, apart from these, are the farms upon which the sturdy can be set to work, corresponding to the Elizabethan house of correction.

Closely connected with this is the classification of the poor, in the Elizabethan code, into the following classes: children of the poor, the adult poor, the sick and the feeble, and, finally, the sturdy vagabond. But the actual carrying-out of this classification was far more effectual in the Elizabethan than in the modern English code. At the present time all the different classes of paupers are confined in the same workhouse. The workhouse in England is neither a school, nor a prison, nor a penitentiary, nor an infirmary, but a curious combination of all of these put together. Nearly all these persons are the very riff-raff of society, persons whose bad character has usually driven them within the walls, persons deserving both of blame and pity. We can easily see, therefore, the importance of making a complete and thorough classification of the inmates. But, even in the large workhouses, this classification is extremely difficult, for they all meet in the chapel and at meals, and, in any case, it is hard to prevent conversation between times.

The Elizabethan code provided also for the responsibility of relations for the support of each other. This still holds good in England, and in many places of the United States, though in the United States there is a wise provision that when the person is a pauper clearly through his own fault, in such a case his relations are free from this responsibility.

Another permanent element is the enforced payment of rates. The act of Elizabeth provides that those who refuse the poor-rate should be brought before two justices of the peace, to show cause of refusal, and if they still remain obdurate they should then be imprisoned. It is almost amusing to see how slowly and with what extreme reluctance the poor-rate was made compulsory in England. It was evident that the ratepayers made a considerable opposition. Under Henry VIII voluntary alms were to be collected among the faithful. These were evidently rather slow in coming in, and a further statute provides that the obdurate ratepayer should be gently admonished by his pastor and church wardens. This was evidently still ineffectual, and under Philip and Mary the obstinate ratepayer was not only admonished by the pastor and church wardens, but was brought before the bishop, as well, to receive admonition. Even the bishop, however, proved ineffectual, and the Elizabethan poor-law code provides that any refusing to pay the rate should be imprisoned. The collectors of this rate were the overseers, and this is one of the few remaining powers still in the hands of the overseers. The overseer in the Elizabethan code had many powers. He collected the weekly rates with the consent of the justices; he was charged with providing work for the children and the adults; in a word, he was entrusted with the general supervision of the inmates of poorhouses. Later on, in the times of the Stuarts, his sphere of action was still further enlarged, and he was entrusted with the task of supervising, not only the poor actually in the poorhouse, but the laborers without it. Later on, however, his powers were curtailed. In the year 1691, it was complained that overseers were sometimes indiscriminate in their giving relief, and a list of paupers had to be drawn up, outside of which none should receive relief, except by the authority of the justices of the peace. The position of the overseer was still further degraded by the law which decreed that if any overseer refused relief, the applicant could arraign him before the justices of the peace to show cause of his refusal. By the celebrated Gilbert's Act, which provided for the incorporation of unions, nearly all the previous powers of the overseer were entrusted to boards of guardians, and at present the only duties of the English overseer are to collect the rates and grant relief in certain emergencies. Here, again, the poor-law code of the United States adheres much more closely to the Elizabethan code, for the overseer still retains many of the general powers of supervision, such as were enjoyed by his ancestor in the Elizabethan code.

The last permanent element we have to consider is that of settlement. The Fourteenth Statute of Elizabeth provides that the justices of the peace must make search for all the poor who have been born, or who have lived in their parish three years. This condition of poor relief is practically still in existence. Even at the present time, the main title that a man has to relief from the union is the fact of settlement, that he was born there, or that he lived there dependent upon his parents, or that he has lived there three years. But in England, this element of settlement is complicated by the law of irremovability, by which, if a person has lived in a parish one year, or if he be only temporarily sick, or a foreigner, then he can not be removed.

Such, very briefly, are the permanent elements of the Elizabethan code. True, it has many defects, but we must remember that it was a tentative measure, and that the evils that it had to cope with were complicated by previous narrow-minded legislators. On the whole, the Elizabethan code was framed in a broad and tolerant spirit, and it certainly recognized that great principle, which was the chief basis of the reform of 1834, that the condition of the able-bodied pauper should be made less desirable than that of the lowest class workingman. It discouraged universal almsgiving, which, without careful discrimination and wide circumstantial knowledge, often does more harm than good, and its object was to secure to the workingman that moral capital which is so important for success in life, the capital of self-dependence, the spirit of initiative. Perhaps it is true to say that the Elizabethan code is almost as remarkable for what it omits as for what it asserts. It says nothing about outdoor relief, about relieving the poor in their homes. Some make the objection that the abolition of State outdoor relief implies one of two things: either starving the poor man, or forcing him into the workhouse, which means, in many cases, breaking up of home and the violation of family ties. But constant experience shows that, when outdoor relief is repeatedly refused, the number of those going into the workhouse diminishes also, and that, in point of fact, outdoor relief is a preparatory school, or initiation, into pauperism. Outdoor relief, with the deadening expectations it raises, is far crueler, far sterner, than the policy which refuses to tempt people away from their own true strength. It is, perhaps, not too much to say that of all the achievements, military and civil, of Elizabeth, one of her greatest, and one that did most good for humanity, was the construction of a poor-law which was practical and elastic.

By thus relieving the destitute, there is no doubt that the State is grappling with a very serious difficulty, which arises from the unequal distribution of wealth. In the Middle Ages, extreme poverty was rare, owing to the greater diffusion and stability of wealth. But conditions are now altered. Capital tends to accumulate in the hands of a few, competition is keener, and many, through no fault of their own, have to fall out of the race. The problem of poverty, therefore, has to be dealt with, in order to avoid the same dangerous discontent and revolutions that threatened the later Roman Republic.

CHAPTER VI

INFLUENCE OF ECONOMICS ON WARS AND TREATIES

DURING the sixteenth and seventeenth centuries, the principles of the Mercantile school of economics generally prevailed throughout Europe. Statesmen regarded the possession of gold and silver as the principal object of their ambition, and since these commodities are limited in quantity, the natural results of such a policy were constant frictions and frequent endeavors, both by commercial and military wars, to destroy the wealth of other nations but one's own.

Most of the wars during these two centuries took their origin from economic causes. Monopoly of the shipping trade, monopoly of commerce with the newly discovered colonies—these were, at first, the real causes of contention. Indeed, the religious wars of Europe, like the Thirty Years' War, and the war in the Spanish Netherlands, had not ended before the economic element seriously intervened, and began to supplant the religious element as an element of strife.

First, there was the rivalry between England and Spain during the reign of Elizabeth. Certainly, there were, as well, religious and political causes. The strong feeling between Protestants and Catholics, the execution of Mary Stuart, and the necessity of preserving the balance of power against Spain, were strong causes. But, even after the removal of these, the wars still continued and were plainly fought out on economic grounds. When Cromwell came to power, he openly avowed that trade with the Spanish colonies was the object of contention. For this purpose, he formed an alliance, first with Holland, and then with France. During the alliance with Holland, Penn Venables made an attack on the Spanish colonies in the West Indies. The attack was foiled, but, by way of compensation, Penn afterwards succeeded in taking the Island of Jamaica, while Blake completely destroyed the Spanish fleet at Teneriffe in the Canary Islands. During the alliance with France, Mardyke, in the Spanish Netherlands, was captured, and Dunkirk was forced to surrender. Nor was the war confined to military tactics alone. Its commercial aspect was still further emphasized by the imposition, on the part of England, of protective duties, hoping thereby to crush the productiveness of Spanish industry in the colonies.

Even when the political rivalry of Spain had declined, her commercial prosperity in the colonies occasioned wars, even as late as the middle of the eighteenth century. It was England's violation of the commercial clauses of the Treaty of Utrecht, and the harshness of the Spanish custom house officers, which occasioned the Spanish and English war during Walpole's administration. At the remonstrances of the English merchants and their supporters, he unwillingly began operations against Spain. The war, however, was carried out in a very half-hearted manner. The dramatic capture of Porto Bello by the six English ships was more than offset by the disastrous failure to capture Carthagena in Spanish South America.

Close on the heels of trade rivalry between England and Spain, came also the commercial rivalry between England and Holland. This also manifested itself during the time of Cromwell. The navigation acts under Cromwell, which limited the exportation and importation of goods between England and Asia, Africa, and

America, to English ships, manned by English crews; the act of 1661, under Charles II, which furthermore insisted that these ships must be owned by Englishmen, were aimed chiefly at Holland.

The navigation acts certainly accomplished their purpose. Holland suffered severely in her trade, and was goaded into a declaration of war. In Cromwell's time, the great naval duel was fought between Admiral Tromp, on the side of the Dutch, and Admiral Blake, on the side of the English. While Tromp won the battle of Dungeness, Blake won the still more decisive battle off Portland.

After peace had been temporarily restored, war again broke out after the navigation act of Charles II. This time the war was more general. All along the Gold Coast of Africa and in North America, there arose hostilities between English and Dutch merchants. In English waters, the English fleet was not so successful as during Cromwell's time. Blake's place had been taken by the less efficient Rupert and Albemarle, while the Dutch Admiral Ruyter was nearly equal to Tromp. At first, the number of successes on either side were about evenly balanced. But the carelessness of the English commanders who, imagining that the war was over, laid up the war ships, allowed the Dutch to sail up the Thames, and to burn the English shipping.

The Peace of Breda was then signed (1667). French jealousy, however, of the Dutch trade renewed hostilities. In 1677, England joined France, under Louis XIV, in the celebrated attack on Holland. Only the intrepid defense made by the Dutch, who flooded their provinces against the invader, and the political sagacity of William of Orange, saved Holland from destruction. Louis XIV was compelled to withdraw his troops. But Dutch trade afterwards became permanently crippled, and her place in the competition for the monopoly of trade and commerce was taken by France.

It was the political supremacy of France, and her aggressiveness, that actually began the great wars between Louis XIV and the greater part of Europe. His early wars were prompted by the desire to strengthen the weak frontiers of France, but his later wars were the result of pure aggressiveness. His invasion of the Palatinate, his arbitrary seizure of certain territories in Alsace, his taking possession of the crown of Spain in behalf of his grandson, his filling the frontier towns in the Spanish Netherlands with French garrisons, were all arbitrary acts that necessitated a war of self-defense, and brought on the Grand Alliance between England, Spain, Holland, and the German Empire against France, and the great War of the Spanish Succession.

And yet, even here, there was present an economic element. Who can doubt but that the union of Spain and France, under one head, would have been vitally prejudicial, not only to the political balance of power, but also to the commercial prosperity and existence of England? In fact, one of the very clauses of the Treaty of the Grand Alliance was the protection of the threatened English commerce; moreover, one of the means by which England tried to strike at France was by an understanding with Portugal to give up the importation of French wines, and, instead, to allow the importation of Portuguese wines. Portugal, on her side, was to allow a free market to the introduction of English woolen goods. It was evidently a case of trying to deal a blow at France by means of a reciprocal monopoly, the first of its kind.

When the war was concluded in favor of the Grand Alliance, its commercial side was again sufficiently demonstrated by the clauses of the Treaty of Utrecht, which guaranteed for a time favorable trade concessions between England and France, and to the former country the peaceful and profitable cession of the colonies of Nova Scotia and Newfoundland.

Gradually, however, the real issue at stake between England and France became more and more apparent. When the attempt to divide the Austrian dominions of Maria Theresa brought on the War of the Austrian Succession, England entered the struggle, and during its course attempted again to deal a blow at French commerce. The termination of the war, also, revealed clearly the undercurrent of the clash of economic interests. Cape Breton was lost to the English, while Madras was recovered from the French.

This growing competition between England and France for the possession of colonial settlements beyond the seas and the wider market that they would thus bring was brought to a head during the Seven Years' War. While on the battlefields of Europe the issues were chiefly political, in other parts of the world the issues were mainly economic. But even the European strife was not altogether devoid of the economic element. Besides the hatred of Austria aroused toward Prussia by the latter's seizure of Silesia, the commercial prosperity of the Netherlands was a very serious cause of contention between Austria and Prussia. Austria wished to revive the commerce of the Netherlands, and for this purpose to promote the formation of an important commercial company at Ostend; Prussia, on the other hand, still insisted on the closing of the River Scheldt, so that the rival port of Antwerp should not injure Dutch trade.

While the question of the economic prosperity of the Netherlands formed one of the important causes of the Seven Years' War, the quarrel between England and France arose from economic questions of a vital and worldwide nature. The prize in dispute was the possession of the colonies in America and India, and the enormous trade and wealth that would result from the possession of those colonies.

During the early part of the fourteenth century, the French had adopted the avowed policy of confining the English to the seaboard of the Atlantic coast, and of establishing, by means of the great waterways, complete communication between their Canadian possessions and those that were in Louisiana. The great valleys of the Allegheny and Tennessee were brought under their control, and, altogether, the French, aided by their strong government at home, were obviously gaining over their English rivals.

In 1754 began the real struggle. General Braddock was sent over from England, in order to destroy the French forts at Niagara, and the other forts as far south as Wabash. Braddock's first move was against Fort Duquesne (Pittsburg). He soon showed himself thoroughly inexperienced in guerrilla warfare. Allowing his army to fall into an ambuscade of Indians in the employ of the French, he himself was mortally wounded and his army routed in 1755.

These disasters were, however, retrieved in 1758. The great English statesman, Pitt the Elder, was then at the head of affairs, and none knew better than he how to choose capable officers. General Wolfe was sent out to take command of the English army. His ability was undoubted, and it was given a favorable opportunity by the exhausted condition of Canada. Montcalm, the French commander, was besieged in Quebec. Apparently, the place was impregnable, but the English, by scaling at dead of night the steep cliffs of the north bank of the St. Lawrence, surprised the French sentinels, and completely outflanked and vanquished the French army. The capture of Quebec was the signal for the general overthrow of French rule in Canada. One after another, Ticonderoga, Niagara, and Montreal became an easy prey. Canada became British, and the Middle States of America were also saved from French domination.

The results were far-reaching. The Teutonic, instead of the Latin civilization, prevailed in the American States. Literature, national law and jurisprudence, national character, and even the form of religion of these States were determined by the English successful resistance against the French. England at the same time became enriched by its permanent possession of a colony remarkable for many valuable productions, and offering to English merchants and traders a most valuable market.

Just about the same time as the Canadian war, the English and French were also fighting out their colonial quarrel in quite another part of the world, namely, in the great Empire of India.

Up to a few years of this time, India had been ruled by a succession of emperors belonging to the Mogul dynasty. The founder of this dynasty was popularly supposed to have been Baber, a potentate who flourished in the sixteenth century, though Baber himself claimed descent from Timon the Tartar, who lived in the fourteenth century.

For a long time the rule of the Moguls was highly centralized, and extended over all the Indian provinces. But a process of disintegration had already begun. The different princes of the provinces began to assert their independence, and the authority of the empire became almost as shadowy and unsubstantial as that of the later Carolingian monarchs.

Besides these internal elements of disintegration, there were also the various foreign trading settlements, of which we have already spoken in a previous chapter. These were chiefly along the coasts. Thus, on the western, or Malabar coast, the Portuguese had established the colony of Goa; the French had established themselves at Hooghly and Pondicherry; finally, the English were in possession of the village of Bombay, on the extreme northwest coast, of Fort St. George in Madras, and of a settlement at Calcutta, on the extreme northeastern coast.

The French, up to 1750, seemed to have made the most progress. The East Indian Company, that had been formed under Richelieu, had received special patronage under Colbert, while Dupleix, the governor of Pondicherry, was an able man, and full of ambition to promote his country's interests.

Opportunity to advance French influence presented itself in the continual petty disputes and fights that were going on between the native tribes. The French backed up one tribe against the other, and by drilling the natives, whom they supplied with instruments of modern warfare, they hoped to secure by this means complete ascendency in India. This policy, however, stirred the English into a course of vigorous action. They espoused the cause of the tribes that were being attacked by the French. At first, the campaign went against the English. Their siege of Pondicherry failed, and even Trichinopoli, in Madras, was placed in imminent danger. But Robert Clive, a dashing young soldier, saved the situation. Abandoning a purely defensive method of warfare, he assumed the aggressive. In 1717, he took the city of Arcot, in the Carnatic, and held it successfully against the most vigorous assaults from the French. Almost at once, the power of the French began to decline. Dupleix had to retire to France in disgrace, and the whole of the Carnatic became settled under English rule.

The next step in the establishment of an English empire in India was the conquest of Bengal. Suraja Dowlah was then the nabob of Bengal. He was a man of savage and fiendish cruelty, but it was greed, more than anything else, that led him to attack the English settlement at Fort William (Calcutta) in 1756. He succeeded, and in the hour of his triumph one hundred and forty-six prisoners were confined in a small room only twenty feet square, and with only two small gratings for ventilation. For only one night were the prisoners confined in this den, but the heat of an Indian summer did its work, and in the morning only twenty-three persons survived.

This massacre roused Clive to put forth his best energies. Marching into the heart of Bengal, he inflicted upon the enemy an overwhelming defeat at the battle of Plassey (1757). This victory placed the English in possession of Bengal, and, together with the victory at Wandewash in southern India by Colonel Coote, practically determined that the English, and not the French, were to be the rulers of India.

Such, indeed, was the real significance of the Seven Years' War. It settled the outstanding colonial question between England and France. The occupation of America by the Teutonic race, and the foundation of the great Empire of India, are events of stupendous, world-wide importance, and they were brought about by the struggle between England and France for the possession of the widest markets.

Even when the Seven Years' War had been terminated by the Treaty of Paris, hostilities were again renewed, about fifty years afterwards, between France and England, and again also the economic element played a part, though not so important as during the Seven Years' War.

In the great wars that Napoleon was waging against the civilized world, there was one power that was always the object of his peculiar dread, and whose destruction was uppermost in his thoughts. That power was England. He instinctively felt that England's destiny, in the present, as in the past, was to preserve the balance of power in Europe against any nation that was becoming too formidable. First, Philip II, then Louis XIV, of France, had been humbled by England, and he felt sure England would again follow the same policy which was so subservient to her best interests. Moreover, his sneering remark, that England was a nation of shopkeepers, clearly showed that her commercial greatness was still an object of jealousy.

In 1806, Napoleon was still on the floodtide of success. The battles of Marengo, Hohenlinden, Ulm, Austerlitz, and Jena had made him victor in Italy, Austria, and Prussia. But one nation had successfully defied his power, and that one nation was England. At the naval battle of Trafalgar, the French fleet had received a humiliating and decisive reverse. This was an injury and an affront that Napoleon was not likely to forget.

In 1806, therefore, he issued the celebrated Berlin Decrees. These decrees placed England in a state of blockade. They forbade all commerce, and any kind of communication, between England and any of his dependents and allies, and ordered the imprisonment of all English subjects found in countries occupied by French troops, and the seizure of English property and merchandise wherever they could be found. These decrees aimed at the complete isolation of England from the rest of Europe. Such an attempt might seem at first absurdly impracticable, but it must be remembered that Napoleon at that time was military master of Europe, and that the secret treaties of Tilsit, signed shortly afterwards, gave him the effective control over the ports of Prussia and Russia.

To these decrees England was forced to reply by a counterblow. In 1807, she issued the celebrated Orders in Council, which curtailed the rights of neutrals, and forbade all intercourse with any port occupied by the French.

Napoleon retaliated by the still more severe Decrees of Milan, which formulated his continental system into a code of law. For years no European port dared openly to admit an English vessel within its waters, under pain of incurring Napoleon's severest displeasure. He even required neutrals to carry a license to trade. One instance of Napoleon's severity, in this regard, we find in his treatment of Pope Pius VII. The refusal of the Pope to expel English subjects from his States and to prevent English ships from entering Papal harbors, was the excuse given for Napoleon's active hostilities against the Holy Father.

England's assertion of her Orders in Council also caused a great deal of distress and annoyance. Her ships not only effectively blocked the French ports, but successfully carried off as prizes many of the neutral

ships.   Incidentally, the United States suffered considerably in her trade and commerce, and the strong tension that resulted between England and the United
States also damaged even the English trade and manufactures.   This was especially the case in regard to the
spinning industries in Lancashire, that were so dependent upon the supply of cotton from America.

Eventually, England came out victorious.   Her ships
became the only carriers of the world.   The Americans
themselves began to respect English blockades, and England, so far from losing her trade, both retained her old
ports and even secured for herself more marts for her
commercial enterprises.

It is curious to observe that, while both the English
and the French governments made a pretense of severely
enforcing their respective blockades, they both made a
considerable revenue by conniving at their violations.
Napoleon, perceiving the hopelessness of enforcing his
decrees, allowed the importation of English goods to
certain licensed holders who, naturally, had to pay a
very heavy price for their license.   In fact, Napoleon
himself was greatly dependent upon English goods.
Even his very soldiers made their march to Russia clad
in English-made top-coats.   England, though not impelled by the same necessity, resorted to the same practice of selling trade licenses, and made therefrom considerable profit.

Such was the nature of the economic war waged between France and England.   It was a war that was,
throughout, marked by the greatest dishonesty and disregard for the rights of others.   But it serves as a useful illustration of the growing importance of trade, as
affecting even the military strength of nations.

In the meantime, there had been waged a war of even

still greater importance to the English-speaking world, and that is the War of American Independence. There can be no doubt that the causes of this war were mainly economic. To none other of her colonies did England allow so much political liberty. It is true that the American colonies were considered to be politically dependent upon the mother country, and that the authority of the governor represented the jurisdiction of the Crown. But the real power was vested in the hands of the popular assemblies. It was they who enacted the laws, and, although the governor could refuse his assent, and thus prevent the passage of a bill, yet their power to fix the governor's salary was a powerful check upon any despotic use of his authority. It was the assemblies, again, that had the power of the purse, levying the general taxes, and appropriating the public moneys for different purposes.

The chief causes of complaint were economic. First of all, England had always prohibited any manufactures in the colonies. They were allowed, indeed, to raise the raw produce, but the manufacture of this into the finished material was to be reserved for English manufacturers in the mother country. This was especially so in regard to woolen manufactures, as these were of great importance, and England was especially jealous of any competition on the part of the colonies.

Also, the colonies were forbidden to trade with any country except with the mother country. In the stringent provisions of the later navigation acts, a very severe blow was dealt at the nascent colonial commerce. It certainly seemed very unjust that the colonies should not be able to send their goods to the market, whether French or Spanish, where they could get the highest price. The fundamental law of supply and demand was hereby absolutely violated, for while, on the one hand, the English demand was not sufficiently extensive to accept all the surplus produce of the colonies, the Americans on their side could not obtain from England all the commodities they were willing to buy. Naturally, a great difficulty was experienced in enforcing such arbitrary laws. Both countries were subjected to heavy protective duties, with the result that the production of wealth was considerably impeded and cut down, both in America and in England.

The colonies were obviously the greater sufferers by this arrangement, but their patience was not goaded into desperation until England attempted to impose upon them an unjust and arbitrary system of taxation. In 1765 was passed the celebrated Stamp Act. This required that stamps, varying in value from two cents to fifty dollars, should be placed upon all legal and business papers, such deeds as wills and insurances, and even upon newspapers and advertisements. The Americans, however, declared that it was an admitted principle that representation and taxation should go together, and that the two had been imposed without their consent, and were, therefore, invalid. In the South, Patrick Henry headed the opposition in Virginia, and successfully passed his resolutions through the assemblies, that no tax could be lawfully imposed without their own consent. In the North, a Stamp Act Congress was formed in Massachusetts, which declared that "the people of these colonies are not, and, from their local circumstances, can not be represented in the House of Commons in Great Britain . and that no taxes ever have been or ever can be constitutionally imposed upon them except by their respective legislatures."

In the face of such opposition, the Stamp Act was repealed. But afterwards, fresh taxes were imposed.
These, also, shared the same fate as the Stamp Act.
Lord North, therefore, in 1770, repealed all the existing taxes except the tax on tea, which, however, was
reduced to the small sum of about six cents a pound.
So thoroughly aroused, however, was the spirit of opposition, that even this tax was resented, as establishing a
precedent, and as embodying the principle expressed in
the king's own words, "There must be always one tax
to keep up the right, and as such I approve the tea
duty."

It was the endeavor to collect this tax that brought
about the famous tea riot in Boston harbor, the first
act in the War of American Independence. The early
stages of the war were fought out on purely economic
grounds. It was a fight for a free market, and for the
exemption from arbitrary financial exactions. Nowhere,
perhaps, can we find a more clear and more dramatic
illustration of the influence of the economic element on
history than the way in which it brought about the rise
of the great American Republic.

CHAPTER VII

THE ECONOMIC ELEMENT IN NATIONAL TREATIES

NOT only in war, but also in international treaties, economics held a very important position. The fifteenth century inaugurated a whole series of commercial treaties, or treaties containing very important commercial clauses. Among the first of these was the celebrated Intercursus Magnus (1496).

This treaty was drawn up between Henry VII of England and the Low Countries. A disagreement had taken place, owing to the circumstance that Philip, Archduke of the Netherlands, had encouraged the impostor, Perkin Warbeck, who laid claim to the English throne. Henry in revenge expelled the Flemings from England. Philip retaliated by doing the same to the English in Flanders. Both countries, however, suffered so severely that they withdrew from hostilities, and agreed upon the treaty called the Intercursus Magnus.

The main terms of this treaty were that there should be free trade between the two countries, merchants being allowed to pass backward and forward on condition of producing a passport; that free fishing should be allowed in English waters, and that merchant ships in stress of storm, or war, could take refuge in the harbors of either nation. Other clauses showed that the union of the two countries was of a defensive character. Thus, enemies' goods were forbidden to enter the territory of either nation, and no hospitality was to be extended to any pirate or privateer. Lastly, certain regulations were laid down regarding trade itself. Trade in foreign bullion was allowed; there was no compulsory sale of goods, and security might be given for debt.

No one can doubt the wisdom of Henry VII in signing this treaty. It secured the Netherlands to his side by the strong ties of self-interest. Perkin Warbeck soon found himself deprived of all resources, and his claim ended in failure. But, beyond all this, the treaty itself embodied principles that lie at the foundation of all commercial prosperity and greatness.

In 1648 was signed the Treaty of Westphalia. This treaty came at the end of the Thirty Years' War, and its main provisions settled the differences between Protestants and Catholics, as well as the territorial position of those countries that had taken part in the struggle. There were, however, one or two commercial clauses, that were afterwards to cause political complications. The Dutch were allowed by this treaty to retain their colonial conquests while at the same time they were secured against the rivalry of the Spanish Netherlands by the closing of the River Scheldt. Not only had this clause the effect of delaying for a considerable time the commercial growth of Antwerp, but it also embittered relations between Charles VI of Austria, and Holland. Charles was anxious to receive the commerce of the Netherlands, but, not venturing to open the Scheldt, he formed the Ostend Company for the purpose of opening up trade with India. This displeased the Dutch, and their side was taken by England, who determined to suppress the company. Thus, hostilities were brought about between England and Austria. After a general European war, in which Austria was supported by Spain, Charles agreed, in the Treaty of Vienna (1731), to dissolve the Ostend Company.

The Methuen Treaty was signed in 1703 between

England and Portugal, during the War of the Spanish Succession. Louis XIV was endeavoring to enforce the pretensions of his house to the Spanish throne, and these pretensions were being obstinately rejected by the Grand Alliance. At first, Portugal was wavering, and it was the Methuen Treaty that secured to the allies her valuable aid. Mr. Paul Methuen, as special ambassador, brought about the treaty which was named after him. It provided that woolen clothes should be admitted into Portugal and that, in return for this concession, Portuguese wines should be admitted into England at a considerably reduced duty.

Commercially, this treaty had important results. English-manufactured woolens began to increase, and the rapid growth of this industry can be estimated by the enormous amount of Brazilian bullion that was imported into England. Politically, this treaty had the effect of cementing the alliance between England and Portugal.

The Treaty of Utrecht terminated the War of the Spanish Succession in 1713. The economic clauses were of paramount importance. They decided some of the outstanding colonial questions between England and France. For England secured Gibraltar, Minorca in the Mediterranean, and Newfoundland, Acadia, and Hudson Bay. At the same time, trade communications were again to be opened between England and France. This last clause, however, was bitterly denounced by many Englishmen as an infringement of the Methuen Treaty, and, as a matter of fact, it was shortly withdrawn.

While trade relations between England and France remained thus suspended, a commercial treaty of a favorable character was signed in 1786 between England

and the United States. This treaty was called the Eden Treaty, after the name of William Eden, afterwards Lord Auckland, who was the chief inaugurator. It provided for a system of reciprocal customs and commercial advantages which were given and received on both sides. The treaty, however, was short-lived, and was followed soon afterwards by the more important Treaty of Amiens, signed in 1803, after the early successes of the Consul Bonaparte during the French revolutionary war. This treaty had the effect, besides making various territorial arrangements, of placing the whole trade of the world in the hands of England. More than ever did English shipping monopolize the carrying trade of the world. Moreover, England was now a greater producer than any other country, and was enabled to fix the market price of almost every commodity. It was this commercial independence and greatness of England that enabled her afterwards to defy the Berlin Decrees, and gave to her such powers of endurance against the power of Napoleon.

The Treaty of Paris (1814), which followed the fall of Napoleon, also contained some important economic clauses. England retained the colonies of Mauritius, Tobago, and St. Lucia taken from the French, and also the Dutch colonies of Cape of Good Hope, Demerara, and Essequibo. The acquisition of the Cape was the beginning of the great English colonial settlements in Africa. Later on, in the same century, came the commercial Cobden Treaty in 1861. By this treaty, certain commercial concessions were made between England and France. While England reduced the duties on French wines and brandy, and abolished those hitherto levied on manufactured goods, the duties that had been levied in France on English imports were also considerably reduced. This treaty was the victorious expression of the doctrine of Free Trade, of which Mr. Cobden was so able an exponent, and not only was it advantageous to the commercial prosperity of both countries, but it also promoted so strong an amity between the two nations that it was not seriously impaired by the downfall of Napoleon III, who had signed the treaty.

Such were the most important commercial treaties that were signed, down to the middle of the last century. They were all so many steps that gradually led up to the present condition of circumstances, when commercial treaties are as numerous, and quite as important, as political treaties. Indeed, the commercial element in treaties now seems to preponderate, and the councils of foreign statesmen have to take into consideration economic questions more, perhaps, than any other subject.

CHAPTER VIII

INFLUENCE OF THE ECONOMIC ELEMENT ON THE FRENCH REVOLUTION

THE French Revolution may be truly considered as the starting point of a new era, not only for France herself, but for the whole of Europe. The Revolution was the result of certain doctrines, that had been formulated even from the time of Hobbes, and were now spreading with very effective results over the whole of the Continent. Such doctrines, for example, as that government is merely the result of a social contract, which can be kept or rescinded according to the will of the people, and that the welfare of the State, as a whole, is of lesser importance than the welfare of the individual, when pushed to their ultimate, practical consequences, were bound to accomplish great political revolutions.

It is true that, even before the Revolution, there were certain monarchs in Europe who were imbued with modern philanthropic ideas, and tried to introduce certain measures likely to ameliorate the condition of the individual living in the lower strata of society. Such, for example, were the enlightened despots like Frederick the Great, Catharine II of Russia, Joseph II of Austria. But these rulers were not thorough. They still believed very strongly in the goodness of personal government, and they little thought of placing political power in the hands of the people.

The French Revolution, however, gave reality and completeness to the new doctrines. Not only was the French monarchy overthrown, but the shock was felt, as well, in all the other European countries. In spite of reactionary tendencies, in spite of the Holy Alliance formed between Austria, Russia, and Prussia to put down any revolution against the established government, the principles of Democracy and nationalization pursued their downward march. In Germany, the Carlsbad Decrees and the influence of Metternich only delayed for thirty years the establishment of representative government. In Belgium, it was the active continuance of the revolutionary principles of France that brought about the formation of a liberal constitutional government. Even such reactionary countries as Spain and Italy were not exempt from the wave of democratic agitation, and were obliged to set up within their borders limited constitutional monarchies. England, also, which had already all the elements of constitutional government, underwent the crisis of the Chartist Riots, and there is no doubt that the rise of the Third Estate in France gave a great impetus to the agitation for parliamentary reform in 1834.

In examining the causes of this great epoch-making event, the French Revolution, we shall find that they were very varied in character. They were of a political, religious, and economic nature. The exclusion of the people from any share in the administration of affairs, the arbitrary way in which the king could enforce his will on the *Parlement,* and the despotic sway of the intendants, who were the ministers and agents of royal power, were certainly causes of complaint. To this must also be added the religious condition of France. While the enormous disproportion between the salaries of the upper and lower clergy made the latter discontented, the prevalence of unbelief amongst all classes of society was removing one of the strongest props of conservatism, namely, the hold of religion upon the people.

Far more powerful, however, than either the political or religious were the economic causes. These were the driving power of the whole movement. No sooner were these in any way relaxed, than the revolutionary movement also began to slacken. And, on the other hand, the events that brought about the revolutionary climax were essentially economic. It will be necessary, therefore, to analyze the material condition of France immediately preceding the Revolution, and then trace the various steps by which the economic condition gradually brought about the abolition of the existing régime and the substitution of a republic for a monarchy.

In France, the greater part of the land was owned by the wealthy, only about one-fourth being owned by the peasants. Even this ownership was not absolutely free. There still remained some of the old feudal obligations in their most vexatious form. In addition to the payment of a chief rent, which was supposed to be a substitution for other services, the tenant had to pay the lord of the manor a certain portion of his yearly crop. There were also certain other obligations, more of a humiliating than a financial nature. The peasant, for example, had to grind his corn in the lord's mill, and to press his grapes in the lord's wine press. At first, these were regarded as favors, rather than as obligations. But the fact that a certain portion of the produce that was thus sent up to the lord's mill and wine press had to be left behind by way of payment, made these favors both vexatious and even burdensome. Then, again, the lord could exercise certain rights, in regard to the property of the peasant, rights that might easily become an instrument of the most odious tyranny and degradation. Hunting and keeping pigeons were strictly forbidden to the peasant, but he had to allow the lord's horses and hounds to gallop over his fields, and the lord's pigeons to pick up grain in his own domain. The peasant was also forbidden to reap and sow his own land, except at stated times. Sometimes, ridiculous customs were even forced upon him, such as beating the water in the castle ditch, so as to keep the frogs quiet. In former times, this condition of servitude and degradation had not, for obvious reasons, caused much discontent. But circumstances then were different. The lord did something in return for all that he exacted, and for his position of domineering superiority. He, at least, acted as the protector of the peasants immediately under his care, and he performed for them the functions of judge, administrator, and police magistrate. Richelieu, however, and after him, Louis XIV, in their jealousy of the nobles, had removed from them those functions, and had entrusted them to a hierarchy of civil servants, called intendants. The nobles, however, while shorn of their usefulness, were still allowed to exact a price for the service that they were no longer able to render.

As though all this were not sufficient, the landlord was an absentee of a most odious description. To live at court was essential to the nobleman's existence. No greater misfortune could be conceived than for him to be exiled from the glitter and sunshine of his sovereign's presence, and to live in the quiet, monotonous exclusion of the country. The king himself required their presence at court, and any lengthy period of retirement in the country would have been construed into an insult. Obviously, court life meant expenditure, and often extravagance, the money for which had to be secured with heartless severity from the wretched peasant.

Nor was the nobleman the only offender. Vast quantities of land were placed out of cultivation by the custom of granting out *capitainaries*. These were large districts of land granted by the king to princes of the blood for hunting purposes. On such lands, even the old manorial rights were swept away in order that the prince might enjoy the unlimited right of preserving and hunting game. Any unfortunate peasant living on a *capitainaire* was absolutely subordinated to the exercise of this right. Not only did the game wander at will over the whole country, destroying the crops, but the peasant was sternly forbidden to engage in any agricultural occupation that might in any way be prejudicial to the welfare of the game. And what added to injury the sting of insult, was that the peasant was forbidden, under pain of the galleys, to kill any of the game that might wander over his property.

Between the cruel and insolent rapacity of king and noble, the condition of many of the peasants was hard, indeed. Yet it would be hardly true to say that the misery was universal. Certain travelers in France spoke very highly of the scenes of contentment and even gaiety that they saw in certain districts, but there is little doubt that, regarding the peasant class as a whole, its material condition and circumstances were such as to cause dangerous discontent.

If we turn our attention from the country to the towns, there also we shall find that the old fetters of the Middle Ages were crippling and galling the commercial activity of the country. All manufactures and trade were practically in the hands of the old medieval guilds. No outsider could carry on any handicraft, unless he belonged to one of these associations. Nor were there any of the old benefits, formerly derived from thus placing the monopoly of production in the hands of a few. Old-fashioned ways were adhered to, at the expense of loss of production, while inventions, even of the most important nature, were impeded by an almost insuperable wall of prejudice.

The result was that, while the upper masters of trades became rich and formed a sort of bourgeois aristocracy, the lower members of the industrial trades were left unjustly in the background. And what added considerably to the bitterness of their lot was the arrogance of those who held the upper position in the same trade as themselves. Distinctions of the most ridiculous kind were established in order to set off trivial grades of precedence. The altitude of a seat in the shop, the number of buckles that could be worn in a wig—such things as these were the stars and badges of the trade aristocracy. It is obvious, therefore, that the jealousy and bitterness of those belonging to the lower grades must have given intensity to the cry for equality and brotherhood of man that was heard so loud during the Revolution.

Having considered the elements of economic discomfort in the surroundings of town and country, we must now consider the economic cause that, more than any other, led up to the French Revolution. This cause was the system of taxation, which violated nearly all the canons laid down by Turgot. The taxes, that is to say, were unequal, they were uncertain and capricious, and they were collected in the most expensive way. This fact, however, will come out in stronger light if we consider, first of all, the nature of the taxation, and then the way in which it was distributed.

First, with regard to the direct taxes, which were as follows: *a.* The *taille.* This was a land tax, levied on all the lands that did not belong to the privileged classes of the nobility and clergy. The reason of this exemption was that the tax was a feudal tax, originally paid by the *villein* in place of granting military service. Since the noble gave military service in person, and the clergy by proxy, they were naturally exempt from this contribution. When, however, the obligation of military service had passed away, the exemption still remained.

The *taille* was of two kinds, being the *taille réele*, or the tax levied on the land, and *taille personnelle*, or tax levied on the profits of land or industry. The latter kind was the most general, the former existing only in Southern France.

In either case, the tax was levied in a very obnoxious manner. It was distributed unevenly and unjustly among the different provinces and districts and parishes, and the same bad qualities attended its levy even on the individuals within the same parish. It was left to the discretion of the collector as to the amount he should collect from the individual. Undue influence, therefore, could often be exerted, and endless lawsuits wasted considerable sums of money.

b. Another direct tax was the capitation tax, to which all were subject. This was really an income tax, and was supposed to be graded according to the wealth of the individual. In practice, however, it fell more severely upon the poor. No very definite regulations being in force, the rich could generally avail themselves of any loophole that the law afforded, whereas the poor and simple were utterly unable to manipulate the machinery to their own benefit.

c. A third kind of direct tax was the property tax. At first, this was one-twentieth part of the income derived from land, but it was afterwards raised to two-twentieths, and during war even another twentieth was added.

d. Amongst the direct taxes might also be enumerated the *corvées,* which meant that the peasants, exclusively, were subjected by statute to enforced labor on
the public roads, and to requisitions for the transport of
soldiers. In one way, this was perhaps one of the most
glaring of all the unjust impositions inflicted on the
lower classes. It meant that the peasants' labors, and
the use of their teams, were not at their service during
the busiest time of the year. The method of enforcing
the obligation was also exceedingly onerous. Much was
left to the discretion of local intendants and military
commanders, and it can be easily imagined that the
soldiers were not over-scrupulous in carrying out the
commands of their officers.

In connection with the *corvées* might be mentioned
also the obligation of providing lodging, washing, and
candles for soldiers who were quartered on them, and
of providing forage for their horses.

Altogether, the burden of the direct taxes and impositions must have fallen very heavily on the shoulders
of the lower classes. It has been calculated that no less
than four-fifths of the peasant's income must have been
sacrificed in the discharge of these burdens. And there
must, also, be taken into account all the incidental acts
of tyranny and humiliation endured from the hands of
minor officials.

We now come to the indirect taxes, which were as
equally oppressive as the direct taxes.

The first of these in unpopularity was certainly the
gabelle, or salt tax. Here again, one of the worst features was the unequal distribution of the tax. While
some provinces escaped with only a light tax, other districts like Provence, Languedoc, and some of the inland provinces of Northern France had to pay about

one-third of the whole assessment. Naturally, the temptation to smuggle salt from one province to another was irresistible. And in spite of a whole army of revenue officers, large quantities were actually so smuggled. So great, indeed, was the profit from this evasion of the law that the transportation of ten pounds of salt beyond a frontier meant the gain of a sum of money equal to the pay of a hard-working day. Nor was it possible to evade the tax by doing without salt, for every household in certain parts of France had to buy seven pounds of salt every year.

Then, there were also the customs duties, levied not only on goods imported from abroad, but on those transported from province to province. Every road and canal in France was barricaded by a complicated system of customs, and the goods thus taxed were not merely wines and spirits, but also ordinary foodstuffs.

Naturally, the results were both disastrous and galling. The cultivation of the vine was discouraged, and the natural laws of supply and demand were being continually violated. Moreover the irritation, caused by domiciliary visits and continual inspections, formed a very intolerable factor in the situation.

Most of these indirect taxes were leased out to Farmers-General, who paid a fixed rent every year, and were then allowed to collect and retain the net product of the taxes. Such a system, it will perhaps be remembered, was sufficiently odious during the days of the Roman Republic. It was still more so during the rapid decline of the French monarchy. The rapacity of the *fermiers généraux* was a hateful burden, and the rich buildings, erected in Paris for their administration, called forth burning denunciations from the impoverished taxpayers.

Having thus passed in general review the impoverished condition of the nation, the obstacles placed in the way of development of manufactures and of all sorts of industries, the hateful economic distinctions between class and class, and, above all, the intolerable condition of the system of taxation, we must now consider how the different elements combined to bring about the Revolution.

Louis XVI, who had ascended the French throne in 1774, was by no means the least worthy representative of the line of French kings. His intentions were good, and he seems to have had at heart, at least, the general welfare of the people. Unfortunately, however, his character was irresolute, and he had not sufficient strength of will to sustain able ministers against the prejudice of the courtiers and of the privileged classes.

His first minister was Turgot. As we have already pointed out, he was the leader of the Physiocrats, and a determined enemy of the restrictions that government had placed upon trade and industry. He instituted a whole series of practical reforms. Liberty of transportation of corn from province to province was allowed, the unjust incidence of the *gabelle* was alleviated, the *corvée* was replaced by a definite tax upon land, while all the old monopolizing trade associations were abolished. Naturally, the opposition on the part of the privileged classes was intense. However popular the measures may have been, the people were not yet sufficiently organized to defend their champion. Not only were the nobles, clergy, and lawyers opposed to him, but even the *Parlement* of Paris, and the members of the king's own household, were bitterly hostile to his reforms.

The king gave way. Turgot was disgraced and dismissed from office, and his place was taken for a time by Necker, a Genevan banker well acquainted with the principles of finance. But whatever might have been his capacity for figures, he was not a statesman.

At first, indeed, he was fairly successful. The publicity that he gave to the public accounts, and his willingness to obtain popular consent for taxation, endeared him to the people. Also, his dexterity in creating loans enabled him to relieve the waning condition of the treasury. He also tried to economize the whole system of administration by removing a great number of highly paid but useless officials, abolishing the system of farming out the taxes, and attempting to remove the heavy tolls on roads, canals, and rivers.

Even though the war between France and England, occasioned by the American revolt, had handicapped his financial endeavors, he was still able to meet the pressing exigencies that constantly occurred. But the privileged classes rose up against him. Like Turgot, he was forced to retire, and the next man who attempted to deal with the financial situation was Calonne. For four years Calonne held the office of comptroller-general. But, in spite of all his versatility and resourcefulness, bankruptcy became imminent. In vain did he try to sustain credit by lavish expenditure of money in public festivities, and the gratification of the greed of hungry courtiers. In 1786, the crisis came. At one extraordinary assembly of the nobles, bishops, magistrates, and officials of the kingdom, Calonne made a public statement of the whole financial condition. He proposed to them the abolition of privileges and exemptions, the reduction of the *gabelle*, the substitution of a poll tax for the *corvée*. Naturally, these proposals excited even still greater opposition, when coming from the mouth of

Calonne, than when they had come from the mouth of
Turgot. Calonne fell, and Necker was once more re-
called to office.

The first thing that Necker advised was to summon
the States-General, of which the Third Estate formed
one integral part. Dramatic, indeed, was this meeting
of the States-General after the lapse of so many years.
It marked the revival of the power of the people that
had hitherto lain dormant, and was the first act of that
great drama by which the people were destined to assert
for themselves the national control that had been
monopolized by king and courtiers. It is a fact of
strong significance that, while feudalism left behind in
its traces the main causes of the Revolution, it also, in
the old power of the *communes,* bequeathed an instrument whereby the ultimate object of the Revolution
could be accomplished by full constitutional means.

Proceedings began with a Solemn High Mass in
honor of the Holy Ghost. After this took place the
formal procession of all the orders of the States-General.
First came the black rows of the five hundred deputies
of the Third Estate; then, the nobility in their scar-
let robes; behind them again, came the clergy divided
into two divisions, the first comprising the dignitaries in
their purple robes, and then, two hundred parish priests
in somber black. Last of all came the king surrounded
by his courtiers.

At Versailles took place the first session of the eventful assembly. A great deal of time was spent in the pre-
liminaries, in deciding questions of etiquette, and in allotting to every one his proper place. Moreover, there
were two questions of formality to be settled, which
were of great legislative importance: first, whether the
three orders should assemble together or apart, and

secondly, whether the representatives of the Third Estate should be equal in number, or whether the Third Estate, following an ancient custom, should have a majority of representatives. Six weeks passed in fruitless attempts to solve these questions. No compromise seemed capable of being effected, so, on June 17, 1789, the Third Estate assumed the responsibility of sitting alone, and declaring itself to be the National Assembly. The move was effective. The king had to give way, and at his request the nobles and clergy joined the deputies of the Third Estate.

In the meantime, economic discontent in the country was necessitating some immediate measures of reform. Owing to famine and drought, the condition of the peasant was becoming absolutely intolerable. Throngs of discontented peasants scoured the country roads, and into the streets of Paris came numbers of ill-clad men of sinister appearance. Riots broke out both in Paris and in the provinces, and, to make matters more serious, the soldiers themselves showed a disposition to side with the rioters. In order to restore tranquillity, the National Guard was organized, and attempts were made to supply the capital with provisions.

At length, matters came to a climax. The National Assembly took upon itself to restore order by removing a whole list of fundamental grievances. All the old feudal régime was completely swept away, and every citizen was declared eligible to all offices and dignities ecclesiastical, civil, and military. *Corvées* and the other feudal services were abolished, the trade associations were dissolved, and all exclusive rights of hunting were completely swept away.

On the 4th of August began the work of forming the new constitution, in which the legislative powers were to be exercised by the nation, acting through the Assembly. Sieyès was the chief legislator, Mirabeau the orator. Sieyès was a democratic priest, a versatile logician, and a fecund framer of theories and constitutions. Mirabeau was a count of haughty and imperious temper, which was little under control. He was also venal, and ambitious to be a minister. But, in the main, he was faithful to the king, and was the leader of the moderate party which could alone ward off the Revolution.

With the judicial and purely political measures passed by the Assembly, we need not delay, but the financial and economic changes demand consideration. Necker, still the financial administrator, was the organizer of the economic changes. As money was urgently needed, he had again recourse to the old expedient of raising loans. Credit, however, was exceedingly bad, and expenses were continually increasing. The necessity of finding employment for the unemployed, for the purchase of corn with which to feed the people, and for maintaining the National Guard, were incessant drains on the treasury; at the same time, the people, since the outbreak of the Revolution, had failed to pay any taxes. As a desperate remedy, Necker then proposed a contribution from each person's income, to be assessed on his own valuation of his property. Even this failed, and nothing was left but to accept the revolutionary scheme of Talleyrand, who pointed out the boundless estates of the Church.

After broaching the theory that the Church was not the absolute owner of its domains, but only an administrator, Talleyrand proposed that the Church property should be seized and placed at the disposal of the nation. In spite of the protests of the clergy, the proposal was carried out. On December 19, 1789, Church property was thrown open for sale to the amount of four hundred million francs. Purchases, however, were very few, and, after an interval of three months, various municipalities themselves purchased the estates, intending to sell them over again and thereby reap a handsome profit. In the meantime, paper money was issued that had the value of bank notes. These assignats, as they were called, could be realized in Church lands according to the amount of their face value. They were also declared legal currency, and it was made a capital crime not to receive the assignats at par.

The results were fatal. The assignats rapidly depreciated in value. Many speculators, availing themselves of the liberty of purchasing Church lands for a merely nominal price, could cut down the timber, make what profit they could out of the movable property, and then decamp. At the same time, as inevitably happens under such circumstances, the bad currency drove out the good, while trade and commerce were utterly prostrated. In vain were more assignats put in circulation. This only hastened the impending ruin. For want of the necessary revenue, the Assembly then had recourse both to a poll tax and to a new land tax, which only caused public discontent, without substantially relieving the exchequer. Then, together with this, came the unpopularity incurred by interfering with the combinations of workmen, and by the injury done to the public workshops. Chronic discontent everywhere prevailed, and while starvation and misery were pinching the lower classes, the work of the Assembly could not but be a failure.

Gradually the reins of power passed from the hands of the Assembly into those of the extreme radical party. The people had by now been goaded into an attitude that was prepared to acquiesce in any extreme. In 1791, the National Assembly was dissolved and its place taken by the Legislative Assembly, over which the king had very little power. But even this very limited form of monarchy was finally removed, and on September 21, 1792, the Republic was formally declared.

The reader will not fail to have noticed, all along, how potent were the economic factors in bringing about this Revolution. While the poverty of the nation and the burden of taxation were arousing the people into agitation, and causing the rapid dismissal of one minister after another, it was the representatives of the *communes,* the Third Estate, who brought about the first few steps in the direction of the overthrow of the established order. Those very *communes,* that were such an important economic factor in the Middle Ages, were once more galvanized into life. But while formerly they were the buttresses of royal power, they now became the instrument of the people's rights.

From now, new forces appear on the scene. The passions of the multitude, the ability and political ambitions of such party leaders as Danton and Robespierre, and finally the military genius of Napoleon ruled for a few years the destinies of France. Not until the empire was fairly settled did the economic element begin once more to assert its influence both on the internal organization of France and on the warfare between France and England.

CHAPTER IX

A GENERAL SURVEY OF THE CONNECTION BE-TWEEN THE ECONOMIC ELEMENT AND RECENT POLITICAL EVENTS

DURING these opening years of the twentieth century, economic activities have not ceased to occupy an important position in the politics of the world. The enormous growth of industry and commerce, the ever-increasing power of money, the preponderance of political influence in the hands of the leading classes, have all combined to make the economic factor a paramount consideration. A cursory survey of some of these economic activities, however, will show that there are no new influences at work, but rather, that the domain of the old economic activities has become considerably widened.

The question, for example, of government interference with industry and trade looms now more largely into view than it did even in the sixteenth and seventeenth centuries. Only a few years ago a great political crisis in England was brought about by the question of Free Trade. Mr. Chamberlain pointed out that the adoption of Free Trade, in its entirety, was mainly responsible for the decline in British industry and trade. He proposed, therefore, to introduce a system of preferential tariffs and a small tax on foodstuffs. At once, there took place a division in the cabinet which was followed by the withdrawal from office of some of its most important members. At the same time, an important weapon of attack was given to the succeeding Liberal ministry that came into office in 1905. For, even the prime minister, then Mr. Balfour, showed himself slightly in favor of Protection, though not to the same extent as Mr. Chamberlain. Evidently, a government that begins office by adopting Free Trade, pure and simple, and then ends by modifying some of its more important tenets, places itself in a weak position. And in point of fact, this prepared the way for the strong Liberal reaction of the last few years.

In Germany, also, Free Trade has become an important factor in politics. During the last imperial elections, the cry of the Social Democrats was, "Down with a protectionist policy which injures the vital interests of many millions of people!" On the other hand, there is a very strong Agrarian Party that wishes for an absolute system of Protection. So strong was the influence of this party, that it probably had a great deal to do with the resignation of Count Caprivi, the Chancellor, in 1894. That such was the case might be gathered from the speech of the German Emperor, who, after expressing his solicitude for the important agricultural interests of East Prussia, declared that his wishes had been thwarted.

Nor in Germany alone does the question of Free Trade reign paramount, but throughout all Europe as well. Free Trade versus Protection is a dominant factor in international politics.

The famous Eden and Cobden commercial treaties proved only the beginning of a new era of international intercourse. The bonds of the Triple Alliance between Germany, Austria, and Italy have been still further strengthened by reciprocal commercial treaties. Furthermore, for two years and a half, there have been carried on negotiations of the same kind between the German Empire and no fewer than seven nations, namely, Belgium, Italy, Servia, Russia, Spain, Austria-

Hungary, and Switzerland. Then, shortly afterwards, a special tariff was arranged between Germany and Russia. No one can fail to see how these different treaties must very seriously affect the relations between the different powers.

In the United States, also, the retention of the tariff duties is one of the main disintegrating principles of the Republican Party, and at the same time a determining factor in foreign politics. In a preceding chapter, it has been shown how the navigation acts are injurious to the interests of British shipping and possibly may cause friction between the two countries. But the tariff system is even a still more potent factor for weal or woe. One notable instance of this was the McKinley Tariff, which, by its extreme protectiveness, created a very strong feeling of animosity in England.

Another aspect of government interference with trade is its attitude generally toward the great activities of industry, manufactures, and trade, as well as toward combinations of masters, or of employed. In regard to manufactures, the general tendency of government has been to interfere in behalf of the employed. Both in England and in America, various ordinances have been passed regulating child labor, the hours of work, and the sanitary conditions surrounding the workman. Also, regulations have been made regarding the compensation of workmen in case of injury and regarding their rights of organization.

While, in England, combinations of workmen have their rights distinctly laid down by law, in America they are allowed greater freedom of action. On the other hand, America is showing a greater tendency to regulate such associations as trusts and combines.

Some of these, by their selfish trampling upon the interests of minor business concerns, and by their corrupt influence in politics, have already occasioned an agitation for government control in the interests of the public.

While, however, the different governments are comparatively slow in interfering with these combinations, their control over banking and currency systems is fully admitted and enforced. They regulate the supply and quality of the coinage, and they authorize the issue of paper currency in the interests of the community. Also, generally speaking, no bank can be established without the permission and a certain supervision on the part of the State authorities. To a certain extent, the government can also control the amount of bullion that must be kept in the country. This has already been done in England by the provision that the Bank of England must keep its reserve up to a definite figure. And in other ways, the same end is accomplished by the endeavor to provide that the exports shall not be too much in excess of the imports.

While government manipulation of the finances has important results on the internal prosperity of combines, still more significant does it become in regard to foreign loans. Almost every government has by now contracted a considerable amount of debt, not only with its own subjects, but also with the subjects of other nations. One notable illustration of this we have in the enormous loans made by French bankers to the Russian Government. These loans were made in reality not by the bankers themselves, but by their clients, who comprised a large portion of the middle class. Naturally, the prosperity of Russia became partly identified with that of France, which would have bitter cause to regret any untoward incident which might bring Russia into a state of bankruptcy. Although the sympathy, or collision, of financial interests affects primarily only the people, yet in these days of representative government natural tendencies must be taken into account.

Indeed, it was the stern necessity of the consideration of the financial welfare of the people at large that brought about the war waged by Japan against Russia. The causes of the war were the question of Free Trade in Manchuria and the occupation of Korea. Russia's vexatious and humiliating treatment of Japanese merchants in Manchuria had deeply wounded Japan, while it was vitally necessary for the existence and well-being of Japan that her surplus population should be allowed to occupy Korea. The natural products of Japan are not sufficient for her own maintenance, and just at the door of Japan lay the country of Korea, apparently destined by Providence to become her colony, abounding both in minerals and in fertile crops of wheat, rice, cotton, and fruits.

If, again, we consider the recent revolution in Russia, we shall find that its causes are mainly economic. The fact that the peasant is cut off from the land, and that, owing to heavy taxation, he can not even enjoy the fruits of what he has, is largely accountable for the discontent throughout the country. At the same time, the constantly recurring strikes throughout the Russian Empire testify to the profound economic discontent of the workingman, which gives strength and force to the political agitations. Indeed, it was mainly the recognition of those very serious causes of weakness that impelled Russia to come to terms with Japan as readily as she did.

Although there have been no colonial disputes between other nations of such gravity as to cause open warfare, yet considerable tension between nations has been caused by conflicting spheres of activity in foreign parts. The Monroe Doctrine in the United States shows her fear and jealousy of any outside intervention in South America. The ill-will aroused in France some years ago by the English occupation of Egypt, the jealousy aroused in England by German settlements in China, and later in the Persian Gulf, show that there still remains some of that same expansive colonial activity that caused the colonial side of the Seven Years' War.

Then, again, the constant discovering or formation of new trade routes is ever changing the relative commercial importance of countries and cities. What could be more important than the formation of the Panama Canal? Not only will this important undertaking have the effect of bringing together the commercial activities of the United States on the Eastern and Western coasts, and of competing more successfully with the ever-rising Japanese trade in the Pacific, but it will also produce very important political results. It will tend to check the tendency of Mongolian civilization to travel eastward, and will enable the old European civilization to pursue its onward march toward the West. In Europe, again, the completion of the Simplon Tunnel will have the effect of strengthening French influence in Italy, much in the same way as the St. Gothard was promoted by certain German States, for the purpose of strengthening German influence in the Southern Peninsulas. The importance of this new tunnel on the future of Austria will also soon show itself in tangible results, for now she will be brought more immediately in contact with the Far East.

It is no exaggeration to say that the relative position

of nations is now determined more by economic than by military factors. Money, not the sword, is now the preponderating force. Even socially, this fact is admitted. Great merchants can penetrate into the charmed circles of royalty, and are admitted on terms of intimacy with the highest in the land.

We may now conclude by saying that the importance of economics as a factor in the making of history has been fully proved and illustrated. From the days of the struggles between the Plebeians and Patricians, down to the late agrarian revolution in Russia, the power of the economic factor has been steadily growing until at the present day it controls not only the relations between nation and nation, but also the earthly weal or woe of toiling humanity.

INDEX

www.ingramcontent.com/pod-product-compliance
Lightning Source LLC
Chambersburg PA
CBHW070627290526
45790CB00001B/29

* 9 7 8 1 4 8 3 9 9 7 3 9 1 *